Culture and Politics

Culture and Politics

An Introduction to Mass and Elite Political Behavior

Oliver H. Woshinsky
University of Southern Maine

Prentice Hall, Englewood Cliffs, New Jersey 07632

Library of Congress Cataloging-in-Publication Data

WOSHINSKY, OLIVER H.
  Culture and politics : an introduction to mass and elite political
behavior / Oliver H. Woshinsky.
  p.   cm.
  Includes index.
  ISBN 0-13-311366-3
  1. Political participation—United States.   2. Political culture—
United States.   3. Collective behavior—United States.   4. Elite
(Social sciences)—United States.   I. Title.
JK1764.W67   1995
323′.042′0973—dc20

94–29316
CIP

Acquisitions editor: *Charlyce Jones Owen*
Editorial/production supervision: *Judy Hartman*
Cover design: *Wendy Alling-Judy*
Buyer: *Bob Anderson*
Editorial assistant: *Nicole Signoretti*

© 1995 by Prentice-Hall, Inc.
A Simon & Schuster Company
Englewood Cliffs, New Jersey 07632

Printed in the United States of America
10 9 8 7 6 5 4 3 2 1

ISBN   0-13-311366-3

Prentice-Hall International (UK) Limited, *London*
Prentice-Hall of Australia Pty. Limited, *Sydney*
Prentice-Hall Canada Inc., *Toronto*
Prentice-Hall Hispanoamericana, S.A., *Mexico*
Prentice-Hall of India Private Limited, *New Delhi*
Prentice-Hall of Japan, Inc., *Tokyo*
Simon & Schuster Asia Pte. Ltd., *Singapore*
Editora Prentice-Hall do Brasil, Ltda., *Rio de Janeiro*

To Pat,
who read every word and encouraged me in every way,
with love and admiration.

Contents

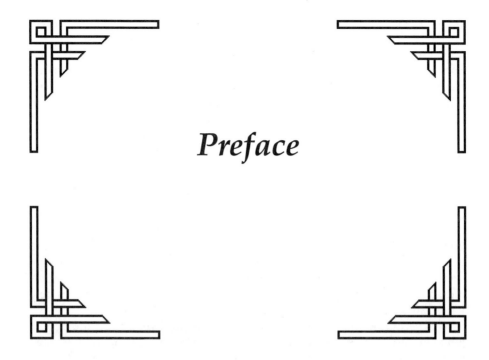

Preface

Soon after arriving in Scotland on a research sabbatical in 1993, I read with bemused detachment a local journalist's anecdote that suggested serious Scottish–English animosity. After finishing his column for *The Scotsman* late one night, the gentleman in question left for home from the newspaper's offices in central Edinburgh. He was soon stopped on his way by a gang of boisterous thugs.

"Are you English?" they asked him threateningly.

"Do I sound it?" he replied, with false bravado.

They let him keep going, but he repeated this little story next day to an English colleague on the newspaper, and *that* journalist began to take taxis home, instead of walking, after late-night sessions at the office.*

I might have found this incident mildly amusing a few years ago, when I didn't know a Scottish accent for a Cockney one. Certainly, most Americans would have trouble seeing what the fuss was about. (They're all Brits, aren't they?) Yet in the early 1990s, at a time when seemingly similar peoples were killing themselves with zealous ferocity in two dozen places around the world, the incident seemed depressingly symbolic. It represented the ubiquitous nature of the potential for violence in human affairs, even among people who seem much alike on the surface. Each of us can think of a dozen examples, if we reflect a bit.

*This episode is recounted by Ewen MacAskill, "Divisions which Are All in the Mind," *The Scotsman*, February 20, 1993, p. 8.

John Jenkins, the black mayor of Lewiston, Maine, tells one such story. Some years ago he arrived at Bates College in tiny, lily-white Lewiston fresh from his home in the inner city of Newark, New Jersey. He noticed with amazement the serious level of dislike that separated students from local residents. "Townies" deeply resented "Batesies," who reciprocated that sentiment with equally strong feeling. Jenkins found these differences incomprehensible. As he told students of mine in 1994: "I was naive, but I thought to myself, 'What's for them to quarrel about? They're all white, aren't they?'"

Conflict lies at the heart of politics—and differences, real or imagined, lie at the heart of conflict. Once people define themselves as "us" and differentiate themselves from others whom they see as "them," this distinction, no matter how ludicrous it may appear to an objective outsider, will lead to conflict and thus inexorably to politics (which is nothing more nor less than society's way of dealing with conflict). This inevitability of conflict and politics, and the varying political patterns that different cultures create to deal with conflict, represents a central theme in the pages that follow.

A second key theme derives from the first and centers on the people who get into politics. It examines those who spend more time than average in this conflict-ridden activity, a business that most people in most places at most times in history prefer to shun. These political activists make our policies, structure our institutions, and make life-and-death decisions for the rest of us. It will clearly pay us to learn something about their nature.

I once heard Tom Allen, a 1994 candidate for Governor of the state of Maine, explain to a questioner how he had "decided" to get into politics:

> It was never a question of *deciding*. Politics was always a central part of my life. When I was growing up, half of our dining-room table was covered with my father's City Council documents, and the other half was taken up by my mother's League of Women Voters papers. As a result, we always had to eat in the kitchen! For me, politics was just natural; it was always a normal part of life, not something you made a conscious decision about.

Many of my students nod their heads in vigorous understanding as I tell this story. Yet others can't fathom why anyone would devote even a second of time to politics. In every society only a minority of people fall into the first camp. Few devote serious amounts of time and energy to political endeavor. These few will consequently have an enormous impact on the political process, on policy outcomes. Who they are and what they are like is of serious consequence. My attempt to answer these questions constitutes the secondary theme of this text.

This book aims to provoke thought and stimulate the beginning student to think about politics in an analytical—and animated—manner.

Along the way I do introduce some of the key concepts in political science, but I must emphasize the word *some*. This work doesn't pretend to be comprehensive or definitive. I purposely avoid extensive definition of terms, enumeration of authors, and methodological discussion of approaches. I wish primarily to convey some sense of the endless excitement and fascination of politics. If students find themselves hooked by the drama of political life, they can then move on to explore advanced texts, those that include the systematic discussion of political science as a formal discipline and give proper attention to all the appropriate terms and structures.

This book, then, is for beginning and intermediate students in a variety of introductory political science courses. It will provide much thought in most undergraduates. It will also engage their attention, so that they will *want* to think about something. But it should not be read alone or taken as the final word on politics.

Only by reading for themselves a wide range of authors will good students get a sense of a field and the myriad ways of studying that field. A short book like this allows instructors to assign other texts that cover different topics altogether or that take different approaches. The good teacher will, of course, ask students to read books that supplement and complement, or even contradict, this one. The good student who wishes to explore beyond these pages will find, in the modest set of footnotes provided here, a way to begin delving into any subject that takes his or her fancy.

Although this book is short, its gestation period was long. In a real sense, it has taken me all of my life to write it. My early interest in politics owes much to my parents, who took me as a boy to my first political convention in 1948. My interest in the quirks and oddities of cultural variation also owes much to them. When you grow up in conservative, rural Vermont in the 1940s with a radical, Russian–Jewish father and a mother who spent the first twenty years of her own life as a Methodist missionary's daughter in northern China, you either grow up confused or deeply interested in cultural variation—or maybe a little of both!

My beloved uncle, the late Richard Hanson, encouraged my teenaged interests in history and public affairs, and another uncle, Perry Oliver Hanson, who spent a lifetime working for the United Nations, served as an inspirational role model. My aunt, Margery Day Hanson, made sure during my high school days that I remembered the importance of reading much and writing well. She then helped me attend Mount Hermon School, where those lessons were reinforced every day with crusading zeal.

Oberlin College broadened my horizons and started me along the road to a lifetime in the study of politics. I was fortunate to study under some remarkable teachers, including John D. Lewis, Ewart Lewis, George Lanyi, Thomas Flinn, Robert Tufts, and the legendary Aaron Wildavsky, then just beginning his impressive academic career. This group, along with other great teachers from that time, helped launch the careers of a star-studded Oberlin mafia of political scientists, a group that has made its mark on the profession in a hundred ways.

A short stint at Columbia's Russian Institute after Oberlin served me well, decades later, when I spent a semester teaching in the Russian city of Archangel. My perspective on politics, doggedly behavioral, took final shape during several happy, if grueling, years at Yale University. I would like to think that this present text reflects the insights of such Yale luminaries from that time as Robert Dahl, Robert Lane, Harold Lasswell, Charles Lindblom, Joseph LaPalombara, James David Barber, Fred Greenstein, and Sidney Tarrow. I also gained much from my classmates of that era, such as David Caputo and Robert Putnam.

To my long-time friend, colleague, and mentor, James L. Payne, I owe much. Over the years we have learned together, worked together, and argued together. I owe him an enormous intellectual debt, as any reader of this book will soon realize, and I remain in awe of his focused intelligence—even if the end to which he is currently applying that intelligence, libertarianism, leaves me sputtering in dismay.

A number of people have read and commented on parts or all of the various drafts, which preceded this version of *Culture and Politics*. I am deeply grateful to their generous donations of time and opinion. In particular, I wish to thank Karla Fuchs, Rob Laskey, Judith Ritchie, Juanita Gable, John Garrett, Michael Williams, Richard Maiman, and William Coogan. I owe profound thanks, in more ways than I can say, to the latter two gentlemen. We have spent over two decades as colleagues and friends, yet I never cease to delight in conversing with them about politics—or about most other topics, for that matter. Without their inspiration and support over the years, my development as a political scientist and as a human being would surely have suffered.

At a crucial point William Field provided some immensely useful research assistance, as well as trenchantly insightful comments on various parts of the manuscript. James Funston gave me some much-needed advice about publishing practicalities and manuscript presentation. I also benefitted enormously from the written comments of Prentice-Hall's reviewers: Joseph Lepgold, Georgetown University; John Nickerson, University of Maine at Augusta, and Richard Matthews, Lehigh University. I am grateful to Maria DiVencenzo for her enthusiastic response to my manuscript proposal. Suzanne Ingrao did a superb job of copyediting my submitted manuscript, and Judy Hartman was a pleasure to work with during the technical process of converting that manuscript to book form.

Without generous support over the years from the University of Southern Maine (sabbatical approval, research grants, teaching exchanges, reductions in course load), I could never have produced this book. I would also like to thank the University of Edinburgh's Political Science Department—Chris Allen, in particular—for providing me with a quiet space, access to all facilities, and collegial company, thus making my latest sabbatical experience productive and fascinating, just the way it's supposed to be.

Pippa Norris, who first suggested that I spend time in Edinburgh and helped open those doors for me, has been important to me in many other ways as well. Over the years our many conversations about politics have kept me both informed and stimulated. I have learned much from her and find her an inspiring colleague, teacher, and researcher.

I am grateful to several generations of students at the University of Southern Maine, who put up with the ideas I have developed here and always gave me the benefit of their (often vigorous) reactions. This work is truly "classroom tested." I have propounded these concepts in formal settings to a variety of students and have benefitted immeasurably from their comments—both positive and negative.

I reserve my final thanks for two special people. My son, David, may not recognize his contribution here, but his happy presence in my life for twenty years has given me the satisfaction, self-confidence, and peace of mind to embark on a variety of quixotic projects, including this one. My wife, Patricia Ellen Garrett, to whom this book is dedicated, has been a tower of support from start to finish. Her judicious critiques, her sensible suggestions, and most of all, her enthusiastic backing gave me the strength to improve the manuscript and carry the project forward, even during those times when I was ready to chuck it all and change careers for good. I offer her my sincerest appreciation for that much-needed reinforcement.

Naturally, I alone am responsible for all errors of fact and interpretation, which, despite the best efforts of most of the aforementioned, remain in the work. I urge conscientious readers to help me cut the error rate in future editions. Please send your reactions and corrections to me at the Political Science Department, University of Southern Maine, 96 Falmouth Street, Portland, Maine 04103. Many thanks!

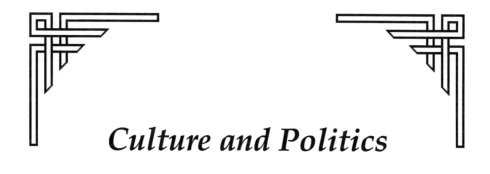

Culture and Politics

1

The Impact of Culture on Politics

People behave, from one place to another, in remarkably dissimilar ways. Brazilians bear hug when they meet friends. The French shake hands formally, and the Japanese bow. Transferring the behavior of one culture to another can produce dramatic misunderstandings. Bear hugging a Japanese businessman would hardly improve your chances for a contract. Fail to shake hands with a Frenchwoman each time you meet, and she will see you as a boor and a cad.[1]

Ian Robertson has written amusingly about the variety of human behavior.

> Americans eat oysters but not snails. The French eat snails but not locusts. The Zulus eat locusts but not fish. The Jews eat fish but not pork. The Hindus eat pork but not beef. The Russians eat beef but not snakes. The Chinese eat snakes but not people. The Jalé of New Guinea find people delicious.[2]

---

[1]For an engaging account of the social significance of body language in different cultures, see Roger E. Axtell, *Gestures: The Do's and Taboos of Body Language around the World* (New York: John Wiley & Sons, Inc., 1991).

[2]Ian Robertson, *Sociology* (New York: Worth Publishers, 1981), p. 63.

Anecdotal accounts of human diversity can be fascinating, and they can also make a serious point. It pays to understand the variety of human mores, because every social pattern impinges in some way on politics. Candidates for office in Japan or France don't throw their arms around constituents while campaigning; in Brazil they do. Try it in Japan, or fail to do it in Brazil, and you will get nowhere in your bid for office.

In the same manner, what you eat (far-fetched though it may seem) will influence your political fortune. Imagine a politician in Israel known to dine on roast pig. Or an American politician who admits to loathing hot dogs and apple pie. George Bush had to claim that he loved pork rinds in order to win the trust of Texas voters, and Bill Clinton is known to enjoy that quintessential American food, the Big Mac. Had these men ever admitted, early in their political careers, that they preferred locusts and snakes to good old American food, they would never have had political careers, and none of us today would have heard of them.

P. J. O'Rourke, the flamboyant American journalist, once described some harrowing (though hilarious) adventures in Lebanon for his best-seller, *Holidays in Hell*. One day he and his guide roamed the countryside looking for a farmer he was supposed to interview.

> It's hard to know what your driver is doing when he talks to the natives. He'll pull up somewhere and make a preliminary oration, which draws five or six people to the car window. Then each of them speaks in turn. There will be a period of gesturing, some laughter, much arm clasping and handshaking, and a long speech by the eldest or most prominent bystander. Then your driver will deliver an impassioned soliloquy. This will be answered at length by each member of the audience and anybody else who happens by. Another flurry of arm grabbing, shoulder slapping and handshakes follows, then a series of protracted and emotional good-byes.
> 'What did you ask them?' you'll say to your driver.
> 'Do they know of your friend.'
> 'What did they tell you?'
> 'No.'[3]

Cultures vary. People differ radically from each other, depending on where they live and how they have been raised. People are emphatically *not* "just the same the world over," as the old cliché would have it. And as human behavior varies from one culture to another, so too does political behavior. The direct, straightforward American manner of asking questions would get nowhere in a Lebanese village. Just as obviously, a "straight-talking" American politician would fail miserably in a bid for office there. On the other hand, the bombastic, circuitous, and loquacious style of Lebanese interaction would produce career disaster for any American politician dim enough to adopt it in the United States.

---

[3]P. J. O'Rourke, *Holidays in Hell* (London: Pan Books, Ltd., 1989), p. 36.

POLITICS AND CULTURE

Politics everywhere reflects the culture of a time and place. This argument under-pins the perspective of modern political science. To understand politics anywhere, you must first understand the culture within which political acts are embedded.

An intriguing item once appeared in my local newspaper: "In the Tonga Islands it is a compliment for a young man to say to a young woman, 'Oh, fat liver full of oil, let us go and watch the moonrise.'"

Can you imagine using that line at a Saturday night fraternity party? It would prove a dismal failure in U.S. culture. The current American ideal of beauty is often expressed in that famous cliché, "You can never be too rich or too thin." Studies consistently show that the vast majority of American women consider themselves "too fat," when in fact most of them are not, by any reasonable standard, overweight.[4] But in a culture that glorifies slenderness, those who deviate even slightly from the reign-ing ideal of beauty see themselves (and indeed, are seen by others) as dis-advantaged.

As it turns out, most cultures have fairly rigid notions of attractive-ness, and those notions vary widely. Many societies prefer heftier body types than those admired in the West. A thin woman, attractive by American standards, once told me that growing up in West Africa in a missionary family, she was shunned by the young men of her village. Her plump sister, however, was considered stunning, and men came from miles around to offer her father many cows for the privilege of making her their bride.

As this example suggests, attractiveness, however defined by a partic-ular culture, is an asset. Study after study has shown that benefits accrue to "attractive" people—that is, to people deemed attractive by the standards of their specific culture. Compared to others, attractive people are better liked, believed to be more intelligent, and prove more likely to get and hold any given job.[5] They not only receive "undeserved" benefits from life, they avoid its worst punishments. For instance, these same studies show that attractive people are less likely than others to be arrested; if they are arrested, they are less likely than others to be convicted; and if they are con-victed, they are less likely than others to serve time in jail. To cap this

[4]According to a recent survey, "three-quarters of American adults are not overweight." See "Losing Weight: What Works, What Doesn't," *Consumer Reports* 58 (June 1993): 347–52. See also Morton G. Harmatz, "The Misperception of Overweight in Normal and Underweight Women," *Journal of Obesity and Weight Regulation* 6 (1987): 38–54; and Marika Tiggemann and Esther D. Rothblum, "Gender Differences and Social Consequences of Perceived Overweight in the United States and Australia," *Sex Roles* 18 (1988): 75–86.

[5]For a recent summary of these findings, see Robert B. Cialdini, *Influence: Science and Practice*, 3d ed. (New York: Harper Collins College Publishers, 1993), pp. 140–42; see also David G. Myers, *Social Psychology*, 4th ed. (New York: McGraw-Hill, Inc., 1993), pp. 473–76.

process of injustice, even when attractive people do go to jail, they spend less time there than the other convicts![6]

Continuing this examination of attractiveness, we know that Americans prefer tall to short and white to black. As we would expect, therefore, when a white and a black person, equally qualified, apply for any given job, the white person is likely to be chosen.[7] Similarly, a tall person is more likely than a short person to be given a job, even when both hold the same credentials.[8] Indeed, this pattern is so powerful that in the entire history of American presidential elections, a candidate clearly shorter than the other has won office only four times.[9]

Deviation from a culture's norm of beauty is hardly fatal to our life chances. Still, it represents a modest hurdle. It subtly detracts from one's career potential. On an individual basis, it must be dealt with, compensated for. Consider famous people (the short Napoleon, the plain Eleanor Roosevelt, the handicapped Toulouse-Lautrec or Stephen Hawking) who have achieved brilliant success despite falling seriously short of their society's attractiveness norms. We can also think of individual examples, from among people we know, who are successful but not especially attractive, or—on the contrary—attractive but not particularly successful. "History" (and by implication, social science) "knows probabilities but not certainties," writes Stephen White,[10] reminding us that there are few rules of human behavior that don't allow for a number of exceptions.

Still, social science prefers generalization to exception, rule to deviant case; that is, attractiveness is an advantage. On the whole, those who come closest to their culture's ideal of beauty will, other things being equal, be better rewarded than others (with whatever that culture's idea of reward might happen to be—money, cows, penthouses, or poems written in their honor).

Those who doubt this point might ask themselves why one rarely sees an unattractive popular singer—especially in these days of MTV. Did nature really contrive to distribute musical potential only to those with

---

[6]See the evidence cited in Myers, op. cit., pp. 354–55.

[7]See, for example, Richard Jenkins, *Racism and Recruitment: Managers, Organizations, and Equal Opportunity in the Labour Market* (Cambridge: Cambridge University Press, 1986), pp. 116–88. See also Andrew Hacker, *Two Nations: Black and White, Separate, Hostile, Unequal* (New York: Ballantine Books, 1992), especially his discussion of black-white differentials in income and employment in the U.S., pp 93-133.

[8]For a summary and critique of the literature, see Wayne E. Hensley and Robin Cooper, "Height and Occupational Success: A Review and Critique," *Psychological Reports* 60 (1987): 843–49.

[9]The Clinton victory over Bush in 1992 may provide a fifth case. On paper, both candidates were listed as six feet, two inches tall, but most observers gave Bush a half-inch advantage over his challenger. This marginal difference does little to undermine the generalization that Americans like their leaders to be tall, since both men stood well above the height of the average middle-aged American male (around five feet, nine inches). Now if Perot (five feet, four inches) had won the election, *that* would have represented a serious deviation from the pattern!

[10]Stephen White, *Political Culture and Soviet Politics* (London: Macmillan, 1979), p. x.

pretty faces? From among the many talented singers available, generally, we elevate to musical stardom only those people who also happen to meet our standards of beauty. The same point applies to a host of other social positions. Why are news anchors uniformly pleasant to look at? Is there really some correlation between looks and the ability to read from a teleprompter? Clearly, we can find thousands of excellent reporters in any country. Hundreds of these would be more than able to read aloud the day's news for us. From among this group, however, only the best-looking are chosen for this straightforward task.

You may be wondering: What on earth does this have to do with politics? The answer is simple. Politics is not some arcane ritual divorced from the life of society. It is intertwined in the most integral way with all other social activity. *Political activity cannot be considered apart from society as a whole*, any more than blood can be considered apart from the body in which it circulates.

Political behavior reflects the culture in which it occurs. If a given society adulates strength, it will reward strong individuals. All social leaders in that culture, including political decisionmakers, will be aggressive. (Even those who aren't will strive to appear so, if they wish to achieve social status.) If a society prefers friendliness, it will choose amiable, cooperative types for all leadership posts, from president on down to head of the local animal shelter. Pugnacious types in that culture will work at toning down their rough edges—or risk being ostracized.

Ruth Benedict found this precise pattern when she examined various North American indigenous peoples in the 1920s. The Pueblos, a peaceful and cooperative bunch, chose relatively weak, nonauthoritarian individuals to head their group. The Kwakiutl, on the other hand, an aggressive lot, chose their toughest and most assertive members for leadership positions.[11]

The simple *politics-reflects-culture* axiom explains a good deal about politics everywhere. In a highly religious society, for example, political leaders will be emissaries of God on earth. Witness the doctrine of the divine right of kings in the Middle Ages. Witness the political power of an Ayatollah Khomeini in the ardently religious Iran of the 1980s. By way of contrast, in a nonreligious (or antireligious) society (say, Russia under Marxist rule), political leaders too will be nonreligious or antireligious. In reverse, deeply religious people in a nonreligious society will rarely gain political power. They will most often be scorned and treated as outcasts, even persecuted as subversives.

In a moderately religious society like the United States, political leaders must be moderately religious—or at least believed to be. They must be

---

[11]See Ruth Benedict, *Patterns of Culture* (New York: The New American Library, 1934), esp. pp. 62–120 and 156–95. On the relation between cultural values and societal leadership patterns, see also Ruth Benedict, *Tales of the Indians* (Washington, D. C.: U.S. Government Printing Office, 1931), Margaret Mead, *Sex and Temperament in Three Primitive Societies* (New York: W. Morrow & Co., 1935), and David Riesman, *The Lonely Crowd: A Study of the Changing American Character* (Garden City, NY: Doubleday & Company, Inc., 1953), pp. 191–217.

seen going to church, invoking God's will, praying publicly. Imagine the doleful fate awaiting the first presidential candidate bold enough (or foolish enough) to admit: I don't see much evidence for God's existence. In my humble opinion, prayer and churchgoing are a colossal waste of time, and I won't insult the intelligence of the American people by pretending otherwise. No such political leader exists in the United States today, nor should we expect one in the foreseeable future. On the other hand, excessive piety also works against someone seeking to rise in mainstream American politics. Many Americans feel uncomfortable around people who give voice regularly to intense religious fervor. Truly devout people rarely gain political power in the United States, thus joining atheists at the fringes of American politics.

Political activity, then, reflects cultural expectations. This proposition, used as a starting point, yields any number of useful predictions. We can confidently assert, for instance, that Americans will not soon elect any nonreligious person to the presidency. We also feel confident that they won't elect any clearly unattractive person to the Oval Office.

We must qualify and expand this last point. Remember the Tonga Islander's appreciation of fat? We can well imagine that the Tonga political leader is a large, burly fellow. (Indeed, I once came across a photograph of him and his wife, both towering over Great Britain's Queen Elizabeth, who was touring the island during a royal visit.) What one culture considers attractive, another may find distasteful. What, then, will an elected American president look like?

To begin, he will be a man—for reasons to be explained shortly. He will be tall—for reasons already explained. He will not be bald—Americans like men with a good head of hair. Indeed, in the history of this country (or at least since wigs went out of fashion), only two balding men have ever attained the presidential office. One was a national hero—General Dwight David Eisenhower. The other was something of a fluke: Gerald Ford. Through an odd chain of improbable events, Ford became president without ever facing the American electorate.[12] When he did try to win the voters' approval, in 1976, he lost a close race against Jimmy Carter, a man with a stylish head of hair. These two exceptions out of thirty-five presidents in the post-wig era do nothing but reinforce our conclusion: Men lacking in

---

[12]Ford was the beneficiary—the only one so far—of the 25th Amendment to the U.S. Constitution, ratified only in 1967. This amendment set up a way to fill any vacancy that might occur in the vice-presidency. The amendment was put to use in 1973, when Spiro Agnew resigned from that office after corruption charges against him surfaced. President Richard Nixon then nominated Ford, minority leader in the House of Representatives, to replace Agnew, and Congress approved the appointment, making Ford vice-president. When Nixon himself resigned from the presidency a year later to avoid facing impeachment charges over the Watergate scandal, Ford acceded to the White House—having never faced the American electorate. Only residents of Michigan's Fifth Congressional District had ever voted for Ford before he gained the presidency.

hirsute qualities will rarely make it to the top of the American political ladder.[13]

On another point of personal appearance, the president of the United States must be relatively thin. He certainly must not be overweight. Americans are so fanatical on this point that we can lay down this simple law: Anyone over ten percent heavier than average for his height and build will not be elected president. Think of all the significant presidential candidates we have seen in recent years: Jesse Jackson, Al Gore, Jerry Brown, Bob Dole, Jack Kemp, Pat Robertson, Ross Perot. To a man, none is overweight. (When Ted Kennedy decided to run for president in 1980, he went on a diet and lost fifty pounds.) Among presidents themselves, none has been clearly obese since the days of William Howard Taft (1909–1913), who, at 300 pounds, stands out as an exceptional case. Exceptions can always occur, but we don't want to bet on them. Given the facts of American culture and the pattern of recent history, we can only conclude that it is advantageous to be thin if you harbor presidential ambitions.

Another matter of external appearance is crucial if you wish to become president. You must possess a friendly smile, one which gives you the appearance (at least) of being amiable and possessing a good sense of humor. Americans value these traits. Not all presidents have them, but most presidential contenders work at *appearing* to possess them—especially in recent years with the need to enhance one's television image uppermost in politicians' minds.[14]

Once into the spirit of this discussion, we can generate dozens of additional qualifications for candidates to the U.S. presidency. Among other requirements, for example, they must be (or at least seem to be) happily married and must have produced at least one healthy offspring. Nearly all our presidents fit this description. Only Buchanan was a bachelor. All other presidents were married, and most fathered several children.

American presidents, then, will be tall and well proportioned, possess a good head of hair, and show good teeth in a friendly smile, which they will display on all occasions. They will also have a supportive wife and at least one adoring child. To summarize: How many small, bald, overweight,

---

[13]Every ambitious politico is well aware of this phenomenon. More than one has addressed himself to the "misfortune" of hair loss. Within the last two decades, at least two senators who harbored hopes for the presidency undertook hair transplant treatment: William Proxmire and Joseph Biden.

[14]No one would quarrel with the assertion that television has stiffened the attractiveness requirement in all realms of American life, especially for those who must meet the public in their job—and that's one of the prime requirements for politicians. In short, the need for presidents to meet some kind of societal photogenic ideal has grown markedly in recent years, although I contend that it has never been absent from our history. The shrewd George Washington, for example, knew well the benefits of presenting an attractive image. He purposely made sure that he was always seen riding on a large white horse—to enhance his overall stature. (You will find no paintings of him on a steed of grey or brown.)

scowling, single, childless men do you know with a serious chance at reaching the Oval Office?

What happens in politics, as these examples illustrate, cannot be divorced from what happens in the rest of society. *A culture's deepest held values will be expressed in all its social institutions.* If society glorifies attractiveness, and if attractiveness is defined by height, hair, and smile, then those who are tall with nice hair and a cheerful grin will be advantaged in the struggle for political power.

WOMEN AND POLITICAL POWER

I have tried to use some amusing examples to get your attention. They may seem frivolous, but the principle they illustrate is profoundly important. Let us now apply it to a serious phenomenon. Our discussion of the attractiveness of U.S. presidential candidates focused entirely on men. The reason is obvious: We cannot generalize about the ideal features of a successful female presidential candidate. Not only have we never seen a successful woman candidate for president, but through the 1992 election we have not even seen a serious *potential* woman candidate for president!

Some might argue this last point. Here's how I justify it. Let's define "a serious potential candidate" as anyone whom knowledgeable political observers would, one year before the next presidential election, place among the twenty people most likely to attain the Presidency. Under this admittedly loose definition, it is difficult to name *any* woman who might have *ever* qualified. Perhaps Pat Schroeder or Elizabeth Dole in 1987 would have made someone's list at numbers nineteen or twenty. Perhaps (though less likely) Shirley Chisholm might have made someone's list in 1971. But that's about it. The rule is clear. To be a serious candidate for president of the United States, even in this current era of feminism, you must be a man. (As I write these words in mid-1994, not one woman is being seriously suggested by anyone as a likely challenger to Bill Clinton in 1996.)

This absence of women at the very top of the political ladder is hardly a fluke. We don't find many women at the next rungs down either. No vice-president has ever been a woman. Only one vice-presidential *nominee* (out of roughly a hundred major party nominations) has ever been a woman—Geraldine Ferraro in 1984. We have never had more than four women in the Cabinet (out of ten to fourteen members, depending on the year), but the average number over the last twenty years has been two. (Before that, during the preceding 180 years, it was roughly zero.)

This pattern continues. No women can be found among the 101 justices named to the U.S. Supreme Court during its first 191 years. The first woman (Sandra Day O'Connor) reached the Court in 1981, and the second (Ruth Bader Ginsburg) twelve years later in 1993. (That makes two women currently on the nine-member Court—two out of the 108 Justices who have served since 1789.) The U.S. Senate has, over the past forty years, averaged two women members out of a hundred, although it had by mid–1993 reached its highest number ever: seven. The U.S. House of Representatives saw twenty to twenty-five female members (out of 435) from most of 1970 to 1990. (Before the 1994 elections, that number was approaching fifty— roughly, eleven percent of the total.) As late as 1994, the country had never had more than four women Governors in office at any given time (out of the fifty states). The total number of women in all state legislatures never attained the twenty percent level until 1993. The story continues in this vein; few women are in power, right down to school boards and town councils throughout the land.

Because women comprise the majority of the electorate, their drastic underrepresentation in nearly every political and governmental body is one of the more striking facts of American political life. To see this point more clearly, go back thirty years—or fifty. In those days, women were practically invisible in American politics.

They were, we must note in fairness, invisible in the political systems of all other countries as well. Except for the occasional oddity of a powerful queen, women were missing from positions of power everywhere in the world until well into the twentieth century.

This absence of women from the structures of power is a vital political fact. After all, a number of studies suggest that when women do reach decision-making positions, they make different choices from those made by men.[15] For one thing, their energy is devoted to different issues. They work for day care funding, health services, and improvements to education rather than on tax policy, roadbuilding, and defense. They also vote differently from men. They show more support for social welfare programs and less for defense expenditures and business subsidies.

Whether you prefer these positions or not, the task of political analysis is to understand how politics works, and the point here is simple: *This dramatic absence of powerful women produces clear effects.* We as citizens get more conservative public policies than we would get if women were represented at something like their number in the population.

This phenomenon—the paucity of political women—is a central issue that touches us all. As students of politics, we must devote some time to

---

[15]For a good summary of this literature, see Rita Mae Kelly, Michelle A. Saint Germain, and Jody D. Horn, "Female Public Officials: A Different Voice?" *Annals of The American Academy of Political and Social Science* 515 (1991): 77–87. See also Debra Dodson and Susan Carroll, *Reshaping the Legislative Agenda: Women in State Legislatures* (New Brunswick, NJ: Center for the American Woman and Politics, 1991); Susan Carroll, Debra Dodson, and Ruth Mandel, *The Impact of Women in Public Office* (New Brunswick, NJ: Center for the American Woman and Politics, 1991), esp. chap. 5; Sue Thomas, *How Women Legislate* (New York: Oxford University Press, 1994); and Joni Lovenduski and Pippa Norris, *Gender and Political Parties* (London: Sage, 1993).

understanding why it occurs. That means we must return to the concept of culture. It would be utterly impossible to explain the lack of women in power without reference to American norms, values, and social expectations. In other words, we must consider the broader culture within which U.S. politics take place.

Notice that if we try to understand this issue by examining narrower frameworks—the world of professional politics, for instance, or the realm of law—we get nowhere. Women aren't legally forbidden to run for political office. The political parties don't have rules preventing women from competing for nomination to public office. Voters don't even punish women who run for office by voting for their male competitors. When a man and a woman run against each other for any given office, studies show that (other things being equal) the man has no particular advantage.[16]

As far as law and politics go, then, women may freely compete for and win party nominations, go on to contest elections for office, and suffer no negative voter reaction when they do. Why, then, don't we find as many women *inside* politics as we do *outside* it, among the electorate?

Scholars have developed dozens of theories to explain this well-known phenomenon. We would need an entire book to account fully for it.[17] Yet one variable stands out as a central inhibitor of women's political activism. That is a simple but deepseated norm of American culture: Women, not men, have prime responsibility for the duties of homemaking and childrearing. Nowhere is this statement written down as law, but deeply implanted cultural beliefs have a stronger effect on human behavior than laws, which themselves are merely a reflection of those cultural beliefs. It will pay us to examine this norm and its many ramifications.

First, let's acknowledge it: Support for this norm is diminishing rapidly. We are all familiar with the changing relationship between men and women in our times, with the decline of traditional gender roles and norms. Still, the idea that women are homemakers and childrearers continues to maintain a significant hold on our society. But *even if it didn't*, I am going to argue, its near-universal acceptance in the recent past goes a long way toward explaining the small number of powerful women in the United States of the 1990s.

Why? Let us begin with a straightforward assertion: *power takes time to accumulate.* You have to work your way up the hierarchies of influence. Just as no one springs full-blown into the presidency of General Motors, so no

---

[16]See, for example, the evidence cited in R. Darcy, Susan Welch, and Janet Clark, *Women, Elections, and Representation* (New York: Longman, 1987), pp. 51–57 and 75–77.

[17]Many books already exist on the subject. Among the more useful, see Darcy, Welch, and Clark, op. cit., and Vicky Randall, *Women and Politics* (New York: St. Martin's Press, 1982).

one leaps from obscurity into the U.S. Senate.[18] Those who reach the upper levels of the American political system need first to attain education, status, and wealth and then convert those assets into the skills that produce political clout.

Many skills are needed to become a political leader: speaking ability, self-confidence, and persuasiveness, to name a few. You also need a variety of resources. Wealth is perhaps the most obvious one. Having good connections is another.

But of all the resources needed to become influential in American politics, two are especially crucial for explaining the predominance of men over women at the upper levels of power. First, you need a good deal of *time* to develop those political skills, mentioned previously, that are crucial to political success. You also need time to convince a broad public segment that you actually have those skills and should be rewarded for having them.

In other words, you don't graduate from high school and get elected senator. You have to study for and earn a college degree, then work for and attain a graduate degree (typically in law), then win a seat on some local or regional body (city council, county board of commissioners), then spend some time in the state legislature, go on to win a statewide office (attorney general, lieutenant governor), then perhaps gain your state's governorship or a seat in the U.S. House of Representatives, and finally after several years in one of these latter posts, make your bid for a U.S. Senate seat.

Naturally, there are other ways up the ladder of power, but all of them have this in common: They take time, and they don't come easily.

The difficulty of attaining political success leads to the second key requirement for gaining that success: *motivation*. There are few accidental powerholders in this world. *Those who get power want it and want it badly.* Consider the enormous expenditure of effort it takes to follow the previous scenario for political success. To be willing to exert yourself doggedly onward for years in order to rise to some serious level of political influence, you must be deeply motivated. That is to say, you must be career oriented, focused on making your way in the world, and willing to suffer those "slings and arrows of outrageous fortune," which are always associated with the bruising career path you have chosen. You must eat, sleep, and breathe politics—for years and years, from young adulthood to middle

---

[18]Well, almost no one. Exceptions do occur, on occasion. One of the most dramatic was the election of Joseph Biden to the U.S. Senate from Delaware in 1972. At the time he was twenty-nine years old, and his entire political experience prior to that date consisted of two years on the Wilmington (Del.) City Council! In fact, Biden was so young that he did not turn thirty until two weeks *after* his election to the Senate and had to keep reassuring people during the campaign that he would be old enough to take his seat if elected. (The U.S. Constitution forbids anyone under thirty from serving as a U.S. senator, although it doesn't prohibit voters from *electing* someone under thirty to the Senate.)

age—to have even a reasonable chance of arriving at the upper-middle to upper levels of the political power hierarchy.[19]

Now who is likely to start out in young adulthood with that orientation? Consider the U.S. political hierarchy as it currently exists (the mid–1990s). Given the time it takes to reach a serious level of political power, we can see that few powerholders will be much under forty years of age.[20] Of course, there will be many exceptions, but let's focus on the norm. The median age of the average powerholder in the United States today is somewhere in the range of forty-five to sixty years.

We start, then, with this age factor. You are going to be middle-aged or older before reaching serious political power. And this power doesn't just come and tap you on the shoulder. You need to make an intense commitment of your energies and resources for years and years if you wish to gain power. You don't, in other words, spend twenty years as an accountant or an architect or an assembly-line worker and then suddenly decide to become governor or senator. Or to put it more accurately, if you do decide to make that kind of midlife career decision, you have little hope of fulfilling it. If you haven't decided on a political career path by age thirty (or better still, by twenty or twenty-five), you aren't likely to rise far in politics.

I can think of one modest exception to this point. A person can occasionally trade power in some other line of work for political clout. A few people manage to make these lateral transfers from some other activity into political positions of real power; General Eisenhower, Ronald Reagan, and even Ross Perot are good examples. These people represent the world of the military, celebrityhood, and business. Going further back into the past, we can find similar examples: George Washington and Andrew Jackson from the military, for instance, celebrities like Horace Greeley or Will Rogers, and businessmen like William Randolph Hearst and Wendell Wilkie. All converted their fame from nonpolitical achievements into political influence of one kind or another *without* spending decades in the political process itself.

These seeming exceptions, on close examination, do little more than support the basic rule: You *still* must start early in life if you wish to attain political power. After all, these people who moved into politics from nonpolitical careers had first gained power for themselves in *another* key decision-making arena of society. All had clearly started early in life down the road toward power attainment. All had been obliged to struggle upward

---

[19]On the energy needed to move forward in politics, see James L. Payne and Oliver H. Woshinsky, "Incentives for Political Participation," *World Politics* 24 (1972): 518–46, esp. pp. 518–21.

[20]By "powerholder" in the United States, I am referring essentially to the president, vice-president, Cabinet and sub-Cabinet officers, House members, senators, Supreme Court justices, federal judges, governors, state legislative leaders, big-city mayors, top lobbyists, top political aides, and top media people.

for years in their chosen profession. All needed decades of perseverance to reach a point at which they could trade the resource of power in their own career path for power in the world of politics.

These "exceptions" merely underline, then, the main proposition. *Political power is rarely attained without two or three decades of grueling effort,* beginning usually during the ages of twenty to thirty.

We must confront one additional fact before putting this argument together to explain why few women are currently found in positions of political power in the United States. A number of studies have shown that the average person's value system (his or her outlook on life) is shaped, roughly, during ages fifteen to twenty-five.[21] It will, of course, vary considerably from person to person. Furthermore, beliefs, once developed, aren't permanent; most people undergo modest changes in their thinking during the course of life. Still, the bulk of evidence suggests that after age thirty, at the latest, most of us will not deviate seriously from the central perspectives on life that we developed by that age.

By thirty, that means, most of us are pretty well set in our views on politics, religion, and society. We are liberal or conservative, feminist or traditionalist, religious or agnostic, rigid toward minorities or tolerant. For most of us, those perspectives developed early and often unconsciously, came to be understood and expressed between ages fifteen and twenty, then matured and hardened in the following decade. By thirty, we have a full-fledged world outlook and cling to it for the rest of life. With these facts in mind we conclude by simple mathematics that Americans aged about fifty today began to absorb their essential view of gender roles some time in the late 1950s.

Let us now put all of these points together. Average powerholders in the United States today are forty-five to sixty years old. These people must have *decided* to start seeking power in their twenties. Their basic outlook on life started being shaped ten years before that—in their teens. The vast majority of people who currently hold power today, then, came of age between 1950 and 1970. Imprinted on their brain cells are the ideas that dominated that era. And what were those ideas? Whatever else we associate with that time, it was characterized by traditional norms about the division of labor between men and women. It was the era of suburbia and the baby boom. Men were to have careers, whereas women were to raise children and keep house. Public activities (like politics) were for men, whereas private activities (the home) was the proper sphere for women.

---

[21]See, for example, Angus Campbell, Philip E. Converse, Warren E. Miller, and Donald Stokes, *The American Voter* (Chicago: University of Chicago Press, 1960), chap. 7; and M. Kent Jennings and Richard G. Niemi, *Generations and Politics: A Panel Study of Young Adults and Their Parents* (Princeton: Princeton University Press, 1981), chap. 4.

"The past is a foreign country," said L.P. Hartley. "They do things differently there."[22] It is always hard to enter the mind-set of another era, but we must try. Although it may seem incredible, women were *forbidden* to enter most law schools as late as the early 1970s. Women were legally *forced* to take their husband's name upon marriage. They could not get credit in their own names. Single women could not obtain mortgages to buy houses. These examples could continue for pages. The National Organization for Women (NOW), a crucial pressure group for women's rights in our time, was not even founded until 1966. No one noticed the event. NOW hardly entered national consciousness until the 1970s. *Ms. Magazine* published its first issue in 1972. The first woman elected governor in her own right (not as the spouse of some famous politician) was Ella Grasso of Connecticut in 1974.

People coming of age in the 1940s, 1950s, and 1960s—that is, those people most likely to be at the height of their political careers in the *1990s*—would have developed their political and social beliefs at a time when current feminist ideals stressing women's equality with men were hardly imagined by the average American citizen, male *or* female. Indeed, the precept that men have careers and women raise children was perhaps *at its height* when Americans who are currently middle-aged first came of political and social consciousness.

This cultural outlook, deeply ingrained in the children of the 1950s, gave a tremendous power advantage to the young men of that time over young women. A female baby boomer, by ages fifteen to twenty, would have accepted the norm that her social duty was to get married and start raising children. She might someday expect to "get a job," primarily to "help out" with family expenses, but she was rarely expected to *have a career,* especially not in any walk of life involving competition for power.

In only a few work areas was the 1950s woman actually allowed a career. We know those specialties as the "caring" or "nurturing" professions (teaching, nursing, secretarial help). They symbolized an extension of the "primary" female role and, as such, presented no threat to men. These jobs derived from activities centered on the home, from the woman's role there as nurturer, caregiver, and helper. Most men didn't want these jobs, so women moved into them. Indeed, men encouraged them to do so.

Teenage males, by way of contrast, had been raised in the expectation of spending their entire lives building careers. At the least, they knew that they had to prepare for a life of continuous work outside the home, work in the paid labor force, in order to support a family (that is, wife and children).

Society taught these norms to most young people in the 1940s, 1950s, and 1960s. True, not everyone conformed. Some women raised in the 1950s sought careers and attained power. Some men of that era stayed home and

---

[22]Hartley, *The Go-Between* (London: H. Hamilton, 1953), Prologue, p.9.

raised children. They were the exceptions, however. The vast majority of people raised in that time behaved as the norms of that day dictated. Men finished school and went right to work. Many pursued careers associated with power—in the world of business, the military, law, or politics. Women raised children and shunned careers—except in a few traditional areas that never lead to societal power. (Quick! Name a famous librarian. Name a renowned nurse. Name a celebrated fourth-grade teacher. Get the point?)

These norms and work patterns devastated women's chances of ever reaching political power. First, they made women feel that the world of politics was for men only; hence, they simply stayed out of it. Furthermore, the skills that women developed from the activities they did engage in (childrearing) were not, in any obvious way, directly transferable to the world of politics. Knowing how to potty train a two-year-old does not help you learn to give a rousing political speech. Knowing how to teach a six-year-old to read doesn't help you become an expert on defense policy. Knowing how to cook macaroni-and-cheese doesn't help you learn the subtle art of winning party nominations.

Finally, the time and effort that women had to put into the years of childbearing, childrearing, and homemaking insured that they would be unable to devote much attention to the world of power gathering until it was essentially "too late." That is, if a woman in her early twenties started having children and had three or four (as was the norm for 1950s families), she would probably find herself in her early forties before her last child had entered the teen years and become reasonably independent. If she *then* decided to embark on a career that might lead to a power position, notice how greatly disadvantaged she became, in comparison to her male contemporaries (also in their early forties) who had been doggedly pursuing that very career path for the last twenty years.

Of course, the knowledge gained by women in those intervening years counts for something. Maturity and experience are assets that can be converted into skills that are useful in the struggle for power. But even with the best efforts and the best will in the world from well-wishers in society, any person, male or female, just starting out to achieve something at forty-two is at a severe disadvantage compared with another person of forty-two who has been pursuing that same objective since age sixteen (or twenty-three or twenty-eight).

This chain of reasoning suggests that by the time some woman, who doesn't decide until her forties to get into politics, starts to amass a serious amount of influence, she will be reaching, roughly, age sixty or older, a time when most people are more likely to be thinking of retirement than of continuing the difficult struggle for political power. Furthermore, voters and party activists (especially in youth-obsessed America) may start looking for a younger candidate to fill whatever job the sixty-year-old woman has her eye on.

In short, even if a middle-aged women successfully gets past her early socialization into traditional gender roles, completes her decades of childrearing with some reasonable level of energy left to embark on her own career, and even if she does quite well at developing that career, she is *still* likely to arrive too late at the threshold of power to be able to make the leap over that threshold and into real power itself before deciding, or having the matter decided for her by a fickle electorate, that she is "too old" to be promoted any further up the rungs of the political ladder.

As if these facts weren't harsh enough, we must add yet another array of grim data. The older any population gets, the more likely it is that its members will fall by the wayside, succumbing to a variety of illnesses that either kill them or force them out of serious competition for power. These are statistical generalizations, but overall they hurt women badly in the struggle for upward political mobility. Let's say it takes twenty-five years on average to go from the day you receive your law degree to the U.S. Senate. If you get your degree at age twenty-seven, you will become senator at fifty-two. Few healthy Americans of age twenty-seven die before age fifty-two. Most don't even get seriously ill in that time frame.

But if you don't decide to start law school until age forty-two (when your children are grown), then you don't get your law degree until age forty-five, and you don't get to the Senate until you are seventy! Now many more Americans die, or become seriously ill, between forty-two and seventy than between twenty-two and fifty. Simply on the basis of these cruel facts of illness and mortality, we would expect that many fewer women than men would get to high levels of power, *if* women start their careers twenty years later. And we have already shown that they are likely to do exactly that, if they were born in the United States some time between 1945 and 1970.

Notice how far we have come. We have gained some serious insights into a key political pattern, by following a simple line of reasoning.

> Cultures affect politics.
>
> Specifically, cultures affect politics by implanting deep-seated norms into people's heads, norms that affect how people behave in the social world.
>
> One deep-seated norm in American society of the 1940s and 1950s held that men and women were to play different roles in life, men seeking careers aimed at giving them wealth, power, fame, and status, and women staying at home to raise families.
>
> This gender-division norm from the 1950s explains why men dominated American politics in the 1980s and 1990s.

This example illustrates the power of a social analysis that begins by focusing on culture.

WOMEN AND POLITICS: A NEW ERA

Incidentally, we can use this same approach to explain a dramatic new trend on the American political scene. The era of few women in American politics is coming to an end. Indeed, we are now witnessing the definite emergence of women onto the political scene and their rise to the upper level of American institutions. The 1990s appears to be the decade when women finally gained a serious share of political power.

Why have women gained their recent clout in politics? To answer that question, we must return to the same reasoning we used to explain why women were rarely found in politics in earlier years. If the norms young people absorb in their teenage years traditionally helped men and hurt women in the long-term struggle for political power, then changing those norms could make the playing field level. And changing norms is exactly what happened.

Even before the mid–1960s, some Americans had started questioning traditional gender roles.[23] Traditional attitudes began seriously eroding by 1970, and by the mid–1970s the modern feminist movement was in full swing. Indeed, by the 1980s it was taken for granted by the majority of Americans that women should have legal equality with men, that they had the right to pursue careers of their own, and that governments should work to obliterate the most egregious forms of gender discrimination.[24]

Given this development, we fully expect to find, as time goes by, an increasing number of women at the upper levels of all prestigious, power-wielding institutions of American life. Specifically, we can even predict that by the time women who were around fifteen in 1975 reach fifty, the number of women in serious positions of political power will look a great deal more like equality than it does now. That means keep a sharp eye out for the year 2010!

Just to be cautious, I'll predict numerical gender equality at all levels of American politics by the year 2020. I will also predict an increasing number of women in political power as each year passes between now and then.

We don't have to wait long to check on this prediction. Just in case it doesn't pan out, however, I have an explanation at the ready. Change is a law of life, but no trend is irreversible. The drive toward a redefinition of woman's traditional homemaker role could peter out or reverse itself, depending on future social, economic, and cultural developments, which

---

[23]The most famous and influential example of this questioning came in 1963 from Betty Friedan in her groundbreaking and eloquent plea for feminism, *The Feminine Mystique* (New York: Dell Publishing Company, 1963). For a survey of efforts on behalf of women's rights in this era, see Susan M. Hartmann, *From Margin to Mainstream: American Women and Politics since 1960* (New York: Alfred A. Knopf, 1989), esp. pp. 48–71.

[24]On recent American attitudes toward gender equality, see the data reported by Virginia Sapiro, "Feminism: A Generation Later," in *Annals of the American Academy of Political and Social Science* 515 (1991): 10–22.

no one can foresee. Perhaps the Dan Quayle-Pat Robertson perspective on these matters will gather steam and overwhelm the forces of the Hillary Clintons and Donna Shalalas. I doubt it, but stranger developments have occurred in history. Who would have predicted the rise of fundamental Islam in the Middle East, setting back for decades the cause of women's rights in that region? I am personally betting on the advance of gender equality in the United States (and everywhere else, for that matter), but ultimately only time will tell.[25]

Before closing this discussion, let us note that in describing social phenomena, the analyst must be objective. The job of the student of human behavior is to observe and explain with impartiality. The goal is to achieve a dispassionate analysis. In describing the circumstances that traditionally restricted women to powerlessness, I was hardly advocating their desirability; I was trying to understand and explain reality. If a cultural norm affects political outcomes in important ways, political analysts would be remiss in failing to inform their readers.

It is important to note that there exist few universal generalizations about human behavior. A given pattern today may or may not exist tomorrow. That depends on what caused the pattern and on whether or not those causes change. Change the cause of some human behavior, and you will change the behavior as well.[26]

These propositions apply specifically to the issue under discussion: gender equality. The cause of male political domination lies in the gender norms of our culture, which have been undergoing change. We should hardly be surprised to see these new norms produce a different set of effects. Our societal values once favored men; now they stress equality. They insured male domination of politics in the past. Now and into the foreseeable future they encourage a trend toward male-female sharing of political power.

Whether one hates or supports this development, it exists and it produces important political outcomes. Our job is to describe and explain. Powerful women were scarce in the past because of traditional cultural norms. Powerful women are more numerous now and will be much more numerous in the future because of modern cultural norms. If you wish to understand American politics—past, present, and future—you have to know these facts.

Now if you want to reverse or quicken the trend, that's another matter altogether. You must then get involved in politics and work to achieve your

[25]For a chilling vision of a different future from the one I imagine, a future in which American women lose all rights and become oppressed slaves, read Margaret Atwood's grim novel, *The Handmaiden's Tale* (Boston: Houghton Mifflin, 1986).

[26]Of course, change may be a long time in coming, especially if the original cause has existed for decades and has had time to create deeply embedded attitudes and behavior patterns. See the discussion in Chapter 6 of this text ('The Persistence of Culture').

goals. The analyst's job is not to teach what your goals should be, but to help you understand the world as it is. What you wish the world to be is your own business. When you start trying to change the world to match your own desires, you become a political participant, an activist, and part of the very world that analysts like me work to explain. If you take that route, I wish you the best of luck as you set off to realize your aims. In the meantime, I shall get back to the task at hand: explaining the world of politics as it currently works.

SUMMARY

Norms—deepseated beliefs about how people should behave—produce a powerful effect on society. When most people in any culture share a norm, they will act in a manner congruent with that norm. Norms, to put it simply, influence social behavior. It follows that any norm in any culture will influence political behavior, since all behavior is intertwined. We cannot separate social from economic from political activity.

This chapter has provided several examples of the way cultural norms affect politics. These examples merely scratch the surface. We could multiply them indefinitely. To understand the wellsprings of political action, we must learn the norms that underpin human thought. When we see any given pattern of political behavior, we must ask what cultural outlook has produced that particular way of dealing with political issues. This perspective, one that owes much to the insights of *cultural anthropology*,[27] will guide our thinking as we move forward to learn about the many, varied forms of political behavior.

[27]For the classic expression of this perspective, see Benedict, *Patterns of Culture*, op. cit. For a recent summary of the approach, see Michael C. Howard, *Contemporary Cultural Anthropology*, 2d ed. (Boston: Little, Brown and Company, 1986).

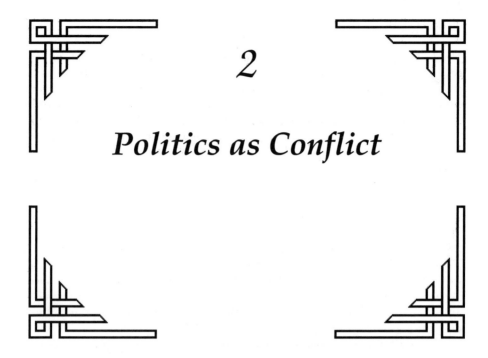

2

Politics as Conflict

All Americans have sat entranced through some electrifying political soap opera. For those of us intrigued by politics, it almost seems as if political elites stage these dramas every so often solely for our personal amusement. Who can forget the time Anita Hill took on Clarence Thomas and the Senate Judiciary Committee? Or the summer when Oliver North took on the entire U.S. Congress? Or the House Judiciary Committee's impeachment hearings on Richard Nixon? And those with long memories can happily recall that exciting melodrama, "the Army–McCarthy hearings," when Senator Joseph McCarthy battled the world communist menace *and* the U.S. Army at the same time (a death-defying feat, politically, which explains why he ended up being soundly trounced and sent off into oblivion).

Many of us, on the other hand, have sat on numbingly hard benches well into the night, trying to stay awake as we watched our town council debate the funding of a new waste disposal system.

POLITICS AS DRAMA

These differing experiences teach us that the world of politics is wildly diverse. It encompasses a bewildering array of activities. These can range from emotional scenes of the highest drama to dreary subcommittee arguments over soybean subsidies.

Although politics can vary from the dramatic to the dreary, most of our attention focuses on its exciting, peak moments. These times of high tension take a variety of forms. Senators and witnesses at a congressional hearing in our era may occasionally lose tempers, speak sharply, even yell. In the nineteenth century Senate confrontations took on a more dramatic form. Senators frequently came armed to the legislative chamber. In a famous 1856 incident, Representative Preston Brooks of South Carolina charged onto the Senate floor and with his cane severely beat Senator Charles Sumner of Massachusetts.[1] Journalists today sometimes accuse committee chairs of "browbeating" witnesses. Note, however, that a nineteenth century committee chair once drew a pistol, pointed it at a disliked witness, and shouted, "If you say another word, sir, I shall blow your head off!" Now *that's* real browbeating.

The United States hardly holds a monopoly on politics as drama. Its political life is positively genteel compared to that in other countries. Deputies in Colombia, on the very floor of the legislature, call each other names, throw inkwells, overturn wastebaskets, bang on tables, and encourage catcalling or cheering from partisans in the balcony.[2] In the newly formed Russian Republic, the heckling of speakers with whom you disagree is common. In a celebrated recent incident the prime minister was jostled and shoved as members of two opposing factions scuffled with each other for control of the microphone.[3]

Of course, political struggles in many places go far beyond even these relatively minor confrontations. As South Africa neared the end of its discredited *apartheid* system, blacks struggling for future political control killed each other regularly on the streets of tension-ridden townships. Saddam Hussein bombed Kurdish and Shiite villages in an effort to consolidate his hold on power in Iraq. Serbs systematically raped Bosnian Muslim women in an effort to win a war through demoralization of their foes.

The drama of politics can quickly turn from spectacle to tragedy. As these examples suggest, the distance is short from an engrossing clash of ideas to bloody battles between vengeful rivals.

Although politics, like any human activity, does have its serene, ordinary, and even dull moments, its central characteristic springs from its confrontational drama. And what produces this drama? The answer is simple: conflict. In essence, politics is about conflict and how people deal with con-

---

[1]Brooks believed Sumner had maligned his cousin, Senator Andrew P. Butler, also of South Carolina, during a Senate debate on slavery. Brooks swore to uphold his cousin's honor and disabled Senator Sumner before dozens of horrified witnesses. Sumner never fully recovered from the beating.

[2]For a description of the way legislators operate in Colombia, see James L. Payne, *Patterns of Conflict in Colombia* (New Haven, CT: Yale University Press, 1968), chap. 11 ('The Colombian Congress'), pp. 238–67, esp. pp. 246–48.

[3]See the description of this incident in the *New York Times*, December 4, 1992, p. A–3.

flict. If there were no human conflict, if we all agreed with each other all the time, we simply would not have politics. Political activity occurs when people and groups *fail* to agree with each other. When people with disagreements take action to gain their opposing ends, thereby clashing with each other in ways that affect society as a whole—*then* you have politics. And you have politics everywhere and at all times, because conflict appears everywhere and at all times, because people disagree with each other everywhere and at all times. Politics derives from the fact that people are always working against each other to achieve incompatible goals.

THE NATURE OF CONFLICT

Not all conflict, of course, is political. Every culture arbitrarily defines some conflict as nonpolitical. Two young men fighting outside a bar at midnight is not normally seen as a political act. A husband and wife shouting at each other is a family drama with few obvious political implications. But in China today those events might be considered political. They imply nonsocial behavior, which is a crime against the state. Participants might be sentenced to many hours of community service and forced to attend a number of "political education" sessions.

Any conflict, then, can assume political ramifications. Bar fights and marital disputes aren't usually considered political in the United States. But if gangs of young men started fighting each other with guns outside dozens of bars every evening in dozens of cities, *then* demands that political leaders do something would quickly surface. If enough husbands and wives shouted at each other and then went on to seek divorce, groups would quickly spring up to make divorce easier to obtain. Just as quickly, other groups would surface to oppose "this immoral breakdown of traditional social values." Street brawls and family tiffs *can*, in the right condition, become the stuff of politics.

It would appear that conflict between individuals or groups, escalated even slightly, will take on political overtones. Since conflict is common, its escalation is also likely to be common. Hence, the ubiquitous nature of politics.

Let us take one step back and ask an obvious question. Just why is *conflict* common? This question can be addressed in several ways. At the level of metaphysics, philosophers and theologians have sometimes asserted that evil is inherent in human nature. If that were true, severe conflict would be forever inevitable. There wouldn't be much we could do but get out of the way as people killed each other. At the level of chemistry some scientists have underlined the power of hormonal imbalance. The idea is popular in some quarters that excessive testosterone produces male violence. If chemical deficiencies cause human conflict, we might want to urge governments to fund research on "aggression-dampening pills" to insure future world peace.

Another way to explain conflict borrows from the insights of *social psychology*. To understand conflict, using this approach, start with a simple fact: Human beings are incredibly complex organisms. Each of us differs from everyone else—in our skills, our goals, our life outlook, and our self-identification. Close friends, even siblings, have different aims in life, differing views about what is good and true and desirable. They disagree, argue, and sometimes clash violently. Think how well *you* get along with your sister or brother—or cousins or father or mother! Can you think of any large family gathering that hasn't produced its tensions and disputes?

Now if even close relatives can clash sharply, how much more likely is it that unrelated individuals, raised in wildly different cultural settings under strikingly different childrearing methods, will see the world in dramatically contrasting ways?

Consider the disparity between poor urban blacks and wealthy white suburbanites. Or between southern fundamentalist conservatives and northern Jewish liberals. Or between Bosnian Serbs, Croats, and Muslims. Should it surprise us that people in radically different groups will seek mutually exclusive goals, each using means considered illegitimate by the other side? Should we be astonished that they will regard each other as operating outside the boundaries of "common humanity" (as people in each group have been raised to imagine it)?

Add to this recipe one additional ingredient. Resources in this world are scarce, needs are many, and wants are unlimited. Almost none of us get all of the goodies from life that we desire and think we need; most of us are continually striving for more. Since there is only so much to go around, your getting more often means I get less—or at least I often perceive it that way. And of course, my imagined dislike of you for (supposedly) taking what I deserve is exacerbated by any actual difference between us—in race, language, ritual, or religion.

In short, since people differ from each other and seek different goals using different means in a universe of scarce resources, they are, on a regular basis, bound to collide. Confrontation and conflict are inevitable. Politics therefore also becomes inevitable. *Politics within any nation is nothing more than the process whereby that society confronts and deals with the implications of conflict among its citizens.*[4] Where you have conflict, there you will have politics. And since you will always have conflict, if this view of human nature is correct, you will also always have politics.

---

[4]We could add that conflict at the international level is nothing more than the process whereby the world community confronts and deals with the implications of conflict among nations (or conflict within a given nation that touches, or is defined as touching, the interests of one or more other nations of the world).

James Madison expressed this perspective best in his famous essays on political life, which form part of the work we know today as *The Federalist Papers*. "What is government," Madison asked, ". . . but the greatest of all reflections on human nature?"[5] And Madison's view of human nature is dark. People in his eyes are self-interested, quick to promote their own goals, and suspicious of others' motives. "If men [*sic*] were angels," he declared, "no government would be necessary."[6] But since human beings are not angels—that is, since they forever want more than they currently have, constantly strive to get it, and resent others competing for the same ends—they will always be in conflict with each other. Hence, says Madison, they need government (that is, politics) to help them sort things out and prevent the continual violence of individual confrontation that produces anarchy.

"In this world nothing can be said to be certain," claimed Benjamin Franklin, "except death and taxes." He might well have added politics to that list. One can't avoid conflict in human affairs. Neither, therefore, can one avoid politics.

Not all conflict produces politics, as we noted previously. Society does not intervene every time two or more people clash. It may ignore some conflicts altogether—usually by defining them as nonpolitical. When two isolated individuals disagree in Western nations, it is usually said to be a matter for the law, not for politics. And conflict between family members is viewed in many societies as a private matter.

Still, any conflict has the *potential* to become political. Society may, any time it chooses, define any conflict as an issue for the public agenda. Spouse battering and child abuse—forms of conflict within the family—were once treated as strictly "private" issues. Many past societies allowed the most powerful male in each household to control family members through physical and emotional intimidation. The Romans, for instance, gave fathers the power of life and death over their children up to the age of sixteen. Society used to shut its eyes to within-family brutality. It was able to do so by accepting the myth that what occurred inside the family was irrelevant to those outside it and therefore not a fit subject for political decision making.

Western political systems have in recent decades consciously decided to define within-family conflict as political. This decision justifies the possibility of state intervention. Spouse battering and child abuse, for instance, are now illegal. Violation of the law can bring police and court action. By redefining some types of family conflict as political, society has in effect reduced the power it traditionally granted to the dominant family member. Sweden has perhaps gone farthest of all nations in this direction. Its govern-

---

[5]Madison's celebrated words occur in Federalist Paper Number 51. For this specific quote, see Alexander Hamilton, James Madison, and John Jay, *The Federalist Papers*, with an introduction and commentary by Gary Wills (Toronto: Bantam Books, 1982), p. 262.
[6]Ibid.

ment has decided to make illegal *any* corporal punishment of children. (In other words, don't spank your children in Stockholm. They may haul you before a court of law.)

DEALING WITH CONFLICT

Conflicts that seem at first to have only personal implications can enter the political process in strange, often roundabout ways. A favorite way for Americans to resolve disputes, as I suggested earlier, is through legal action rather than politics. As a result, U.S. citizens have an inordinate number of lawyers. That is to say, Americans produce a significant number of technicians skilled in conflict resolution, because we choose to confront each other formally in courts over issues of disagreement. That is our cultural pattern. In other cultures, people might (a) ignore the conflict, (b) work it out between themselves, (c) use a council of elders or a neighborhood self-help group to resolve it, or (d) simply fight it out.

Oddly enough, this American use of law instead of politics to deal with conflict has itself produced a debate within American politics. Some observers are now suggesting that Americans have "too many lawyers." They argue that we live in an "excessively litigious" society, that lawyers cost all of us a good deal of money. They claim, among other things, that lawyers encourage frivolous lawsuits, which waste society's resources of time, energy, and cash. Lawyers also (this brief against the legal profession goes on) persuade juries to make absurdly high awards to winners of malpractice suits, thereby driving up insurance costs and thus forcing doctors to multiply the number of medical tests they perform. The very method that American society evolved to deal with conflict (turning to the law instead of politics) turns out to be politically controversial in its own right.

All conflicts, then, even those that seem merely personal, can lead to politics. Through the political process, society confronts and deals with conflict it can no longer ignore. Note that *dealing with* conflict does not necessarily mean *resolving* it. Many societies exacerbate conflict through the political process, eventually insuring the escalation of natural human disagreement into bloody armed confrontation between fanatically opposed groupings. Other societies "deal with" conflict by suppressing it. The use of strong governments to repress dissent has been common throughout history.

Another way to deal with conflict is simply to deny that it exists. Turkey for years denied that it had a restless Kurdish minority. It called its Kurds "mountain Turks" and refused to consider the legitimacy of their efforts at regional autonomy. Likewise, Greece today denies the existence of a Macedonian minority. People in the Greek province of Macedonia "are Greeks, period," say government spokespersons, and by implication have no legitimate right to any special political claims on the Greek government.

Defining issues as nonpolitical is one of the principal ways whereby American society deals with political conflict. Like Greeks and Turks, Americans often close their eyes to the conflict between themselves and a nearly invisible indigenous group, Native Americans. In addition, conflict between workers and the owners of capital is also frequently denied. (Indeed, capitalist ideology usually suggests a close harmony of interest between these two groups.) In other cases, the United States simply defines certain types of conflict as "illegitimate," not suitable issues for the political process. Conflict between husband and wife, as we have seen, was long denied as a proper subject for the realm of politics. Another issue once defined as politically irrelevant was society's treatment of its gay and lesbian members.

All societies define some conflicts as nonpolitical. All societies deny the very existence of other conflicts. As analysts of the political scene, our job is not to swallow any society's political line on this topic, but to examine the implications of these definitions and denials. To deny that a particular conflict is politically legitimate is itself a political statement. It means that the groups being denied access to the political process can legitimately be ignored—or worse, repressed—if they do attempt to force themselves into the political process.

The very act of denying that some aspect of life is political is itself a profoundly political act—and often a clever political maneuver, one might add. Deciding what is or is not political is the ultimate political action. Not until society defines an issue as political does it allow the machinery of government and the focus of the political elite to be brought to bear in deciding that issue's fate. In American society, we decided a decade or two ago that spouse abuse was a political issue. We are currently in the process of deciding whether the treatment of gay people is a political or private matter.

Exacerbation, repression, compromise, or *denial*: These are the four ways by which societies tackle conflict. They result in four different political styles, which we might call: *conflictual, suppressive, cooperative,* and *disconnected.* We shall later examine what societies look like when they stress one or another of these approaches to conflict. For the moment, however, let us examine some additional evidence on the inevitability of conflict in human affairs.

THE INEVITABILITY OF CONFLICT

I have argued that politics is inevitable because conflict is inevitable, and that conflict is inevitable because people differ seriously from each other in wants, aims, and beliefs while living in a world of scarce resources. Working toward opposing goals, people naturally find themselves at odds with each other. Once people find themselves at odds, a natural human tendency works to increase the intensity of any conflict: Most of us see our own goals as "right" and "proper." What *we* want is "the morally correct thing." Armies rarely march off to war without believing that "God is on our side."

Human beings have a wonderful ability to rationalize their desires as ethically proper. A famous scholar once defined "political man" *[sic]* as someone whose inner needs were "displaced onto public objects and rationalized in terms of the public interest."[7] Man or woman, liberal or conservative, most of us operate by this principle. We develop a way to explain our subconscious drives that makes them sound morally legitimate, as if fulfilling some higher purpose and not just our own base satisfaction. This moral certainty about the rightness of our own goals, carried into politics by each participant (who there confronts others with differing goals but equally certain of their own rectitude), always insures a serious level of political tension in all societies.

We can all recall examples of this tendency to see our own goals as moral. Do we all not believe that we personally pay too many taxes and receive too few government benefits? And don't we all know people who should be paying *more* taxes and receiving *fewer* benefits? There are too many "welfare cheats" out there, or "fat cats" avoiding taxes. Unfortunately, *they* are thinking the same thing—but applying it to us! No wonder we come into conflict.

Members of congress exemplify this tendency to rationalize individual desires as universal truths. Most Americans are convinced that the federal government is "too big," its taxes "too high." To cut taxes, we need to cut programs—and most Americans also agree with that. The problem is that no Americans want their *own* programs to be cut. So members of Congress are under intense pressure to cut programs—in all other members' districts, that is, but not their own. They are instead under intense pressure to keep and even add programs that benefit constituents in their own district. No wonder it's impossible to cut government spending.

One of the great advocates of tax cutting and deficit reduction is Senator Phil Gramm of Texas, prime sponsor of the famous 1986 Gramm-Rudman-Hollings Act that was supposed to wipe out federal government deficits by 1991. Yet even this famous opponent of government largesse is a zealous supporter of a seemingly absurd $190 *million* tax subsidy for wool and mohair producers. Why should the U.S. government pay people to produce mohair wool? Because, apparently, most of those who benefit from this subsidy happen to live in Texas and coincidentally are Gramm's own constituents. If even a cost-conscious crusader like Phil Gramm succumbs

---

[7]Harold D. Lasswell, *Psychopathology and Politics* (Chicago: University of Chicago Press, 1930), p. 75.

to this attitude of "do favors for those who elect me," who could be immune from these pressures?[8]

This pattern of congressional politics is best seen when it comes to cutting defense spending. Almost everyone agrees these days that we have a "bloated" Defense Department. Furthermore, most of us expect a "peace dividend" now that the cold war is over. A good way to save money and cut government spending, in theory, would be to close down some of our military bases. We don't need as many as we once did, given the demise of our archenemy, the Soviet Union. Besides, some of those bases were nothing but unnecessary porkbarrel nonsense in the first place. So the argument goes. Under these conditions, we can all agree: Let us by all means shut down some military bases.

Now a natural question arises: Which military bases, specifically, should be closed and which should be kept open? The answer, for each member of Congress, is simple. *Your* base is outmoded, superfluous, and redundant. It must be closed. *My* base is efficient, essential to the national defense, and on the cutting edge of modern military technology. It must be kept open.

Few events in politics are more amusing than the spectacle of our nation's lawmakers running for cover when the base closure issue appears. The close observer of politics then delights at an extraordinary alliance. Hidebound conservatives, who believe that all government programs must be abolished immediately, suddenly find friendship with liberals, who castigate the Pentagon for excessive waste and greedy militarism. All factions in Congress unite on this one point: We must defend all military bases that are essential to insure continued world peace, international security, and the American way of life. Coincidentally, all bases that meet this definition just happen to be in these particular politicians' districts.

The inconsistencies of other people are always amusing—especially when the other people are politicians. The rest of us must not feel superior, however. We don't act any differently from the way members of Congress do. Indeed, our political representatives reflect popular desires quite well. They do what we urge them to do. Think, after all, how you would react if your senator came back from Washington and argued that a military base in your town was *indeed* outmoded, a waste of taxpayer money, and a candidate for instant mothballing? Would you send this person a check and volunteer to work on her reelection campaign?

To bring the point closer to home, how would you feel if politicians you knew started campaigning for immediate closure of your state university system? They might make their case on the grounds of "good fiscal management;" it would help balance the state budget. Or they might claim

---

[8]On Gramm's support for wool and mohair producers, see Mary McGrory, "Wool vs. Voluntarism," *Boston Globe*, August 13, 1993, p. 17.

that state support for university education was incompatible with a free market system. Whatever their reasoning, politicians who took this "bold and principled" stand would lose their jobs at the earliest opportunity. Why should we expect politicians to be any more noble than the rest of us?

The point is not that politicians are being hypocritical and venal when they defend projects deeply desired by their constituents. They, like the rest of us, quickly come to believe in the validity of the programs that serve their goals. Students and teachers believe in the universal value of education. Police officers believe in the importance to society of law-enforcement activities. Business leaders are firmly convinced that lowering the capital gains tax is good for national economic growth. Workers believe that everyone benefits when the minimum wage is increased. In other words, whatever serves our interest we quickly define as part of God's plan for the universe.

Just as we can persuade ourselves of the morality and wisdom of our own aims, so we often imagine that the goals of other people are illegitimate—even immoral or evil. That is especially true when their goals get in the way of our own. We rarely consider people to be goodhearted, just, and wise when they are blocking progress toward something we desire. Since our own goals are right, those who oppose us must be wrong. This attitude can quickly lead to rationalizing the legitimacy of violent acts against others (government crackdowns, street riots, lynchings). Unfortunately, the people you oppose are thinking about you in exactly the same way. You are an immoral evil-doer preventing them from attaining their own cherished aims. If most humans reason this way, no wonder conflict (and politics) is inevitably present in all societies.

One additional factor, uncovered by some quirky experiments in social psychology, explains the inevitability of conflict. It appears that simply dividing people into groups, however random and meaningless the basis for the division, creates a feeling of group loyalty. In short order there develops what social psychologists call ingroup bias and outgroup prejudice. "The mere division of people into groups," writes Walter G. Stephan, "leads to biased evaluations [by in-group members] . . . and to discrimination . . . against out-group members."[9]

In a typical piece of research Tajfel and associates gave some boys a meaningless task to perform: estimating the number of dots on a piece of paper. After making several estimates, each boy was randomly categorized by the experimenter; some were told that they were "overestimators," while others gained the label "underestimator." When later asked to assign rewards to other boys whom they had never met, each boy was more generous to fellows who shared his label than to those in the other category.

---

[9]Stephan, "Intergroup Relations," in Gardner Lindzey and Elliot Aronson, eds., *Handbook of Social Psychology*, Vol. II, 3d ed (New York: Random House, 1985), p. 613.

Additional research showed that the boys retained this tendency toward ingroup identification and outgroup hostility even when informed that their label had been randomly assigned to them.[10]

In another experiment Jane Elliott, an Iowa schoolteacher, divided her third-graders into "brown-eyed people" and "blue-eyed people," suggesting some superficial reasons why they should distrust each other. Before long, each group had come to develop a strong collective identity—along with a clear dislike, bordering on hatred, for the other group[11].

In a similar experiment, Zimbardo divided a class of students randomly into "jailers" and "prisoners" to study role-playing behavior. These students were to simulate the conditions typical of a modern prison. Although Zimbardo had planned to have the experiment last two weeks, he was forced to cancel it after just six days. The students had gotten too zealously into their respective roles. "Guards" were acting like callous brutes toward the clearly hated "prisoners." The "prisoners," ordinary students who had been locked up and treated as convicts, began showing all those signs of psychological breakdown and pathological confusion typical of people who, in real life, are subject to feelings of utter helplessness in totally controlling institutions.[12]

In the most famous study of this type, Sherif and associates divided boys in a summer camp randomly into two groups, and encouraged them to compete against each other in every manner of activity. A state of near-war soon existed between the two sides.[13]

The power of these experiments lies in the meaninglessness, the artificiality, of the original groups. All participants began as nearly identical members of the same society: young, white, suburban, and middle-class. In several experiments of this type, two additional variables were held constant: Participants were all of the same age and sex. These extremely similar people were then divided into components that had no societal basis whatsoever. The randomly constructed groups did not represent people of dif-

---

[10]H. Tajfel, M.L. Billig, R.P. Bundy, and C. Flament, "Social Categorization and Intergroup Behavior," *European Journal of Social Psychology* 1 (1971): 149–78; and M. Billig and H. Tajfel, "Social Categorization and Similarity in Intergroup Behavior," *European Journal of Social Psychology* 3 (1973): 27–52.

[11]This experiment is described in David L. Watson, Gail deBortali-Tregerthan, and Joyce Frank, *Social Psychology: Science and Application* (Glenview, IL: Scott, Foresman and Company, 1984), pp. 186–7. Dozens of experiments have shown this tendency of people to form in-group bonds and out-group hatreds, even when group membership occurred on a purely random basis. See especially Fredrik Barth, ed, *Ethnic Groups and Boundaries: The Social Organization of Culture Difference* (Boston: Little, Brown and Co., 1969), esp. ch. 1. For a summary of some of this literature, see Myers, *Social Psychology*, op. cit., pp. 389–91 and Stephan, "Intergroup Relations," op. cit., pp. 599–658, esp. pp. 609–16.

[12]See the description of this experiment in Myers, op. cit., pp. 193–6.

[13]Muzafer Sherif, *In Common Predicament: Social Psychology of Intergroup Conflict and Cooperation* (Boston: Houghton Mifflin, 1966).

fering religion, race, region, ethnicity, or language. They represented exactly nothing.

Randomness in the selection of group members, along with similarity in the original pool of participants, insured that each group was as alike to the other group as it is humanly possible for any two groups of people to be. Furthermore, the goals set for these groups were wholly artificial. One task was estimating dots on a piece of paper. The boys in summer camp played competitive games. The very word "game" suggests that fun, not violence, ought to be involved. The group that Zimbardo divided into jailers and prisoners knew all along that the distinctions were entirely arbitrary and that what they were doing was simply play-acting.

Despite identical composition, meaningless goals, and an artificial situation, groups in these experiments still came to develop the strongest sense of animosity toward each other. Members of each group came to see themselves as comrades and intimate friends, while developing contempt and hatred for members of the other group. This animosity led participants to dehumanize and stereotype opposing group members. Eventually, threats and even acts of violence became common.

Remember again that these groups had no basis in historical, economic, or social reality. The hated and despised outgroup members differed in no way from those in the ingroup. If these arbitrary and artificial divisions can produce such animosities, should we be surprised to see people of different religions, classes, and races fighting each other, using the most barbarous tactics, throughout the planet?

It appears that the process we have described taps something deep in human nature. We develop strong attachments to those people we spend time with, especially if we work closely together for common goals. These attachments can over time develop into intense, internalized psychological identification. Almost always they imply a contrary, negative orientation toward some set of people seen as opposing our own group's goals. Irrational though they often are, these identifications shape our lives and influence our behavior in vital ways.

You can easily find an example of this process from your own experience. Nearly all of us have attended a school that had a bitter and hated rival. The other school may have been in a nearby city or across town; sometimes it was just down the street. Remember how you used to deride those sad kids who had to attend that sorry excuse for an educational institution? All the time, of course, they were thinking of you in exactly the same way. But now that you come to think of it, was there really any difference between students in those two schools? How would anthropologists from Burma or Zambia describe the difference? Would they even notice one?

No one is immune to this phenomenon. To my discredit and eternal woe, I have been a lifelong fan of the professional baseball team, the

Boston Red Sox. This morbid habit was inevitable, since I grew up in New England, where all residents worth their salt spend summer cheering for the Red Sox and winter explaining why they'll win "next year." I maintain an intense emotional identification with this group, while managing to abominate anything remotely connected to its major historical rival, the New York Yankees. I have experienced extraordinary adrenaline highs (as the Red Sox win crucial games); states of clinical depression (as the Red Sox lose crucial games); and pathologically murderous rages (as the Yankees win crucial games—especially crucial games against the Red Sox).

Now what could lead a supposedly intelligent grown man to behave in this fashion? After all, I don't even live in Boston. Indeed, at one time I lived in New York. And in any case, the difference between these two cities is marginal at best. (Both are large, multiethnic, northeastern American urban sprawls.) Furthermore, both teams regularly change personnel and managers, so that over a three-to-five-year period, they are transformed from one team into quite a different one. Why cheer for the Red Sox today? It is not remotely the same team it was five years ago—let alone the team it was when I was growing up.

Despite this perfect logic, I have maintained my irrational enthusiasm for decades. Early-learned loyalties are hard to shake.

This emotional attachment to a sports team will hardly surprise my readers. It is a serious contemporary social phenomenon. While the reason behind these allegiances may seem flimsy, there's no denying the intensity of the feelings they produce. Opposing fans often engage in violent confrontations. Name calling, pushing, shoving, and fistfights are hardly uncommon when sporting events take place. Everyone knows about the vicious British hooligans whose rioting led to dozens of deaths after football matches at various European sites in the 1980s[14]. In the United States riots broke out in Chicago after the hometown professional basketball team (the Bulls) won the National Basketball Association's championship match in 1992. The most striking example of sports-related violence occurred after a disputed football game between the national teams of Honduras and El Salvador in 1969. El Salvador, having lost, promptly declared war and invaded Honduras![15]

Humans, in short, don't need to use race, class, and religion to excuse conflict and confrontation. Wherever you find groups of people in competi-

---

[14]The game I refer to here as "football" is what Americans call soccer. The rest of the world calls this sport football, while calling *our* game of football "American football."

[15]In similar vein, after Ghana defeated the Ivory Coast in a 1993 football game, disappointed Ivory Coast "fans" brutally beat and killed scores of Ghanaians who had been living in the Ivory Coast at that time.

tion, you will find the intense hatreds that spur serious conflict. No one has made this point better than Madison:

> So strong is this propensity of mankind to fall into mutual animosities, that where no substantial occasion presents itself, the most frivolous and fanciful distinctions have been sufficient to kindle their unfriendly passions, and excite their most violent conflicts.[16]

People will always find reasons, serious or frivolous, to disagree with others. In addition, they will always belong to differing and competing groups. Hence, they will continue to develop strong positive emotions about "their" group, strong negative feelings about the groups of "others."

These identifications will be reinforced by fellow group members, insuring that groups remain separate and hostile toward each other. Although psychologists have figured out some ways to "reduce intergroup hostilities', it seems unlikely that in the near future the leaders of all of the world's contending and contentious groups (including nations) are going to turn power over to well-meaning academics to resolve the world's problems. For the foreseeable future (that is, for as long as you and I are alive) we are going to have a wide range of groups in this world who look at each other with feelings ranging from mild disgust to utter hatred. Quite frequently, they will act on those feelings. These facts mean, very simply, that we are always going to have social conflict, hence political conflict, hence . . . politics.

CONFLICT RESOLUTION

Many people find this news depressing; I prefer to see it as realistic. True, we can't soon expect to see the millennium—a time of peace when people break swords into ploughshares and lions lie down with lambs. But the news is not all bad. Politics and conflict may be inevitable, but the *violent and bloody* resolution of political disputes is not. We have all heard clichés about "the art of politics," or "politics as the art of compromise," or "politics as the art of the possible." These aphorisms may be tired and banal, but they do suggest that politics can be something more than a war of all against all. It can involve skilled participants adept at the process of diplomacy, negotiation, and compromise. Political disagreement can, in short, be resolved peacefully.

Indeed, political arguments are *usually* resolved in nonviolent ways. While violence is the most spectacular and noticed way to bring political conflict to some kind of resolution, it is rarely the most typical way. Let us

---

[16]Madison in Federalist Paper Number 10; see Hamilton, Madison, and Jay, *The Federalist Papers*, 30

consider the options. When groups of people realize that they oppose each other in a struggle for one of life's scarce resources, they can do several things. First, they can work at resolving the problem peacefully—through discussion and then compromise. That is a common and familiar method for dealing with conflict.

Second, one group can defer to the other's wishes—either through a desire to placate (possibly in the hope of future good will), or more likely through a fear of the other's power. Defer to the other group today to insure your survival for tomorrow. You can also defer to another group's wishes out of guilt, that is, a belief that you are responsible for their unhappy circumstances and should try to make amends. This reasoning surely affected white, middle-class Americans in the 1960s, as they frequently deferred to, instead of opposing, the demands of black Americans (thus producing civil rights laws, affirmative action programs, and the like). It is also possible to defer to the wishes of another group because you come to understand and agree with their aims. Americans who supported rather than opposed the Viet Cong had come to take their perspective on Vietnam ('a war of national liberation') instead of the standard perspective of the American government at the time ('a struggle to thwart communist aggression').

There is a third way to deal with conflict. Both groups may back off. Each may wish to avoid confrontation, because each fears the other's power. The case of the United States and the U.S.S.R. both backing away from war against the other during the 1945-to-1990 period illustrates this pattern. Groups or nations may also back off from armed conflict because their desire to achieve their aims may not be so intense as to be worth making the sacrifices that are certain to be necessary with the outbreak of violence. Or they may back away from conflict because within-group schisms are so great that neither group can muster the kind of unity necessary to undertake armed confrontation with some likelihood of success.

Finally, groups may fail to confront each other in any violent way, because both fear a more powerful third group. This third party might be displeased by conflict between the other two groups and might be willing to take repressive steps to prevent it. That situation existed in Yugoslavia. We can now see that Serbs, Muslims, Croats, and other nationalities were eager to clobber each other during the cold war era. They refrained from doing so, however, because all those groups were cowed by a more powerful one: the state-controlled, communist-dominated, Yugoslav Army—especially when it obeyed the orders of strongman dictator, Marshall Tito.

SUMMARY

We can find other reasons to explain why most people usually live together peacefully. However it happens, people do find ways to confront and tackle the inevitable conflicts of social life without resorting to armed confrontation. We shall later pay special attention to one type of political system (the polyarchy) in which the vast majority of political conflict is resolved without recourse to serious violence.

This issue of violence raises perhaps the most vital question in the whole realm of political science. Just when does social disagreement produce open warfare between political opponents? Conversely, under what conditions can the myriad natural disputes between individuals and groups be handled by means other than violence? Why, in short, does political conflict sometimes and in some places erupt in hideous brutalities, but not at other times and in other places? These central questions, lying at the heart of any serious political analysis, are matters to which we now turn our attention.

3

Political Cultures and Conflict

What do you do when the Supreme Court makes a decision you don't like? Yawn and turn to the sports pages? Let me rephrase the question. What do Americans in general do? What actions can citizens take when the Court makes a series of decisions they detest?

When I ask students that question, they come up with a range of answers, which include the following options:

> March outside the Supreme Court building in Washington, waving signs and banners to demonstrate anger at the decision.
>
> Write letters to newspapers, call radio and TV stations, and contact political leaders to express disagreement with the Court's policies.
>
> Join with like-minded citizens to elect a president who will appoint different justices to the Court. Work also for the election of U.S. senators who support judicial appointees you like and oppose those you dislike.
>
> Work to bring a lawsuit before the Court that makes the best case possible for changing the justices' past policy decisions.
>
> Pressure Congress to rewrite the law—or more drastically, to begin the process of rewriting the Constitution itself.

You can surely think of other options in this vein. American citizens can undertake a number of peaceful, civil, legal, and procedural activities to change the result of Supreme Court rulings. They do, in fact, undertake these activities regularly. Furthermore, political action of this sort often works. Over the years concerted group efforts have succeeded in changing Supreme Court policies on such key political issues as government intervention in the economy, racial integration, abortion, and prayer in the schools.

VIOLENCE AND JUDICIAL POLICY DISAGREEMENT

Most Americans would stop the discussion at this point. They would be satisfied with having dealt with the question of how citizens can respond to an abhorrent Court decision. Yet disagreement with judicial policy can be approached in a radically different way.

Consider what happened a few years ago in Colombia. A group of citizens came to dislike the policy decisions of that nation's Supreme Court. One day several armored cars raced up to the Court building, and out poured masked men wielding submachine guns. They raced into the building, fired wildly at everyone in sight, and ended by killing over half the Court members. Although police pinned them down, several managed to escape, never to be apprehended or punished. Now *that's* a different way of responding to political disagreement!

A third type of response is possible. In Russia during Marxist rule courts simply ratified and reinforced the line of policy laid down by the nation's communist elite. Hardly to our surprise, justices were neither mowed down by thugs nor placed under the pressures of peaceful political protest. Instead, citizens simply accepted judicial decisions in the most docile way, no matter how much they disagreed with their impact.

To understand the political process, we must broaden our perspective. We must open our eyes to patterns that differ radically from our own. We in the West assume that political disputes will be settled in a *non-violent* and relatively *open* manner: nonviolent in being resolved through discussion and voting; open in allowing all (or at least many) interested parties to participate in the discussion and voting. Politics just doesn't work that way in most places.

Take the case of Lebanon. It seemed to be the rule from 1974 to 1989 that whenever a group of Lebanese disagreed with some other group (or with their own government), they took up arms against their opponents and killed as many as they could lay their hands on. In that unfortunate nation a war of all against all went about as far as it could go—or one might have thought so, until Yugoslavia's explosion onto the scene of international consciousness. Despite apparent progress toward ethnic harmony in the cold war era, this latter country has recently torn itself into shreds—having gone, it seems, completely psychotic. Its many ethnic groups have committed unspeakable atrocities against each other, culminating in the systematic raping of the other side's women. This horrific behavior was surely carried to new lows by Serbian forces against Bosnian women in the early 1990s.

Colombia, Lebanon, Yugoslavia: The political history of each country shows a land soaked in blood. Political disagreement goes beyond heated debates and contested elections. It ends, more often than not, in perverse and murderous physical confrontations.

Outside observers recoil in horror at these ghastly events. From our seemingly secure vantage point, we see them as barbaric and immoral. Given our own political perspective, we also view them as shocking exceptions to the way politics "normally" works. Yet these countries and their way of conducting politics are hardly atypical. This manner of dealing with conflict has been much more common throughout history than has ours.

Consider the country of Haiti. Since it gained independence in 1803, it has suffered over 100 revolutions and coups d'état. It can expect, on a regular basis, the violent overthrow of its current rulers. (The military action that toppled President Jean-Baptiste Aristide in 1991 should have come as no surprise to the world diplomatic community.) Consider Rwanda and Burundi. In each nation rival tribes confront each other: the Hutus and the Tutsis. Fighting in Burundi between these two groups left over 100,000 dead in 1972–73; a similar outbreak of hostilities in Rwanda caused an even greater number of deaths in 1994. Consider Afghanistan, Cambodia, Peru, or Liberia. In each country so-called rebel forces have spent years fighting each other and the existing government in bloody, take-no-prisoners warfare.

The levels of mind-numbing violence that occur regularly in one place or another surpass our ability to comprehend. In El Salvador, a country not much larger than Delaware with a population less than the city of New York, 50,000 people died in a civil war from 1982 to 1992. The same war created 1 *million* refugees. If violence at that level ever occurred in the United States, it would produce 2.5 million American dead! Fifty million *more* Americans would be wandering homeless, living in refugee camps, or fleeing abroad.

That scale of disaster is almost impossible for us to imagine. What political disagreement among Americans could produce such intensity of hatred, such naked animosity, as to lead to devastation on that scale? Yet the situation was, if anything, worse in Tadjikistan. With a population about the same as El Salvador's (5 million), that country managed to produce, in a mere ten months (1992–1993), about the same number of dead and displaced people as it took the Central American republic seven years to "achieve." Another national tragedy occurred in Nigeria in the late 1960s. A civil war there led to mass starvation. Perhaps 2 million out of fewer than 60 million Nigerians died as a result of political hostilities. Similar conflict in the United States would produce over 8 million dead.

The United States has hardly been immune to domestic barbarism. Our Civil War (1861–1865) was one of the most gruesome on record. It produced

500,000 deaths in a nation of 35 million people. An outbreak of domestic hostility on that scale today would give us 3.5 million American dead.

In all this discussion we haven't even mentioned the two most brutal societies of all time: Nazi Germany and Stalinist Russia. Both regimes were responsible for the deaths of tens of millions of people, most of whom were helpless, ordinary citizens. Such large-scale atrocities are nearly impossible for the average mind to grasp. As Stalin once said, "One death is a tragedy. A million deaths is a statistic."

It almost seems as if nations have been competing against each other throughout history for the title of Most Barbaric Country. A recent prime example of this atrocious activity is continuing in the country formerly known as Yugoslavia. The several-sided civil war raging there since 1991 has produced, among other cruelties, 150,000 Bosnian dead out of a population of merely 4 million. (That figure, to give it perspective again, equals 7.5 million American corpses.)

Closer to home, pockets of political violence exist in supposedly stable Western countries as well. Bloodshed aimed at making a political statement erupts regularly in Northern Ireland, the Basque region of Spain, and the French province of Corsica, not to mention Los Angeles and other American cities.

In short, the use of violence to gain political ends is hardly unusual in human affairs. Indeed, violence is probably far more common than other tactics mentioned earlier, which Americans take for granted as central to the political process: the free and peaceful expression of opinions, wide-ranging and unimpeded discussions involving give-and-take and compromise, voting, majority rule, and minority rights.

Violence, then, is an intrinsic element in the political process of many nations. Another common worldwide pattern is authoritarian rule. For much of history, tyrannical governments have imposed their will on cowed citizens. Popular input into the policy-making process has almost always been kept to a minimum. The ideal citizen in oligarchic systems is not outspoken, but obedient. A docile population is expected, and force is used to guarantee that outcome. Citizens learn to obey the will of a unified set of rulers, often led by a tyrant who brooks no opposition.

Americans frequently show surprise when encountering these regimes. We profess incomprehension at why they exist. We can't fathom, for instance, how Saddam Hussein remained in power after humiliating defeats in two wars, first against Iran and then against allied forces in the Gulf. George Bush kept American troops from taking Baghdad and toppling Hussein on the typically American assumption that, after seeing this humiliating loss, the Iraqi people were bound to rise up and overthrow him. They would surely express popular indignation at the evils he had forced them to undergo over the years. Why waste American lives to achieve an inevitable result?

Bush turned out to be wrong, but most Americans undoubtedly shared his assumptions. We have trouble understanding blind obedience. We can't fathom passive acceptance of hated conditions. In the same way, we have trouble understanding why Germans continued to follow Hitler right to the bitter end, despite all the evils he had clearly foisted on them.

I once saw first hand how authoritarian regimes operate, while I lived for a few months in the Russian provincial city of Archangel in 1990. The streets were kept in appalling shape during that bitter winter. Sidewalks were clogged with snow and ice. Walking, even in the center of town, was a constant gamble. Salt, chemicals, even dirt seemed unknown to the local authorities. The slipperiness underfoot was constant. Dozens of people daily took serious tumbles. Many sustained real injuries: broken bones, twisted ankles, concussions.

On one particular day in February when an early, unexpected thaw was followed by a sharp drop in temperature, the entire city resembled nothing less than a polished skating rink. Forward movement could be achieved only by slowly shuffling the feet and grabbing any stationary object nearby. I took an hour that day to go from residence to work, a trip that normally took twenty minutes. Yet when I complained to colleagues and acquaintances about the dangerous state of city walkways, they replied merely with embarrassed smiles and half-hearted shrugs. No one expressed shock or anger. No one suggested a possible remedy. I simply encountered passive acceptance of these appalling conditions. The cultural norm appeared to be *close your eyes to the social ills around you, bear them as best you can, and keep your mouth shut.*

We can well imagine the reaction of Americans to these conditions. By midmorning the mayor's office would be deluged with angry complaints. They would arrive by way of telephone, personal visit, and fax. Radio talk shows would be bombarded with telephone calls from irate citizens suggesting (a) how to deal with the problem, and (b) what city officials could do to themselves in the meantime. Political rivals of the current city leadership would appear on television to bemoan the sorry state of affairs in the local administration.

These publicly voiced criticisms would continue, increasing in volume and number, until city officials provided relief in the form of snow removal, salting of streets, and similar measures. If city officials failed to act promptly, they might suffer future political defeat. Other city officials in later years would then pay closer heed to complaints of this sort.

This scenario is commonplace in Western nations. Chicago Mayor Jane Byrne actually lost her bid for re-election in 1983, a few months after a snowstorm had immobilized the city. It took days to get life back to normal, and Chicago residents blamed her for the tortoise-like cleanup. Many thought her dithering and ineffectual leadership was personally responsible for the slow pace of snow removal by the Public Works Department. One can never prove these things precisely, but the affair clearly hurt the mayor's image, and she did lose the election that followed soon after.

We can well imagine the popular reaction to government incompetence in a country like Lebanon or Liberia. There are parts of Peru where the government can't repair roads. Work crews would be attacked by armed guerrillas—members of the virulently antigovernment rebel group known as Shining Path. Government shortcomings in violence-prone places lead to extreme antisystem behavior. As a result, ironically, the government can do little to make incremental improvements, even if it wished to (and of course, often it does not, preferring instead to concentrate on *wiping out* those forces that criticize and oppose it).

UNDERSTANDING A COUNTRY'S POLITICS

What can we make of all this? First, we see that politics varies dramatically from place to place; it is not always peaceful, and it is not always democratic.

Second, we know from the discussion on culture that political actions never occur in isolation. They reflect and exemplify society's deepest-held values. Political patterns cannot change overnight, because the entrenched norms and expectations of a culture are embedded in the people's consciousness. Only thoroughgoing sociocultural change can produce any comparable political change in the life of any nation.

To understand a country's politics, then, we must first grasp its culture. But once we do understand a pattern of politics, we are well placed for understanding both past and future patterns, since political change occurs only after cultural change, and cultural change occurs only slowly.

This perspective suggests the value of severe realism when viewing the world's political scene. It is unlikely that a country will quickly change its customary mode of dealing with conflict. Iraq will not become a peaceful democracy in one day. On the other hand, the news is not all bad. For example, Britain will not tomorrow break down into warring factions as did Bosnia. Cultures are stable, as are the political processes that reflect them.

Finally, this discussion suggests that, while different cultures deal with political disagreement in different ways, the number of ways for dealing with conflict is not infinite. Far from it. Political processes everywhere operate within a small number of political styles. Let us temporarily label three of these styles authoritarian, pluralistic, and anarchic. The former Soviet Union and Hitler's Germany both stand as prototypes of authoritarian politics. Most Western political systems are regarded as pluralistic. And a range of countries exhibit the anarchic, chaotic violence we have already associated with Colombia, Lebanon, Tadjikistan, Liberia, Peru, and the remnants of Yugoslavia. (A fourth style, parochial politics, less common in our age, is discussed in Chapter 4.)

Within each style of politics, variations will naturally occur. Among pluralistic systems, for example, the French have several political parties, while Americans have only two. This fact, however, is minor compared to the broader pattern. Both countries allow freedom of speech and press, while encouraging competition among diverse groups for the right to control government and shape public policy. Anarchic systems also differ on the surface. Struggles in Bosnia reflect ethnic hatreds, while conflict in Peru may reflect class and ideological divisions. Still, the result of these differing conflicts is the same. Thousands of people are murdered in a continuing armed struggle to dictate political outcomes.

It is true that these "minor" differences between similar countries will appear great to those who live in them. The closer you get to any phenomenon, and the more you know about it, the more it appears unique. Some scholars have spent a lifetime explaining the differences between countries as similar as Sweden and Norway, say, or the United States and Canada. Whole books have been written on these topics.[1] Yet an introduction to politics must start with the broadest distinctions. It is critical that we learn what the major political systems look like. Only then can we go on to describe the subtle differences between similar nations within the same category.

At this introductory level where we must make broad and basic distinctions, it makes sense to imagine a few options for the primary political pattern of any culture. We can begin to understand the options available to any society by focusing on a simple question. What is that society's "normal" method for dealing with conflict? I have a short answer to the question. (The rest of this book represents the long answer.) Societies deal with conflict in one of four principal ways: *negotiation, repression, war,* or *denial.* Depending on which style they stress, they end up with *pluralistic, authoritarian, anarchic,* or *parochial* political systems. All polities today tend to adopt one of these political styles for dealing with conflict. To understand these styles is to know how politics in the modern world actually works.

Of course, any categorization simplifies reality; after all, most nations are complex entities. Any country's political process will contain elements of all four principal styles for dealing with politics. In the United States, for instance, where negotiation is the primary means of settling political disputes, strong elements of denial are also found. In addition, violence is not unknown in American politics. We see examples of it every day: from confrontation between prolife and prochoice partisans at abortion clinics to

---

[1]On U.S.–Canadian differences, for example, see Seymour Martin Lipset, *Continental Divide: The Values and Institutions of the United States and Canada* (New York: Routledge, 1990). On Swedish–Norwegian differences, see David Klingman, *Social Change, Political Change, and Public Policy: Norway and Sweden, 1875–1965* (London: Sage Publications, 1976).

clashes between police and blacks in urban ghetto areas. Even Americans have used repression as a political tactic. We all know about the rule of fear, which kept African Americans "in their place" in Southern states during the many decades from the Civil War to the modern civil rights era. Over the years groups defined as "subversive" have had their mail opened and telephones tapped by the F.B.I. And some argue that our treatment of illegal immigrants today also contains a strong dose of political repression.

Just as we can find exceptions to the normal U.S. pattern of dealing with conflict, so too can we find exceptions to typical political behavior in other places. We could find nonrepressive examples of dealing with political strife in even the most repressive regime. And no system operates entirely through anarchic clashes of armed citizens. Even in Lebanon at its worst, some groups at least occasionally tried to resolve differences through discussion and compromise rather than by way of guns. No nation stands out as an "ideal type."

Nonetheless, our understanding of world politics will improve if we think of most nations as *tending toward* one operating style. That style can be considered their preferred, or most common, method for confronting that central human fact: the inevitability of social conflict. Yes, all nations use all four means for dealing with conflict, but most nations stress one of those means over the others. Because it is so important to know how nations deal with conflict, it makes sense to characterize each nation by the particular means it chooses to stress when confronting conflict.

Numerous typologies exist for characterizing political systems. The categories you use depend on the questions you ask. If, for instance, you are interested in how political parties operate in various countries, you could divide the world's nations (as of 1994) into categories such as the following:

-No-party systems (Cuba)
-One-party systems (China)
-Two-party systems (United States)
-Few-party systems (Canada, Australia)
-Multi party systems (Italy, Holland)
-Weak-party systems (Dominican Republic)[2]

Or, if you are interested in the relationship between economic systems and politics, you could describe nations in the following way:

-Feudalism (twelfth century France)
-Pure capitalism (United States, nineteenth century)

[2]See, for example, Joseph LaPalombara and Myron Weiner, eds., *Political Parties and Political Development* (Princeton, NJ: Princeton University Press, 1966), Seymour Martin Lipset and Stein Rokkan, eds., *Party Systems and Voter Alignments: Cross-National Perspectives* (New York: The Free Press, 1967), and Maurice Duverger, *Political Parties: Their Organization and Activity in the Modern State,* 3d ed. (London: Methuen, 1972).

-State capitalism (Franco's Spain)
-Modern ("mixed-economy") capitalism (United States, currently)
-Welfare-state capitalism (Norway, Denmark, currently)
-Socialism (Russia, pre–1990)
-Dependency economy (Guatemala, Ivory Coast, currently)[3]

You can also divide countries into "big" and "small," or into "industrial" and "agrarian," and so on.

The categories you develop will spring from the issues that interest you. My typology of nations derived from a focus on conflict. I chose that focus because of conflict's centrality to the political process. There are many other ways to get a handle on politics. You can find literally dozens of typologies for categorizing countries. As you confront this and other theories for explaining politics, you must always ask whether they are *useful*. Do they help you understand events in the real world? If the argument that follows doesn't help you understand international political patterns, forget it and look for a better one.

Another question to ask when encountering a set of categories is, How did the author arrive at this typology? In this case, for instance, what led me to conclude that there are exactly four political styles for confronting conflict? I shall answer the question in two ways. First, I arrived at the categories empirically. That is, after years of observing world politics, I gradually concluded that what I was seeing justified a fourfold division of political systems. Some nations seemed perpetually in a state of internal warfare, while others rarely resorted to violence in making political decisions, even though they allowed citizen disputes and disagreements to be widely aired. Still other nations turned much of the time to dictatorial rule, and some denied or ignored conflict altogether. After years of watching world politics, I came to feel that a fourfold categorization of systems clarified the various political processes out there.

These categories developed, then, through intellectual trial and error. One can find another way, however, using logic and theory, to arrive at the same conclusion. Start by asking, What are the key variables that influence the way a given society handles conflict? I asked that question and came up with two factors: (1) the degree of *cultural homogeneity* within that society, and (2) its level of *citizen activism*. The intensity of political conflict depends largely on these two influences.

---

[3]See, for example, Barrington Moore, *The Social Origins of Dictatorship and Democracy: Land and Peasant in the Making of the Modern World* (Boston: Beacon Press, 1966), and Theda Skocpol, *States and Social Revolutions: A Comparative Analysis of France, Russia, and China* (Cambridge: Cambridge University Press, 1974).

Cultural homogeneity is clearly crucial for understanding conflict levels. The more alike people are, the more likely they are to get along. At the least, they probably won't do major physical damage to each other. So we must ask, as social observers, whether citizens in a given polity share the same outlooks, norms, and values. Do they see each other as similar, as sharing a common perspective? In societies where people vehemently disagree about basic beliefs, a potential for animosity is created, which can produce high levels of violence. A culture of this sort will experience frequent turmoil and political instability.

Residents of Germany in the middle of the seventeenth century could not agree on which religion constituted the one true path to salvation. As a result, they fought the devastating Thirty Years War. Some historians believe it took the country 200 years to recover. White Americans in 1860 did not agree on whether black Americans could be legally defined as property and kept as slaves. The ideological split on that central issue led to our bloody Civil War. The economic and political consequences of that conflagration are still being felt.

By way of contrast, Sweden stands out as a strongly unified society. Nearly all Swedes are of the same race, ethnic group, and religion. Nearly all support a full-fledged welfare state, espouse a strong work ethic, and express support for equal treatment of women. They disagree only on modest matters—whether small increases or decreases should occur in governmental expenditures, for example. Like Swedes, the Japanese stand out as a homogeneous people. The vast majority represent the same race, ethnic group, and religion. Most Japanese agree on key social values: the importance of work, the centrality of the family, and the idea of sacrifice for the group. Given this cultural cohesion in Sweden and Japan, we are hardly surprised to learn that neither nation has seen serious political unrest for decades—certainly nothing threatening the stability of their post-World War II political systems.[4]

These brief sketches suggest that cultures divided on central values will differ dramatically from cultures that are homogeneous. As analysts, we need to know the degree to which people in a given place see eye to eye. Do they think more or less the same? Do they agree, more or less, on the same values and customs? Or do they live "worlds apart," even if geographically connected?

---

[4]On the cultural homogeneity of Sweden, see Michael Roskin, *Other Governments of Europe: Sweden, Spain, Italy, Yugoslavia, and East Germany* (Englewood Cliffs, NJ: Prentice-Hall, Inc., 1977), pp. 12–41. On cohesion and consensus in Japan, see Karel van Wolferen, *The Enigma of Japanese Power: People and Politics in a Stateless Nation* (New York: Vintage Books, 1990). Although he argues that Japanese unity is "rigged," "artificial," or "imposed by elites," van Wolferen nevertheless demonstrates its definite existence.

Knowing the degree of cultural homogeneity is necessary, but not sufficient, for understanding a nation's level of conflict. We must also know whether its citizens *act* to secure their values. If you disapprove of your next-door neighbors' behavior, but you keep your mouth shut, nothing will come of this disagreement. If you express your contempt for them periodically, you can expect, at a minimum, an escalation of verbal conflict. Your initial condemnation may lead only to a heated comeback. If eventually you make a habit of flinging barbs at your neighbors, they may respond with angry tirades. Shouting matches become inevitable and will grow into shoving, pushing, and eventually full-fledged fighting. Finally, one of you may even resort to weapons.

Social scientists call this process "the escalation of violence." Deadly force won't be used after the first verbal exchange, but mutual bitterness will build as arguments continue over central issues. One or both sides will ultimately lose control and in anger, will turn to violence.

Speaking your mind to your neighbor is only one kind of action, and a mild one at that. Social activity can be much more dramatic. For example, let's say everyone on your street is a Christian, and you and your neighbors normally attend one of the local churches on Sunday morning. You will consider the neighborhood peaceful and harmonious.

Now imagine that three houses in the very heart of your community are bought by a little-known sect that practices unusual rituals. As you and your neighbors head off to church, the neighborhood resounds with blood-curdling cries. As you pass by your new neighbors, you see them painted purple and dancing naked around bonfires, while some of them sacrifice live sheep and goats to their gods. What would happen in these circumstances to the peace and harmony of your little corner of the world?[5]

This (not entirely far-fetched) example shows that agreement on social values can be indicated in a number of ways; *speech* is just one. A more dramatic way occurs when people *act* to express their life outlook. The key question then becomes, How active are citizens in any given place when it comes to expressing their deepest values? How much energy do they expend to insure the realization of their strongest desires?

Varying levels of activism can produce quite different political results. If people don't act on their beliefs, those beliefs can hardly have any conse-

---

[5]To forestall the social disharmony that unusual religious practices bring to a community, the city of Hialeah, Florida, outlawed animal sacrifice a few years ago, thus banning a ritual connected with the religion of *Santeria* practised by recent Cuban immigrants. The Supreme Court recently overturned that law, however, declaring it contrary to the U.S. Constitution's "freedom of religion" clause (part of the First Amendment). See *Church of the Lukumi Babalu Aye, Inc. v. City of Hialeah* (1993).

quence in the real world. Imagine a society where people are placid or docile, never opening their mouths about the irksome behavior of their neighbors. Or imagine that people appalled by their neighbors' behavior simply moved to a new section of town. In these cases, the process of escalating violence would never begin.[6] In a society of timid people ("That's not my business"), or tolerant people ("Let them do their own thing"), or people who just don't like confrontation ("So long, Jack; I'm outta here"), cultural heterogeneity wouldn't necessarily lead to namecalling, social friction, and the escalation of tension.

In the United States clashes have occurred regularly for twenty years between prolife and prochoice activists—people with profoundly different perspectives on social issues. Imagine how much calmer the U.S. political scene would be if these militants simply stayed home. They might *think* to themselves, "Oh, how I detest that (prolife) (prochoice) position," but if they actually *did* nothing to implement their attitudes, the intensity of political conflict in the United States would clearly be reduced.

Social analysts, then, must not focus simply on the degree to which nations are unified or fractionalized. They must also learn whether a society's citizens, be they disparate or unified, will take definite *action* to express their values. Societies with an activist citizenry will look very different from societies dominated by passive fatalists.

It is like the old question of whether a tree falling in the forest makes noise if no one is there to hear it. Whether the tree makes noise or not, the *effect,* if no one hears it, *is the same* as if it made no noise. In the same way, your *thoughts* are irrelevant to social life, unless you act on them in a way that affects others. Thus, the political process is deeply affected by the willingness or hesitation of people to act on their beliefs.

Some people remain uninvolved in social life. They appear docile and apathetic. Alienation and cynicism, even fatalism, define their outlook. Or they may be afraid to act, cowed into obedience after years of terror and repression. For whatever reason, a general ethos of passivity exists in a number of the world's cultures. Citizens in those places refuse to involve themselves in their society's political life.

An opposite ethos prevails in other places. An activism norm predominates, in striking contrast to a resigned acceptance of whatever life doles out. People in these cultures are constantly voicing opinions, organizing to achieve aims, and working to convert others to their perspective.

---

[6]See the discussion on this point in Albert O. Hirschman, *Exit, Voice, and Loyalty: Responses to Decline in Firms, Organizations and States,* 2d ed. (Cambridge: Harvard University Press, 1972), esp. pp. 21–29.

Many scholars stress this contrast between fatalism and activism. They see it as a crucial variable for understanding differences between people.[7] I too see it as a major determinant of social action. Individuals in a "participant" culture will work forcefully for their goals. People in a "fatalist" culture will accept what life offers them. The two outlooks could hardly produce more divergent styles. We must take account of this difference in trying to understand the marked variation in national political patterns.

SUMMARY

Let us summarize the argument. To understand why political patterns differ from one nation to another, analysts must pay special attention to two underlying causes. We can describe these causes as follows:

1. The degree of cultural homogeneity within any nation
2. The level of citizen social-political activism within any nation

For simplicity's sake I shall use the words *homogeneity* and *activism* throughout the rest of this book when referring to these variables.

To simplify still further, let us arbitrarily express each variable in dichotomous terms, that is, assume that each variable can take on two, and only two, values. Thus a nation's level of homogeneity can be only "high" or "low." To put it another way, we shall define all nations as possessing *either* a homogeneous *or* a heterogeneous culture. In making this crude distinction, we shall ignore (for the time being) subtle nuances and minor variations among nations in each category.

Using this assumption about the dichotomous nature of homogeneity, we can produce a simple diagram:

Homogeneity among Nations of the World

Type 1: Homogeneous   Type 2: Heterogeneous
(example: Japan)   (example: Lebanon)

---

[7]Psychologists refer to this phenomenon as the "locus of control" issue: Do I control my fate, or does the outside world direct things for me? On the difference between "internal" locus of control and "external" locus of control, see Herbert M. Lefcourt, "Internal versus External Control of Reinforcement: A Review," *Psychological Bulletin* 65 (1966): 206–20, and Herbert M. Lefcourt, "Durability and Impact of the Locus of Control Construct," *Psychological Bulletin* 112 (1992): 406–14. For a summary of the psychological factors that induce political activism, see Lester W. Milbrath and M. L. Goel, *Political Participation: How and Why Do People Get Involved in Politics?* 2d ed. (Chicago: Rand McNally, 1977), esp. pp. 43–85.

What we have done for homogeneity, we can also do for activism. Let us assume that citizens in any given nation will be either active or passive (recognizing again that modest variation can occur within each of these categories). This assumption produces another simple diagram:

Citizen political activity level among nations of the world

Type 1: Active   Type 2: Passive
(example: Sweden)   (example: Nepal)

These diagrams provide visual illustration of our two propositions

1. Political systems reflect either heterogeneous or homogeneous cultures.
2. Citizens everywhere take either an active or a passive role in public life.

Having created two simple dichotomies, we can introduce a degree of complexity. What happens when homogeneity and activism intersect? By combining the two variables into one table (Table 3–1), we achieve a striking result.

Table 3–1 Types of Political Culture

		Citizen Agreement on Basic Values?	
		Yes	No
Citizens Hold Activist Outlook?	Yes	Type 1: Homogeneous/Active (example: Denmark)	Type 2: Heterogeneous/Active (example: Peru)
	No	Type 3: Homogeneous-Passive (example: China)	Type 4: Heterogeneous-Passive (example: Zaire)

Table 3–1 suggests the existence of four political cultures. These can be described, at their most basic, as places where citizens are one of the following:

1. Active within a homogeneous culture
2. Active within a heterogeneous culture
3. Passive within a homogeneous culture
4. Passive within a heterogeneous culture

These four cultures correspond to the four political systems we have already encountered.

1. Nations characterized by pluralism and participation
2. Nations characterized by fragmentation, anarchy, and violence
3. Nations characterized by oligarchical rule (citizens obedient)
4. Nations characterized by imperialist rule (citizens passive and parochial)

These four culture types are central to an understanding of modern-day politics. It will therefore pay handsomely to learn in detail how each one operates.

4

Political Behavior in Four Cultures

HOMOGENEOUS–ACTIVE CULTURES

Type 1 culture (*homogeneous–active*) produces a familiar political system. Its processes lie embedded in a unified culture. Most members of society share a common identity. They see themselves as part of the same group or nationality: Swedish, Costa Rican, Japanese—"us" in some general way (often vague and difficult to explain, but nevertheless deeply felt).

People in cohesive cultures agree with each other, for the most part, on key social values (the work ethic, the dignity of age, the importance of discipline, the need for freedom, etc.). They also tend to act alike. Half the citizens don't wear robes, while the other half wear shorts. Half don't stop work five times a day to kneel in the direction of Mecca and pray, while the other half stops work five times a day to snort coke.

In other words, the bulk of people in homogeneous cultures think and act alike. They see other citizens in the culture as much like themselves, fellow human beings to be respected and supported.

A second characteristic of this culture is citizen activism. Its members take an aggressive role in shaping their environment. They are convinced of their ability to mold reality. They work regularly to influence the external forces that define their lives. They are *engagé*, as Sartre would put it. They struggle with their environment, but feel certain of eventually bettering themselves.

People with this outlook wish more than anything to shape their own destiny. The activist ethos springs from optimism about the chance for progress in this world. Individuals, and even whole societies, can in this view attain their ends, if they just keep struggling to improve and achieve. In a circular chain of reinforcement this activism produces additional optimism about the value of personal effort. Since active struggle toward your goals is more likely to help you attain them than other options you might try (passivity, prayer, luck), people in active cultures learn that activism pays off. They often do achieve their goals. Thus they have every reason to feel optimistic about the value of activism.

Optimism about the ability to improve one's situation leads to a corollary belief. *If things are not as desired, one should work to improve them.* This attitude produces a politically alert and periodically involved populace. When political, social, or economic circumstances bring unpopular results, citizens (imbued with the spirit of optimism, certain they can change this world for the better) will enter the political arena to produce "better" policies. No wonder you hear continual cries of "Reform the system!" and no wonder reform movements of every type spring up in this culture. Only in lands where citizens have learned that it is possible to make real improvements in their own lives do they also believe it is possible to improve the functioning of social institutions, including government.

Homogeneous–active cultures, then, should see a wide range of citizens regularly involved in public affairs, working to achieve the passage of political policies they like and to defeat policies they abhor.[1]

Some analysts have worried that this continuous citizen activism could increase levels of political tension.[2] After all, they reason, as more people get involved in politics, they will represent a wider range of opposing aims and interests. Political issues are often charged with emotion and can be difficult to resolve. The more parties to a dispute and the more varied their perspectives, the more unlikely it is that they will be able to coalesce around peaceful and satisfactory resolutions. We are likely to expect a continuing series of violent confrontations in a culture of political activism.

Although widespread citizen activism does produce violence in many places, it rarely does so in homogeneous–active cultures. When violence does occur there, it affects few people, is short-lived, and fails to put a dent in the rock-solid structures of society. That is because political disputes in

---

[1]See, for example, the portrayal of the United States in Robert A. Dahl, *A Preface to Democratic Theory* (Chicago: University of Chicago Press, 1956), pp. 124–51, and the description of the United States and Great Britain in Gabriel A. Almond and Sidney Verba, *The Civic Culture* (Princeton, NJ: Princeton University Press, 1963), pp. 360–67.

[2]Berelson et al., for example, seem to be arguing that continuously high levels of citizen activism are destabilizing. See Bernard R. Berelson, Paul F. Lazarsfeld, and William N. McPhee, *Voting: A Study of Opinion Formation in a Presidential Campaign* (Chicago: University of Chicago Press, 1954), pp. 305–23. For a similar line of reasoning, see also Almond and Verba, op. cit., pp. 356–60.

this culture rarely cut deep or involve profound value differences; hence, they can be resolved relatively peacefully.

These are generalizations, of course. Political violence can occur in any society. In Sweden that quintessential example of homogeneous–active culture, Prime Minister Olaf Palme was shot to death on a quiet Stockholm street in 1986. Race riots are not infrequent in the United States, Japanese students have been known to arm themselves with helmets and batons before charging police lines in protests over government education policies, and French farmers regularly dump tons of tomatoes or peaches onto major roadways and then clash with police and clean-up crews trying to restore order. These events should not surprise us. Politics touches us all, in ways that are intense and immediate. Even in the calmest of settings people will sometimes react violently to political events they detest.

Nevertheless, when politically inspired violence does occur in homogeneous–active cultures, it rarely threatens the foundation of the regime itself. That is because only a few people, relative to the entire population, engage in it and never for very long. Most citizens can accept the agreed-upon methods for dealing with conflict, and those methods are civil, procedural, "democratic," and peaceful.

Political peace in the homogeneous–active culture rests upon its underlying cohesion. Despite all the political activism, citizens agree on the basics. The similarity of outlook reduces political stress in two ways. First, their political disagreements rarely touch fundamental values. Opposing groups may want a little more or a little less of a particular program. They may even disagree on whether to start some new program or abolish an existing one. But they don't disagree on whether or not to continue working within the existing constitutional framework. And they certainly don't disagree with the proposition that all parties to any dispute have the right to continue living!

In short, political disagreement in this culture is over minor matters. Disputes involve incremental, not fundamental, change. Political tensions rarely rise to the level at which people are willing to beat up or kill opponents to insure their own victory. Although the high level of citizen involvement naturally produces a continuing stream of disagreement and confrontation, clashes occur at the level of policy (a little more or a little less), and not at a deeper psychological level, the level of values and beliefs (all or nothing).[3]

Political disagreement in the homogeneous–active culture rarely produces violence for a second reason: People acknowledge a common humanity in their political opponents. The reasoning goes something like this. Those who disagree with us on the issue at hand are, after all, very much

---

[3]See the discussion on this point in G. Bingham Powell, Jr., *Contemporary Democracies: Participation, Stability, and Violence* (Cambridge, MA: Harvard University Press, 1982), pp. 175–200.

like us in most other ways. We all believe in "the American way of life," or in "France for the French," or in "the specialness of the Japanese,' and so on. We agree, in other words, with our political opponents much more often than we disagree. It makes no sense to treat them as knaves or barbarians. We should instead treat them with courtesy and understanding. We oppose each other today, but we may be allies tomorrow on one of the many issues where we do see eye to eye. Besides, these people are very much like us, except for our modest differences on this one policy. Both we and they face truly serious enemies beyond our borders. Let us act in a manner that allows us to continue living and working with these people tomorrow, even if we oppose each other today on this one specific issue.

This perspective leads opponents to treat each other reasonably. They don't dehumanize adversaries through heated, overblown rhetoric. In an atmosphere of trust and civility, political competitors can seek accommodation and compromise. They thus live to fight (and cooperate with) each other another day. In short, opponents accept the necessity of "agreeing to disagree."

This trait of disagreeing, often vigorously, on details while maintaining a profound level of agreement on essentials stands as the distinguishing feature of the homogeneous–active political system. Political scientists call this phenomenon *disagreement on goals but agreement on the rules of the game.*

HETEROGENEOUS–ACTIVE CULTURES

It is this ability to sustain *moderate* levels of disagreement that is unique to Type 1 culture. Other societies produce either *no* disagreement (a unified elite dictates policy), or exceptionally *high* levels of disagreement, which lead to violence and instability. The latter situation prevails in Type 2 (*heterogeneous–active*) culture. Here citizens are definitely active; they get involved in politics to promote their own goals, to improve their life conditions. Unfortunately, they find themselves in total disagreement with each other concerning basic life values.

Heterogeneous–active cultures are undoubtedly the most interesting. Alas, an old Chinese curse goes, "May you live in interesting times!" "Interesting" is the opposite of "dull," but dull suggests stable and by implication peaceful. Heterogeneous–active cultures, though interesting, are rarely peaceful. They produce high levels of internal violence, sometimes staggeringly high. Let us examine why.

In heterogeneous–active culture we find countries lacking widespread agreement on basic norms, such as rules of the political game, the proper religion, views of justice, the ideal family, definitions of equality, progress, and freedom. You name the subject, and each group in this culture will leap into angry argument with all the others to prove the truth of its own per-

spective. These fundamental divisions concerning life's central values produce a society of fragmentation. Instead of basic unity punctuated by the
occasional modest division, as in homogeneous–active culture, we find in
heterogeneous–active culture a basic disunity exacerbated by a continued
series of *profound* divisions. It is a society of diverse and clearly differentiated people, deeply suspicious of each other and fundamentally at odds
over most of the issues that people care about.

We have seen what can happen when people feel murderously about
each other. Yugoslavia, Tadjikistan, Lebanon, Colombia are places that fit
the pattern of heterogeneous–active culture. Citizens disagree on funda-
mentals. They can't even agree on what form their disagreement should
take. Parliamentary debates, street demonstrations, hunger strikes, guerrilla
warfare—what political actions are legitimate? There are no widely
accepted rules of the game. In any case, opponents don't see politics as a
game at all. It is a deadly serious activity, designed to protect a way of life,
or life itself, against adversaries who would destroy both.

Combatants under these conditions can't risk accommodation and
compromise; that would be consorting with the enemy. Besides, you
couldn't trust opponents to maintain an agreement. Each side believes others will cheat whenever possible for their own benefit, taking advantage of
"our" good will or naïveté. The only true solution is total victory. Destroy
the enemy to insure your own security (not to mention achieving the victory of "truth" and "righteousness").

Politics in heterogeneous–active cultures, then, goes well beyond parliamentary speeches, interest group lobbying, and electioneering. It
includes (as part of its normal process) street riots, mass demonstrations,
illegal antigovernment activity, illegal repression by governments of opponents, and pitched battles between followers of various political movements. Violence is frequent—and expected. It isn't an occasional aberration,
but an ongoing element in the political process.[4]

Even when periods of relative calm prevail, suspicion and distrust
poison the atmosphere. Not only do political opponents fear and resent
each other, but nearly all resent the government as well. It is seen as staffed
by opportunists, who line their own pockets, hand out favors to allies, and

---

[4]James L. Payne first called my attention to the phenomenon of violence as an integral part of
the political process. He used the provocative term "democracy by violence" to express this
idea. See his discussion in *Labor and Politics in Peru* (New Haven, CT: Yale University Press,
1965), pp. 268–72. See also Samuel P. Huntington, *Political Order in Changing Societies* (New
Haven: Yale University Press, 1968).

repress their enemies. Cynicism abounds toward government and toward all politicians (except those of one's own ingroup, and sometimes even then).

Governments in this circumstance are weak. Since no one feels emotionally tied to the existing institutions, leaders can't rely on any goundswell of citizen support in time of crisis. When the French Fourth Republic was on the verge of military takeover in 1958, its leaders called on citizens to turn out in the street to support the regime. No one turned out. The regime fell.[5]

Heterogeneous–active cultures are typically led by weak, divided governments commanding little public support. Hence, they are subject to frequent takeovers: coups d'état, assassination of leaders, peasant or worker revolts, and the like. These events reflect the widespread degree of citizen distrust. First one group and then another will decide that it is more urgent to take power (and insure their own security) than it is to worry about legal niceties. To remain passive is to run the risk that another group will seize control and use the powers of government for its own ends and against yours. All groups *not* in government are therefore in a perpetual state of semirebellion. And groups *in* the government must perpetually act as semi-oppressors, because they can't sit idly by while powerful enemies out there are hatching revolutionary plots against them.

HOMOGENEOUS–PASSIVE CULTURES

A third type of culture behaves in nearly opposite fashion to the previous one. Homogeneous–passive cultures differ from heterogeneous–active cultures in possessing a citizenry that is both cohesive and profoundly inactive. The resulting political style contrasts radically with the type of politics found in such places as Peru, Liberia, and Rwanda.

We have already encountered the phenomenon of social cohesion. In this type of culture citizens look at life in reasonably similar ways and live more or less alike. They agree on key values: the meaning of life, the importance of religion, gender roles, and so on. They think of themselves as one people, a group distinct from others, a nation. Internal disagreements are modest in scope; they rarely touch fundamental values. Citizens are proud of their common heritage, secure in agreement on the key principles of life.

---

[5]France at that time would appear to have been a society moving from a heterogeneous–active to a homogeneous–active state. Its history during the several decades of the Fifth Republic (1958–) shows growing agreement by a majority of French citizens on key social values and institutions. In the 1950s at least forty percent of the population (Gaullists and communists) wanted political institutions different from those provided by the constitution of the Fourth Republic. Today almost no one disputes the desirability of Fifth Republic arrangements.

In this common group identity (this "we feeling" for others within the culture) the people of Type 3 culture resemble citizens in the homogeneous–active culture. They differ, however, in their complete lack of social activism. They are extraordinarily unwilling to form independent groups to work for common goals. When social problems arise they sit on their hands. "Mind your own business" and "Do what the government says" are two deeply ingrained norms.

As a result, spontaneous citizen input into the decision-making process is rare. Organized, independent groups struggling against each other for the power to influence government policy is a pattern that almost never occurs.

Explaining this passivity is easy. It makes perfect sense to avoid political involvement when it will prove fruitless or dangerous. If governments always throw people in jail (or worse) at the first sign of political protest, citizens will learn to abandon all but government-approved political activity. If criticism of government produces no substantive results and furthermore lands you in trouble, you are unlikely to become a government critic. Most citizens in this type of culture will avoid politics altogether; it is too dangerous. Those who do become active will turn out to be staunch supporters of the ruling elite. Homogeneous–passive cultures, then, produce citizens who are either nonparticipatory or cheerleaders for the regime.

A familiar kind of politics emerges from this culture of cohesion and passivity. We often use words like *dictatorship* or *authoritarian* to describe it. The word *totalitarian* was coined to describe its most extreme form. Since all think alike in this culture, it frequently happens that a strong set of leaders, embodying the general ethos, will emerge. Since few citizens are active, few dispute this elite's claim to rule. Since the elite embodies the culture's core values in any case, few *wish* to dispute that rule. Passive acceptance of leaders who embody the received cultural norms is what typically characterizes the political pattern in homogeneous–passive culture.

HETEROGENEOUS–PASSIVE CULTURES

The fourth type of culture (heterogeneous–passive) is probably the least common today, but it has typified many societies in the past. The nineteenth century Ottoman and Russian empires would be examples, as would perhaps India in the 1950s. In this culture (as in heterogeneous–active culture) citizens belong to a variety of unrelated groups sharing little. Within the same state will coexist deeply believing Hindus and devout Muslims, or people who speak languages as divergent as Spanish, German, and Hungarian, or people of black, brown, and white skin color. Given the diversity of people, one would expect great potential for social confrontation and physical violence.

Yet in such cultures, the potential for violence often remains just that: potential only. Or, if it does occur, it remains sporadic and isolated. That is because citizens in this culture share a feature of citizens in Type 3 culture. They are, at heart, passive, quiescent, and docile. Profoundly parochial, these citizens have yet to absorb the norms of "modernity." They don't believe they can mold the environment to their own benefit—or they fear to try.[6]

Most people in heterogeneous–passive culture live in a traditional setting (rural or small town) and carry on an existence that varies little from the way countless ancestors lived for generations. They are fatalists, and they are much more willing than citizens in industrially advanced nations to accept the meager lot that life has thrown their way. They live with a constricted vision and are hardly aware of a broader world stretching beyond the confines of their village, valley, or region. Totally alien to them is the notion that action on their part could affect the deliberation of distant elites. Accepting their role, and soldiering on, is their definition of the way to live.

Holding this outlook, citizens in heterogeneous–passive cultures won't be spending time arguing with each other over proper government policy, nor will they be out in the streets demonstrating against state actions they detest. They won't be on the public scene at all.

We could argue that this docility has (in an odd sort of way) its positive side. A high degree of citizen activity in this type of culture would produce a dramatic rise in the level of political tension. That is because members of this culture resemble members of the heterogeneous–active culture: At base, they differ radically from each other. As long as these differences aren't asserted, they can all live in some degree of harmony. But if citizens start becoming "modern" and acting to promote their values, conflict will increase dramatically, since those values stand diametrically opposed to each other.[7]

---

[6]An excellent description of the difference between "traditional" and "modern" outlooks on life can be found in Daniel Lerner, *The Passing of Traditional Society: Modernizing the Middle East* (Glencoe, IL: The Free Press, 1958), esp. pp. 19–75. See also Alex Inkeles and David Horton Smith, *Becoming Modern: Individual Change in Six Developing Countries* (Cambridge, MA: Harvard University Press, 1974). "Traditional" or "non-modern" citizens are called "parochial" by Almond and Verba, *The Civic Culture*, op. cit., esp. pp. 16–18. Perhaps the best description of the parochial outlook can be found in Edward C. Banfield, *The Moral Basis of a Backward Society* (Glencoe, IL: The Free Press, 1958), esp. pp. 83–101. He dubs this perspective "amoral familism'—a single-minded focus on defending and maintaining the interests of one's immediate family, while ignoring all broader issues and pursuits.

[7]This argument follows a line similar to that expressed by James Davies in his famous "J-curve theory of revolution." Davies, picking up an idea of Tocqueville, argued that revolution and social unrest don't occur when people are hopelessly oppressed or utterly bereft of material resources. Revolutions occur after people have made serious progress toward a better life, but become discontent when improvements don't continue to occur rapidly enough to meet their expectations. In the same way, citizens may become modern (i.e., participationist) and start expressing their political desires faster than the system can accommodate them. See James Chowning Davies, "Toward a Theory of Revolution," *American Sociological Review* 27 (1962): 5–19.

One can speculate that if heterogeneous–passive cultures are to become modern without violence, they must first move toward the homogeneous–passive system and become cohesive. Then a movement toward activism would bring "acceptable" (that is, nonviolent) levels of conflict. Spain in the 1939 to 1974 period might be seen as an example of this pattern. It moved from a heterogeneous–passive society (circa 1945) to a homogeneous–passive society (circa 1975) and thence, under the current parliamentary regime, to a reasonable facsimile of homogeneous–active culture. Of course, to achieve this end, it had to endure the repression of Franco's dictatorship, which forcefully "homogenized" the population by wiping out all opposition to his rule.

The price Spaniards had to pay for achieving homogeneity was high. Whether it is possible for nations to move from heterogeneous–active cultures to homogeneous–active ones without enduring a period of authoritarian government remains a fascinating and vital question.[8]

To return to heterogeneous–passive culture: Its central characteristic lies in its odd conglomeration of unlike people. Most of them live narrow, traditional lives and accept a thoroughly nonparticipationist attitude toward public life. They are governed by a distant set of leaders whom they scarcely imagine influencing. They mind their own business, stick to the way things have always been done, and obey the orders of people who have always given them.

Societies like these operate in the manner of traditional empires. A small elite governs a farflung and disparate set of subjects. This status quo reflects some past pattern of conquest. The relationship is clear between those who were conquered (and who are now subjects) and their rulers. The rulers expect quiet obedience, along with a certain minimum level of support (taxes, road work, military service). The subjects will comply with state directives when necessary, avoid them when possible, and try generally just to keep out of sight. To influence or change the elite is out of the question.

This type of political system has been common. Here are some obvious examples: the Roman Empire, the empires established by Alexander the Great and Genghis Khan, and more recently, the Austro-Hungarian Empire. The Soviet Union, one could argue, was the last of these great world empires.

In the late twentieth century India still bears some resemblance to this pattern. Its population is deeply divided, fragmented into a multitude of diverse subcultures. The potential for intergroup violence is great, but it has

---

[8]For one interesting discussion of this matter, see Robert A. Dahl, *Polyarchy: Participation and Opposition* (New Haven, CT: Yale University Press, 1971), pp. 208–27 ("Postcript"). For a more recent treatment, see Guillermo O'Donnell and Philippe C. Schmitter, *Transitions from Authoritarian Rule: Tentative Conclusions about Uncertain Democracies* (Baltimore, MD: Johns Hopkins University Press, 1986).

been muted, in part, because many Indians are thoroughgoing fatalists. Their attitude produces widespread political apathy. Many of India's current problems, ironically, may stem from growing levels of citizen activism. As more groups turn to politics to achieve their aims, they will come into conflict with other groups radically opposed to those aims, and tensions will soar. Indian politics may already be moving into the heterogeneous–active culture of intergroup confrontation and violent turmoil.

POLITICAL TERMINOLOGY

Readers of this chapter have been exposed to some "strained" vocabulary. To categorize these four political cultures, I tried to use descriptively precise terms. Homogeneous–active, heterogeneous–passive, and so forth— these words, standing alone, pinpoint the central features of each culture. The word homogeneous–passive, for instance, tells you in a nutshell that citizens in that culture think and act alike (homogeneous), but don't participate much in politics (passive). This term is specific and descriptive. It also avoids the emotional overtones of partisan language, being almost clinical in its objectivity.

Despite the advantage of this terminology, the four words, taken as a whole, are cumbersome. They smack of social science jargon, and they also commit a scholarly sin that one should always avoid: inventing new words to describe already-known phenomena. Each culture type has long been familiar to students of political behavior—but under another name. For instance, the homogeneous–active culture sounds a lot like what Americans mean by the word "democracy." And the homogeneous–passive culture sounds a lot like "dictatorship." Why not simply use those common, everyday words and avoid unnecessary, not to mention irritating, jargon?

The trouble with "democracy" and "dictatorship" is that the words are heavily value laden. They raise emotional temperatures. Everyone knows that democracy is good and dictatorship bad. Consequently, every country in the world, it turns out, is a democracy. That is, rulers throughout the globe claim loudly that theirs is an ideal democratic system (no matter what form of government they actually operate). Not surprisingly, they also claim that the government of their worst enemies is clearly dictatorial. Even Saddam Hussein says this. We could argue forever and never agree on which countries are "really" democratic and which aren't.

What we need in a science of politics are terms that are factually descriptive, but emotionally nonprovocative. Terms that meet those criteria do exist for the four culture types already discussed. These cultures have been investigated, described, and labeled by many researchers over the years. While agreement on the meaning of terms is notoriously lacking in the social sciences, and even in this area is by no means unanimous, still the combined effort of many scholars over the years has produced words to describe these four political systems that are widely in use and lacking in obvious emotional stimuli. I plan to adopt these words in the interest of scientific uniformity.

From this point onward, therefore, let us relabel the four culture types.

-Homogeneous–active cultures will be called *polyarchal* cultures, or *polyarchies*.

-Heterogeneous–active cultures will be called *fragmented* cultures, or cultures of *fragmentation*.

-Homogeneous–passive cultures will be called *collectivist* cultures, or cultures of *collectivism*.

-Heterogeneous–passive cultures will be called *parochial* cultures, or cultures deriving from *empire*.

Table 4–1, which is identical to Table 3–1 except for the new terminology, puts the argument into perspective.

All of these terms are in wide usage. Social scientists already know them and even tend to agree on what they mean. The words don't sound as jargonistic as many do in our field. It is therefore worthwhile to use them.

One of these terms—polyarchy—is closely associated with the scholar, Robert Dahl, who invented the term and made it well known through his prolific and seminal writings.[9] The word seems especially appropriate for the dispassionate description of some real-world political systems.

Polyarchy means, literally, "many rule." Dahl uses the word specifi-

Table 4–1   Types of Political Culture

		Citizen Agreement on Basic Values?	
		Yes	No
Citizens Hold	Yes	Polyarchal culture	Fragmented culture
Activist Outlook?	No	Collectivist culture	Parochial culture

[9]He deals most extensively with this idea in *Polyarchy, op. cit.* See also his *Preface to Democractic Theory,* op. cit. and *Democracy and Its Critics* (New Haven, CT: Yale University Press, 1989). The term is also associated with Dahl's early close collaborator, Charles E. Lindblom, but over the years Dahl has been more persistent in writing about the forms, causes, and consequences of polyarchal political systems.

cally to describe political systems in which *many participants are allowed to contend publicly for political power.* Note the relative objectivity of this statement. Dahl argues, and I agree, that we should avoid the term democracy as a description of any existing political system, because the word carries too much emotional baggage. Besides implying some ideal state of affairs in which everyone is happy, it also suggests that, in the system being described, *all people share equally in political power.* That situation has never existed. Indeed, it is doubtful that power can ever be shared equally by any group of people numbering more than a few dozen. So the word democracy, beyond the ideological and emotional difficulties it presents, makes no sense as a description of any large-scale political system in the world today.[10]

Dahl argues, in essence, that we should jettison democracy as a descriptive term and adopt the practical and nonemotional term polyarchy. Polyarchy does, after all, describe the way some real-world political systems work. Nations do exist wherein (1) competition for power occurs; (2) many people can participate in that power struggle without fear for their lives; and (3) responsibility for public policy making is shared by a large and diverse set of actors. Those are the systems Dahl calls polyarchies.

The fit seems obvious between the homogeneous–active culture and the polyarchy. Only in a culture of participants will many citizens get involved in the political struggle and achieve some influence. Only in a homogeneous culture will the conflict resulting from this participation be moderate and restrained, so that competition can occur in an nonviolent atmosphere. Majorities will get their way, but won't ride roughshod over the rights of minorities. Polyarchal culture, homogeneous–active culture: they come to the same thing. Let us use the more common term.

The idea of a fragmented culture is found widely in the literature of political science. The terms *plural society* and *segmented culture* are also used to describe deeply divided nations. This concept is not clearly associated with a single author; several scholars have based their work on the idea.[11]

---

[10]I don't advocate throwing out the term altogether. The word democracy has its uses, especially in suggesting some ideal state toward which political systems should strive. But that, of course, is another matter.

[11]See, for example, Samuel P. Huntington and Joan Nelson, *No Easy Choice: Political Participation in Developing Countries* (Cambridge: Harvard University Press, 1976); Arend Lijphart, ed., *Conflict and Coexistence in Belgium: The Dynamics of a Culturally Divided Society* (Berkeley, CA: Institute of International Studies, 1981); Arend Lijphart, *Democracy in Plural Societies* (New Haven, CT: Yale University Press, 1977); Gabriel A. Almond and James S. Coleman, eds., *Politics of the Developing Areas* (Princeton, NJ: Princeton University Press, 1960); and Kenneth D. McRae, *Consociational Democracy: Political Accommodation in Segmented Societies* (Toronto: McClelland and Stewart, 1974).

Fragmentation: The very word suggests a society that is fractured, riven by noncohesive subgroups. In a culture of social fragments each isolated subculture has little in common with the others. Trust levels are low, conflict levels are high. The literature of political science has frequently described this pattern of deep social cleavage, a pattern I described in presenting heterogeneous–active culture. Since these terms clearly refer to the same phenomenon, let us henceforth use the term fragmented, which is already in wide usage, to describe this society.

Collectivism is also a familiar term in social science discourse, but again it is associated with no particular scholar. It implies a society in which people are unified: They think alike and hold similar values. The word also suggests a certain passivity, a follow-the-leader mentality. Some analysts prefer words like authoritarian, dictatorial, or even totalitarian to describe this culture, but those words are as emotive and value laden as is the term democracy. Collectivist has a neutral, nonpejorative ring to it.

Besides, to label this type of culture dictatorial would be misleading in two ways. First, it is not the only culture that can produce autocratic leadership. Dictators will often be found in parochial cultures; empires usually have their emperors, after all. Fragmented cultures as well produce the occasional autocrat. In the latter case dictatorship occurs when one of the conflicting subgroups wins temporary dominance and imposes its leader over the rest of society. That leader may then proceed to repress or even wipe out his group's internal enemies. Therefore, labeling the collectivist culture as dictatorial would create the misleading and erroneous impression that only this particular culture is likely to produce a repressive, one-person rule.

Furthermore, the use of terms like totalitarian and dictatorship suggest that the people within that system are being ruled against their will, which creates a false impression. Indeed, in collectivist nations most people *accept* the regime willingly. Its leaders and those who staff the system's various institutions are just like everyone else; it's a homogeneous society, after all. Most citizens in this culture don't feel any great desire to revolt and wouldn't describe themselves as living under a dictatorship. Living in a homogeneous culture that stresses social harmony, they may well feel that one party expressing the general will makes perfect sense. The term collectivism, implying submission of the individual to the will of the group, specifically captures this outlook.

The fourth culture type, heterogeneous–passive, is well described by two words: *imperialist* and *parochial*. It's an imperialist culture from its leaders' viewpoint: strong autocrats ruling a farflung patchwork of disparate regions and nationalities. It's a parochial culture from the populace's viewpoint. Most people within the system live in a narrow world of family and village, scarcely even aware that they form part of a larger political community. I shall use either term, depending on whether I refer to elite or mass culture in this system.[12]

In an imperialist culture, one group imposes its will on a large and diverse set of people, keeping them passively obedient and uninvolved with each other. Although the term imperialist has been used commonly since at least Roman times, the empire-building process seems antiquated today. It stands completely out of harmony with current trends. It is defied especially by the recent surge to create ministates that serve as spring-boards for the many minuscule nationalisms. This trend goes hand in hand with the deconstruction of formerly large and heterogeneous political systems. It seems safe to say that the decline of the imperialist (or parochial) culture is in full swing.

DEFINING POLITICAL VARIABLES

Our four cultures differ significantly from each other and, as we would expect, produce four distinct political systems. The political process within each culture can be clearly differentiated from the others on the basis of four variables. Specifically, each system produces a different answer to the following questions.

1. What is the attitude of people in the culture to the inevitable set of *social divisions* that exists in their society?
2. How exactly does society deal with the *conflict* that springs from these social divisions?
3. What is the citizenry's general *attitude toward the state?*
4. How do state institutions operate? What is the typical structure of *government?*

Each culture provides a unique answer to these four queries. Table 4–2 summarizes those answers and, in doing so, illustrates the four basic political patterns of our time.

AVOIDING CULTURAL GENERALITIES

Typologies represent generalizations about reality, yet all generalizations inevitably distort reality too. The world is complex, while intellectual categories are simple. No real-world entity fits perfectly into the little boxes

---

[12]Almond and Verba, *Civic Culture*, op cit., pp. 16–24, use the term "parochial political culture" in a somewhat different way from my usage here. They see it as designating cohesive, relatively isolated tribes. Their term "parochial-subject culture" comes closer to designating the political pattern I am describing.

Table 4–2 Overview of the Four Political Cultures: the Major Characteristics

Polyarchal Culture

1. Attitude toward social divisions	Relative trust prevails between people in different groups; an ethos of tolerance predominates, allowing for expression of differing social, religious, and political values.
2. How society deals with conflict	Low levels of political conflict lead to the acceptance of civil procedures and democratic norms to resolve disputes ("rule of law," open debate, elections, etc.).
3. Attitude toward the state	Moderately strong state loyalty, which falls short of blind obedience but overrides local and parochial ties.
4. Typical structure of government	Longlasting, stable, popular regime; elections determine which elites rule; peaceful governmental turnovers; high participation rates.

Fragmented Culture

1. Attitude toward social divisions	Social groups deeply mistrust each other; they don't acknowledge the legitimacy of their opponents' aims (nor, sometimes, even their right to exist); conflict levels are high, violence is common.
2. How society deals with conflict	No widely accepted procedures for resolving disputes; the basic decision rule to determine who governs is rule of the strongest.
3. Attitude toward the state	State viewed with alienation and hostility; occasionally seen as a means to an end (seizing control of the state allows promotion of one's own interests), but more often seen as a means for enemies to carry on their own nefarious plans for self-aggrandizement and oppression.
4. Typical structure of government	National governments are unstable in form and duration.

Collectivist Culture

1. Attitude toward social division	Citizens deeply fear disagreement and disharmony. They deny or turn a blind eye toward social divisions. Calls for supresion of socially dissident behavior will be widely supported.
2. How society deals with conflict	Social divisions are artificially suppressed by a dominant elite. Remaining disputes are resolved by unquestioning (and fearful) acceptance of authority figures' decisions.

Table 4–2   Continued

3. Attitude toward the state	Strong attachment to state, amounting at times to blind loyalty and unquestioning obedience.
4. Typical structure of government	Long periods of stable, authoritarian (usually militaristic) government, alternating with revolutionary turnover and short periods of political chaos.

Parochial Culture

1. Attitude toward social division	Ethnocentrism prevails; people live within the culture of their own subgroup, hardly aware of other subgroups; when made aware of them, they express fear and hatred.
2. How society deals with conflict	Major disputes resolved by fiat from a unified elite in control of the state apparatus; these central rulers delegate decision making on "minor" matters (i.e., those that don't affect their power base) to traditional subgroup (ethnic, regional, religious) leaders.
3. Attitude toward the state	State hardly acknowledged by those living inside its borders; local and parochial loyalties paramount; subgroup leaders recognize and support the state apparatus, in exchange for modest rewards.
4. Typical structure of government	Oligarchical rule of a unified elite; disputes occur from time to time among members of the elite but are usually resolved within the elite by intrigue or low levels of violence (e.g., assassination).

scholars construct while cogitating in cozy armchairs. Hence, no society exhibits perfectly all the hypothesized traits of a single culture type.

The best we can say is that many real-world societies tend *toward* exhibiting the characteristics of one of these types.[13] Furthermore, we can understand any society better when imagining it as an example of one culture type. The typology is useful; that's all we can ask. It isn't perfect, of course. Some societies may fall between the cracks. Either they have characteristics of more than one type, or they are in transition between two of them. As an example of the former, the old Soviet Union, in the Brezhnev era, had many traits of the collectivist culture—within Russia, an extremely homogeneous place at the time—but it bore significant resemblance to imperialist culture as well, given the wildly diverse set of disparate people living under the regime's control at that time. Current Japan, on the other

---

[13]Recall the earlier *caveat* on this point; see above, pp. 42–44.

hand, illustrates the transitional case. It looks like a collectivist culture and surely was until recently, but it appears to be moving, even if slowly, toward a polyarchal one.

SUMMARY

Given the uncertainty of life and the inevitability of change, these categories must not be seen as rigid absolutes. They are helpful and suggestive ways of ordering a complex reality.[14] The good student of politics maintains an openness and a common sense in using intellectual constructions. Not all societies will be perfectly described by these four terms. Let us use them where they illuminate the political process, but look for other ways to make sense of the world when these terms show an inability to explain political realities.

---

[14]In good social science jargon, we say the typology is "heuristic."

5

The Origins
of Political Culture

Once we accept that different political cultures exist and differ radically from each other, a logical question arises. Where do these differences come from? Why exactly are people alienated from politics and cynical in southern Italy, Colombia, and south central Los Angeles, while they are imbued with a reasonable degree of trust in governmental processes and a participatory spirit in Sweden, Switzerland, and Minnesota?

We can't find easy answers to these questions. Obviously, if we knew how to create stable, peaceful, and participatory societies, we would do so immediately. For decades, perhaps a century, democratizing the world has been a central goal of American foreign policy and the fondest wish of the American public. If the task were easy, we'd have a world of peaceful polyarchies by now.[1] The conditions that give rise to a culture supporting polyarchal politics are complex. They take ages to develop and have a life of their own—immune, it often appears, to outside manipulation. As is frequently the case in history, accidental occurrence, as much as rational planning, accounts for the mix of values that become embedded in the cultural perspectives of any given society.

For example, the way governments decide to collect taxes can have enormous political consequence. In his study of pre-Revolutionary France,

[1]On the difficulty of creating polyarchies by design, see Dahl, *Polyarchy, op. cit.*, pp. 208–27, and Robert Putnam, with Robert Leonardi and Raffaella Nanetti, *Making Democracy Work: Civic Traditions in Modern Italy* (Princeton, NJ: Princeton University Press, 1993), pp. 121–85.

the great nineteenth century French historian Tocqueville showed how a government can lose the loyalty of its citizens and reduce their level of social trust, simply by failing to think through the implications of its tax-collection process.[2] An examination of his analysis will be illuminating.

The process of collecting taxes in pre-Revolutionary France began with an arbitrary decision in Paris. Bureaucrats in the central Finance Ministry would decide that each village in the country would have to raise a set sum of money for that year. This sum varied from one year to the next, so no one could ever be sure just what the tax bill was going to be. Regularity, stability, planning—all became impossible, and villagers knew that the government had created this chaotic state of affairs.

The situation got worse. There were no regular tax collectors. A regional official randomly chose some village resident to collect taxes from his unhappy peers. Each year a new tax collector was appointed. Thus, each person in the village came to be detested by all his neighbors. (How do you like people who knock on your door and ask for large sums of money?) Since these temporary officials were unschooled in tax law, had no official records to help them, and could neither read nor write, their decisions about who owed what to the government were even more arbitrary than the government's decision about how much each village owed as a whole. Human nature being what it is, their decisions would not reflect the "ability to pay," but rather the connections and animosities of local life. A cousin might pay little tax; a village rival would be gouged.

Since no one could tell who would become tax collector and when, villagers learned over the years to be secretive, to remain aloof from each other. After all, if someone knew you well and realized that your affairs were thriving, he could tax you outrageously when his turn came to collect taxes. Villagers learned to be tight-lipped and keep to themselves. Unlike the American pattern of conspicuous consumption, French peasants feigned conspicuous poverty. They learned to let no one inside their homes, in order to avoid the possibility that word of their comfortable circumstances might leak out to the tax collector of the day.

Many of the patterns set up by this absurd system endured for centuries. The French hatred of taxation is legendary, as is their cleverness at evading tax payment. Their wholehearted suspicion of government also dates from this era. Finally, the French villager's distrust of "the others"— that is, peers and colleagues in the community—is also legendary and derives, at least in part, from the prerevolutionary tax system.

Two hundred years after that system was abolished, French villager animosity toward peers was still strong. Laurence Wylie, recounting the year he spent in a small French town, vividly describes these traditional

---

[2]See his classic account of the pre-Revolutionary tax-collection system in Alexis de Tocqueville, *The Old Régime and the French Revolution* (Garden City, NY: Doubleday & Company, Inc., 1955), pp. 125–28.

peasant suspicions.[3] Each villager, for instance, would take Wylie aside and warn him not to trust anyone else in the hamlet. When Wylie pointed out to one of these pessimists that all his experience showed everyone in the village to be honest and trustworthy, his acquaintance snapped,

> Well, there you are. If you listen to all that "the others" say you'll never know the truth. The fact is that people here are honest, as you see for yourself. You have to learn to ignore "the others" if you live here; they can't be trusted. [!][4]

Even to this day, the French maintain a habit of fronting their homes with shabby, decaying exteriors (to fool would-be tax collectors), while spending serious sums of money on interior decoration—which can't be seen by the prying eyes of the outside world.

One could find, for each country, critical historical events like the one Tocqueville discovered in French history—events that helped produce those key values and outlooks embedded in the modern culture. Cultures don't develop overnight, nor do they change overnight. They are the product of a long, slow set of unique historical developments, which often reflect unforeseen, unforeseeable, and accidental occurrences.

VARIABLES THAT DETERMINE POLYARCHY

Robert Dahl has for years explored the conditions that make poly-archy more or less likely. His studies clearly show that certain key variables play a vital role in shaping the political values of people in any given place. His work (and that of others) points to a small number of variables that help determine a nation's culture.[5]

1. *The class system.* If clear and strong class differences exist, differences that present enormous barriers to those wishing to rise from one class to the next, then distrust between socioeconomic groupings will be high and conflict levels will be intense. These societal schisms will prevent the development of social comity and impede cultural homogeneity. People in different groupings will not see each other as equals, to be respected and given equal rights and powers. They will never develop that all-important outlook for stable polyarchy, which asserts: "Yes, we have our differences, but despite everything, we're all in this together and we're all (Americans),

---

[3]Wylie and his family inhabited a village in southern France during the early 1950s. See his fascinating account of this experience in Laurence Wylie, *Village in the Vaucluse,* 2nd Ed. (Cambridge, MA: Harvard University Press, 1964).

[4] Ibid., p. 196.

[5]In the following pages I draw heavily on Dahl's discussion of the conditions necessary for polyarchy in *Polyarchy,* op. cit., esp. pp. 202–07 and the summarizing table on p. 203.

(Japanese), (Australians), (whatever)." The longer the period in which these feelings of class difference exist, the more likely they are to instill social fissures and fractures that make a unified, cohesive culture difficult to achieve.

2. *Level of wealth*. Political scientists rarely unite in their opinions. Their academic disputes rival those of the politicians they study. But if there is one point on which most of them agree, it is this: Impoverished nations are unlikely to develop stable, free, and competitive institutions.

Most wealthy countries become polyarchies, while most poor countries are nonpolyarchal. These assertions can be easily demonstrated. However we measure national wealth, we find that richer lands are likely to be polyarchal, while poorer ones are less likely. As Dahl puts it, "The higher the socio-economic level of a country, the more likely it is to have a competitive political regime."[6]

Just why wealth correlates with democratic or polyarchal behavior patterns is not entirely clear. The process linking the two variables is surely complex, but two reasons quickly suggest themselves. First, wealth produces satisfaction, or at least some degree of contentment. Happy people don't leave their homes to riot in the street. They don't hunt down and kill their neighbors. They don't risk their lives trying to topple governments. In short, people who are even reasonably well-off seem unlikely to act in ways that produce political instability.

Wealth by itself, however, is not sufficient for political stability. If a country's riches are unevenly apportioned, deep resentment between its haves and have-nots may develop, leading to violence. Wealth must be spread fairly *evenly* to insure the survival of polyarchy. The reason is simple: If many citizens are well-off, no group can make a reasonable claim to special rights and privileges on the grounds of being clearly superior. If few people are badly off, no well-off group will develop an excessive fear of "the masses;" hence, no one will work to disenfranchise society's poorer citizens. Only when *most* citizens are reasonably wealthy, then, will a polyarchal culture develop. Otherwise, you are likely to see either elite rule (by the wealthy few) or mass rebellion (by the poor many), and both these situations impede advancement toward polyarchy.

Thus, equality of wealth is as important as wealth itself in laying the groundwork for polyarchy. If many people are well-off and few are impoverished, a sense of general contentment will combine with feelings of social equality. Wealth *and* equality are the two factors that lay the groundwork for mass participation in moderate political activity, a political style that practically defines polyarchal politics.

3. *The beliefs of political activists*. Those who are most active and most powerful in any institution will have the most impact in shaping it. Hence,

[6]Dahl, *Polyarchy*, p. 64.

political activists will have an inordinate impact on the political life of their country.[7] Participants in some places seem shrill, rigid, vengeful. Politics there is unlikely to develop the norms of tolerance, compromise, and respect for majority rule that are associated with polyarchal systems. Where political activists exhibit traits congruent with democratic processes—respect for those you disagree with, support for widespread citizen participation, acceptance of the legitimacy of government decisions you dislike—the entire society's commitment to polyarchal methods of resolving conflict will grow.[8]

4. *Number of distinct and antagonistic subcultures.* We have already stressed this point. In a nation racked by ethnic, racial, and regional hatreds, we hardly expect to find citizens thinking of each other as equals, respecting each other's viewpoint, accepting with equanimity the possibility that members of a competing political group may gain power. In short, the growth of polyarchal norms won't develop where intergroup animosity is high. Few nations with large, cohesive, and dramatically different subgroupings have remained polyarchal for long.

5. *Historical developments.* The events of a nation's past hang heavy over its present and future. Three types of historical occurrence are especially crucial in determining the likelihood of a nation becoming polyarchal.

(a) Independence or foreign control? Foreign domination, especially over a prolonged time, produces conditions especially *un*favorable to polyarchy. The reason seems clear: By definition, if one people is compelled against its will to submit to another, it isn't living in free and open circumstances. If you haven't experienced freedom, you can't easily learn the norms and habits of a polyarchal system: tolerance for enemies, moderated competition for power, and so on. Citizens used to enforced obedience don't gain practice in the give-and-take methods of resolving conflict that are central to polyarchal politics.

Russia offers a prime example of this pattern. For 200 years (roughly 1240 to 1450) Russians lived under the control of a brutal Tatar (or Mongol) empire. Those years helped create a profoundly nondemocratic culture. Most Russians, by necessity, survived by behaving as servile subjects. Their attitude of abject obedience endured long after the end of the Tatar reign. The few Russian leaders whom the Tatars allowed to operate adopted that attitude of cruel arrogance exhibited by their masters from the East. Thus, Russian citizens came to think of themselves as obedient subjects, while Russian rulers defined themselves as ruthless demigods. Those norms, set firmly by the year 1500, have since shaped Russian politics.

---

[7]Political activists are loosely defined as those who spend large blocks of their time in politics, as distinct from average citizens who devote very little time to politics. For a lengthy discussion of activists and their influence, see below, chap. 11.

[8]Robert Putnam explores the effect of elite values on political culture in *The Beliefs of Politicians: Ideology, Conflict, and Democracy in Britain and Italy* (New Haven, CT: Yale University Press, 1973).

Life under the domination of another people will often produce these feelings of fear and servitude that are wholly incompatible with the participationist ethos of a polyarchy. It undermines polyarchy in other ways too. Domination by outsiders can bring feelings of alienation and distrust. People may develop that attitude of negative individualism characteristic of fragmented cultures. ("I'll do what I can to survive; screw anyone else.") Edward Banfield calls this outlook "amoral familism," postulating that it is based on a simple operating rule: "Maximize the material, short-run advantage of the nuclear family; assume that all others will do likewise."[9] Attitudes of this sort, which seem common in many Latin American nations, may be traced to their years of savage oppression at the hands of Spain and Portugal.

In a few special cases foreign domination may *not* undercut the chances for polyarchy; it may even enhance them. That situation occurs when the foreign power itself is a polyarchy—or is developing toward polyarchy. The United States, Canada, Australia, New Zealand, and other formerly British colonies were once under "foreign domination," but have clearly today become polyarchies. The same might be said (perhaps with less conviction) for Puerto Rico, the Philippines, Japan, South Korea, and other lands formerly under U.S. control. Foreign domination, it appears, doesn't *have* to prevent polyarchy.

These examples probably do represent special cases, however, since the foreign power encouraged the development of competitive elections, parliaments, and other trappings of the polyarchal system. Nevertheless, they teach us that foreign domination alone does not undercut the conditions suitable for polyarchy. What counts is *foreign domination as a militaristic–autocratic phenomenon*. It seems safe to conclude that nations that have experienced a long period of *oppressive* foreign rule have found it difficult to advance toward a system of political polyarchy.

(b) Historical accidents and singular events. Chance plays a greater role in our lives, and certainly in the life of nations and in history, than we usually care to admit. How different the history of Europe might have been, for instance, had the winter of 1812 been a mild one and not one of the coldest on record. Napoleon's army might then *not* have been wiped out during his invasion of Russia. What if it had instead survived to keep him master of the Western world? Would that development have impeded the growth of polyarchal conditions that occurred throughout much of Western Europe during the nineteenth century?

In a similar vein, what if the Battle of the Spanish Armada in 1588, which gave Britain supremacy of the seas for generations, had *not* occurred during a violent storm, which handicapped the bulky and hard-to-maneuver ships of the Spanish fleet? A Spanish victory there might have led to

---

[9]Banfield, *Moral Basis of a Backward Society*, op. cit., p. 83. See my discussion of parochials on pp. 57–60 of this text.

Spanish, not English, colonization of North America. Think what a different world we would live in today had that been the case. Would North American politics then have developed along the lines of the political system in Colombia?

And what about the impact of discovering gold in California in 1848? Many historians believe that the American North could not have won the Civil War without the financial benefits of the Gold Rush. It gave the North money to buy weapons and supplies, as well as funds to pay men to fight. It also gave New York bankers enough confidence in the future that they were willing to make loans to Lincoln's government for prosecution of the war. The influx of that gold into the Northern economy generally kept it humming along in high gear instead of faltering during the war, as many had expected it to do. One could argue that this chance discovery kept the United States united in fact and also allowed the abolition of slavery, one of the great impediments toward the development of real polyarchy in North America.

In short, the unforeseen consequences of unplanned and unintended events can have enormous historical repercussions for the shaping of a nation's political culture.

(c) The timing of mass political participation. The studies of Dahl and others show that one variable makes an extraordinary impact on the likelihood of polyarchal development: the conditions under which the bulk of a nation's people enters political life. Roughly speaking, if *suddenly* the mass of citizens in a given nation enters politics, the chances diminish for that nation to become a stable polyarchy.

This point is easily illustrated. Imagine that the United States "liberated" North Korea. Our president would surely announce that North Koreans now had "their freedom," and he would urge them to move forward to fair and competitive elections. Yet even if we (or the United Nations) *guaranteed* them a free election, one would hardly expect to see North Korea operating in the democratic fashion of Norway, say, or Luxembourg in the next year or two—or even in the next twenty years. In the same manner, if the United States decided to "free" the people of Libya from the control of their current dictator, Moammar Qaddafi, one would not expect that country overnight to become a model of pluralistic competition.

Indeed, we don't need to resort to these seemingly far-fetched examples. The United States has in a number of places intervened to "free" various people from their tyrannical rulers, practically forcing them to hold "democratic" elections. American Marines invaded a number of Latin American countries during the early decades of the twentieth century with "democratization" as the prime rationale. In most cases the cure didn't take. The fragile democratic institutions we set up were toppled within a few years (sometimes months), as the typical local pattern of strongman rule or civil war reasserted itself after the departure of American troops.

Polyarchy, in short, takes time. Illiterate people used to obeying autocrats or habituated to following sectarian zealots into deadly warfare against their foes don't suddenly behave like members of the League of Women Voters just because someone out of the blue tells them they are "free" and have the right to participate in "fair elections."

People everywhere continue to act as they always have. If they are used to obeying dictators or using violence against enemies, they won't suddenly confront tyrants or show tolerance to foes the moment they are allowed to vote. People in a collectivist culture, if suddenly given the vote, will likely choose an authoritarian leader who will behave like any dictator and make the cancellation of future elections his or her first priority. In a fragmented culture, first-time voters are likely to be swayed by vocal subgroup leaders. The electorate will proceed to choose demagogic representatives who promise to annihilate each other.

LEGITIMATE OPPOSITION: A NEW POLITICS

As a result of the sudden influx of the masses into politics, elections will produce another dictatorship or another civil war, depending on the culture in which they occur. In either case, polyarchy perishes.

Polyarchies don't develop when an uninformed mass of citizens, not schooled in the habits, norms, and ideals of democracy, are suddenly given the vote. Three historical traditions are necessary to insure the stable construction of polyarchy: (1) a history of political competition, (2) a gradual enfranchisement of the citizenry, and (3) a tradition of mass education.

1. *A tradition of political competition.* This point is crucial. One of the hardest things for any leader to accept, is the existence of legitimate rivals. Over the ages most political systems have tended toward anarchy and fragmentation (as rivals for power tried to kill each other) or dictatorship (as one set of competitors triumphed and imposed their will on everyone else). One of the latest ideas to develop in the history of political systems was the concept of "the loyal opposition."[10]

The fact that a rival faction could oppose you and your group and your interests and *still* be allowed a fair hearing, still be treated as an honorable equal was a radical concept in itself. Even more radical was the idea that that group should be given every opportunity to expand its political powers so as to *supplant* you and your group and your interests, allowing these disputants to control the powers and resources of government, which

---

[10]See the extensive discussion of this point by various authors in Robert A. Dahl, ed., *Political Oppositions in Western Democracies* (New Haven, CT: Yale University Press, 1966), especially the preface by Dahl himself, pp. xi–xix. See also Joseph LaPalombara and Myron Weiner, *Political Parties and Political Development* (Princeton, NJ: Princeton University Press, 1966), pp. 3–42 and 177–200.

traditionally had been in *your* hands. Such an idea has been virtually unheard of throughout most of human history. Not until the eighteenth century did this notion of a legitimate opposition slowly begin to take hold—and it developed only in parts of western Europe and in a few other places populated by the descendants of west Europeans.

To summarize a long history, the idea of legitimate and peaceful competition for the right to govern came only slowly and painfully to be accepted by the ruling elites of a small number of countries. As recently as the late nineteenth century, the vast majority of nations rejected this norm altogether.

It may help you grasp how unusual this idea of the right to compete for and take power actually is, if you remember those familiar images that occur when one president is replaced by another. Most of us can recall the recent inauguration ceremony. George Bush actually walked away from power, as Bill Clinton walked into it. The extraordinary nature of that event can't be overstressed. Smooth transfers of power have occurred but rarely in the history of the world. Imagine Saddam Hussein walking out of the presidential palace in Baghdad to greet his chief rival, Mohammed ben-Abi Hassam (or whoever), wishing Hassam well in his coming stint as national leader of Iraq. Or imagine Chinese communist leaders stepping down from power, after admitting defeat in a national election by, say, the Free Enterprise Party. You need a strong imagination to picture these events, because they can't and won't happen—not in the present cultural environment of Iraq and China and dozens of similar places throughout the world.

Free and open competition in which you can actually lose power is hardly a popular idea for elites. And since elites structure political institutions, competition—an idea at the core of the polyarchal concept—will never happen unless elites accept it. No, we must state it more strongly. The idea must be embedded into the elite value system, so that political activists will actually *defend* their opponents' right to compete, if the idea ever comes under attack.

2. *Gradual enfranchisement of the citizenry.* If legitimate competition is difficult for elites to accept, it would appear even more difficult to be accepted by people unfamiliar with the political process. In nearly all countries today in which the right to rule is determined by free and fair elections, the tradition of legitimate competition developed first at the elite level, then gradually spread to the masses as they were slowly admitted to full political rights and then socialized into the norms of the polyarchal political process.

In other words, if you want to move toward democracy, start slowly. Teach a small number of leaders—society's political participants—the idea of competition. Encourage them to try it, make sure they understand it and learn to abide by its rules: Losers leave office, winners get power, no one wipes out the other. Then after a few years expand the political class a bit, and then some more, and finally open it to all, but open it only after the broader culture has accepted this general habit of competition, only after most people have come to accept that their group will not win every election, that elections must be held regularly, and that deference to the electorate's wishes in each election is absolutely mandatory.

Dahl provides a simple and powerful summary of this process. In the historical sequence most favorable to the development of polyarchy, he says, *"competition precedes inclusiveness."*[11]

3. *An educated populace.* Polyarchy and education go hand in hand. Very few countries with illiterate citizenries seem able to sustain pluralistic competition. True, a well-educated population does not *guarantee* polyarchal politics. Germany in the 1930s, supporting a Nazi dictatorship, had citizens as well educated as those in democratic Britain, France, or Norway. Nevertheless, without a literate, reasonably educated mass base, polyarchy as a system stands little chance of long-term health.

It takes little effort to verify this proposition . Look around the world. The vast majority of highly educated nations are polyarchies or are nations moving toward polyarchy. The vast majority of countries with illiterate majorities are nonpolyarchies: fragmented states for the most part. The correlation between level of education and likelihood of stable political competition is clear and strong. Just why this correlation should exist is not quite as clear, but theories abound. The connection may derive from a fact we have just discussed: The idea of allowing those you hate to compete for the right to gain power is not easy to accept. Education may help make it acceptable, because it expands our horizons, opens our eyes to other ways of thinking and acting. It may lead to greater tolerance for the rights of others whose views differ from ours. It also helps us understand the rationale underlying peaceful competition. If you allow others to seek power without trying to kill them, they may reciprocate, allowing *you* to seek power without fear of being killed. The personal benefits of this system are obvious.

Education also improves one's mastery of the environment, enhances one's life chances, and increases one's overall self-confidence. Self-assured people may be less threatened by those who are different from them; they may be better able to let others share power without fearing obliteration of self as a consequence.

Finally, education may enhance the possibilities for polyarchal politics by producing higher levels of cultural homogeneity. Most educated nations develop a reasonably unified system of education; thus, their schoolchildren learn the same perspectives and absorb the same values. This agreement on values, as we know, is a key requirement for polyarchal culture.

These are all speculations. One can conjure up other reasons as well to explain the correlation between education and polyarchy. The main point is

[11]Dahl, *Polyarchy*, op. cit., p. 203 [emphasis added].

to stress the fact itself and its causal significance. The rule is simple: If you want a polyarchy, you need to provide your citizens with mass education of high quality. Without it, you are going to find that sustaining peaceful political competition is a difficult task indeed.

SUMMARY

The roots of culture lie deep in a nation's past. Some historical developments are congruent with polyarchal norms and values; others are not. Factors that diminish social division, while encouraging individual self-esteem, are most likely to produce a culture capable of sustaining polyarchal patterns of conflict resolution. Thus, where levels of class and subculture consciousness are moderate to low, social conflict can be resolved through civil and procedural methods rather than through violence. Where most people are educated and wealthy, they will feel less threatened and less desperate about the demands of other groups, so they will be able to deal with those demands through accommodation, not confrontation.

In explaining current cultures, we must also pay close attention to accidents of history. Chance events often become justified as right and inevitable. If a government responds to popular pressures only after people take to the streets (France, 1789), a tradition gets set up: If we don't like our government, let's take to the streets. If a leader steps down from power after eight years (George Washington, 1797), another tradition takes hold: No leader should serve more than eight years. The luck of history thus deeply affects modern cultural norms that bear on support for polyarchy.

A key factor in the development of polyarchy is gradualism. Nations can't quickly become full-fledged polyarchies. This system can't exist unless most political activists respect the rights and opinions of others, even to the point of letting those others compete for and hold power. This idea—that legitimate rivals are proper and even desirable—is difficult to grasp, especially for those eager to gain power themselves. Only after that idea has been deeply embedded in the outlook of the political élite is it likely to trickle down slowly to the broader mass of citizens. Thus, it takes years of peaceful elite competition, with a gradual inclusion of more and more citizens into the political framework, before the entire culture is embued with the notion that continuous peaceful competition for power is the only acceptable way to resolve political differences.

A culture favorable to polyarchal politics, then, doesn't happen overnight. Neither do the fragmented, collectivist, or parochial cultures. Values within a culture develop over decades and even centuries as a result of complex social, economic, and historical experience. They are, as a result, deeply ingrained in the minds of those cultures' citizens. These values aren't susceptible to quick and easy change. They are likely to endure—and in so doing, sustain the traditional political patterns that each culture has evolved to fit its psychological style and philosophical perspective. The longevity of cultures is a topic worth exploring in depth—and the subject toward which we now turn our attention.

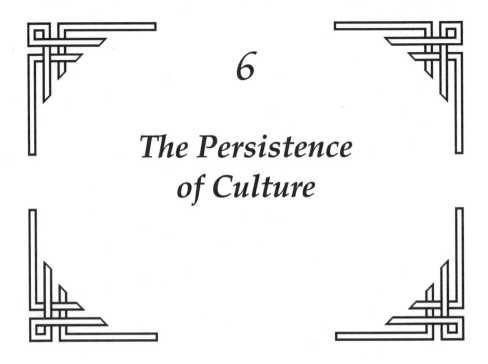

6

The Persistence of Culture

Compare these two comments about Italy, which appeared recently in the *International Herald Tribune*.

> Almost every day, new disclosures link Italy's political and business leaders in a vast web of organized corruption. The scale of wrongdoing has outraged even the famously cynical Italian public, feeding demands for fundamental changes. . . .

> The situation in the Italian Parliament is becoming graver, and the [Cabinet] continues to oppose the inquiry into the Banks Scandal. . . . We live in an age when the people have lost all confidence in those who represent them. . . . They want honest men.

Both comments describe a key element in Italian politics: widespread corruption among political elites. Both argue that this pattern has led to high levels of voter cynicism and an unstoppable demand for radical reform.

THE MORE THINGS CHANGE . . .

Despite their similarity, however, the previous comments differ in one dramatic aspect: They were written one hundred years apart!

The first comment appears on page four of the Tribune's March 4, 1993, edition; it represents their lead editorial. The second comment appears on the same day and on the same page, but with this difference: It is found under the rubric "In Our Pages: 100, 75 and 50 Years Ago," and it is subtitled "1893: Italian Scandals." I reproduced this one-hundred-year-old quote with just one minor change (to avoid identifying its era). The word Cabinet (in brackets in the second of the two previous quotes) replaces the actual words Giolitti Ministry. Otherwise, the passage reads just as it was written in the late nineteenth century. *It would appear that nothing has changed in the broad pattern of Italian politics—except the names of the players.*

This concept is relevant to all countries. Go back a hundred years and you will find people in the United States complaining about the "obscene" power of "petty tyrants" in Congress who wield "excessive" power in committee through the "archaic and irrational" seniority system. American political moralists have been demanding "reform" of Congress to "better reflect the people's will" long before any current reformers, who are making the same demands, saw the light of day.

By the same token, one finds descriptions of the "absolutism" and "barbarity" of Russia's political leaders going back centuries. In 1950 the tyrant Stalin governed the Russian nation. In 1850 it was governed by the brutal Tsar, Nicholas I, who suppressed all dissent with callous cruelty. In 1750 Russia was soon to be ruled by Catherine I ("the Great"), who befriended Enlightenment philosophers like Voltaire, but who attained the throne by murdering her husband and later defeated peasant rebellion with barbarous massacres. One can continue in this vein back through Peter the Great and Ivan the Terrible to the Mongol invasions of the thirteenth century. One must return to the year 1220 or so, to find a time when Russians were ruled with some degree of humanity.

In other words, political systems persist. Take any group of astute political observers and transport them one hundred years back in time within their own country. Once they make allowance for obvious technological differences, they will feel right at home and will understand perfectly what is going on.

We can predict the same would be true if we transported them one hundred years into the future. If we could leap ahead to 2095, what would we see in the United States, Russia, or Italy? Some American reformer will likely be denouncing the excessive power of some "congressional dictator" ensconced at the head of some obscure subcommittee. Some Russian reformer, from exile in Paris or London, will no doubt be denouncing the *real* dictatorship of the Russian leader of that age. And some Italian reformer will probably be denouncing the continued scandal of corrupt Italian legislators, pointing out that the people are "fed up" with the old system and demand its immediate transformation.

Obviously, change is possible, and I could be wrong in these predictions. Yet pattern persistence is the most common expectation. Bet on things continuing to happen as they have in the past, bet on people continuing to behave as they have behaved in the past, and you are unlikely to go broke!

The reason political systems change slowly should be obvious by now. They are based on deep-seated cultural norms, values, and expectations; these in turn shape the personalities and the behavior patterns of all members of the culture. The culture itself came into existence over a period of decades, more likely centuries. It can change over time, but this change will normally occur incrementally, at the margins. In any person's lifetime these changes will appear modest, sometimes barely recognizable. And the more deeply ingrained the attitude, the less likely it is that time alone or merely modest historical change will destroy, or even affect, the attitude. Only dramatic, powerful, long-lasting historical developments are likely to affect the core of a cultural outlook, and events with that type of impact on a nation occur rarely.

We can test the truth of this position by again turning to historical sources. Has American culture changed seriously in the last one to two hundred years? Our first reaction is to say, "Of course!" Many dramatic developments have occurred since the time of Washington or Lincoln. We have gone from an agrarian to an urban society. We have become more tolerant and egalitarian in matters of race and gender. Indeed, we have become more supportive of all minorities. We have become less religious and less puritanical than we once were. But in many essential elements American culture has changed little since foreigners first began describing it at least 200 years ago.

The most famous observer of American mores was the French aristocrat, Alexis de Tocqueville. After an 1831 visit to the United States he returned to Europe and wrote his brilliant social analysis, *Democracy in America*.[1] The book became a runaway bestseller and has been continuously in print ever since. Delving into this work, I am always amazed at its contemporaneity. A modest updating of the language, and the text would read as if culled from the pages of a current newspaper.

Many of Tocqueville's observations sound as if uttered by pop psychologists on the Phil Donahue show or by political reporters during a Ted Koppel interview. American character, says Tocqueville, exhibits "a restless spirit, immoderate desire for wealth, and an extreme love of independence."[2] He goes on, "The passions that stir the Americans most deeply are commercial and not political. . . ."[3] As a result of these traits, says Tocqueville, Americans have become the richest people on earth. Yet even so, the apple contains a worm. Americans "find prosperity almost every-

---

[1]Alexis de Tocqueville, *Democracy in America*, edited by J. P. Mayer and Max Lerner (New York: Harper & Row, Publishers, 1966).
[2]Ibid., p. 262.
[3]Ibid., pp. 262–3.

where, but not happiness. For them desire for well-being has become a rest-less, burning passion, which increases with satisfaction."[4]

How often have we heard Americans described in these terms? We are an ambitious, driven people, worshipping the false God of Mammon (or "the almighty dollar," pick your cliché), never satisfied despite all our wealth. When you hear people talking today in these somber tones, deplor-ing the loss of "traditional American values," just remember: Tocqueville was saying the same thing in the 1830s. And he was hardly the first to make those observations.

Let's take another instance in which Tocqueville captured something enduring in American culture. Imagine the way new immigrants to the United States feel when they arrive in the 1990s—especially those used to orderly, even oppressive, regimes. Would their reaction be different from that of Tocqueville in 1831?

> No sooner do you set foot on American soil than you find yourself in a sort of tumult; a confused clamor rises on every side, and a thou-sand voices are heard at once, each expressing some social require-ments. All around you everything is on the move: here the people of a district are assembled to discuss the possibility of building a church; there they are busy choosing a representative; further on, the dele-gates of a district are hurrying to town to consult about some local improvements; elsewhere it's the village farmers who have left their furrows to discuss the plan for a road or a school. One group of citi-zens assembles for the sole object of announcing that they disapprove of the government's course, while others unite to proclaim that the men in office are the fathers of their country.[5]

The chaos and color of American life has always played a large role in this culture. Like most patterns in American society today, it's not something that sprang up just last week.

The America that Tocqueville observed sounds familiar to us today in myriad ways, right down to the mundane aspects of everyday life. Note, for instance, how he described something as ordinary as the format of an American newspaper:

> In America three quarters of the bulky newspaper put before you will be full of advertisements and the rest will usually contain political news or just anecdotes; only at long intervals and in some obscure cor-ner will one find one of those burning arguments which for us [in France] are the readers' daily food.[6]

[4]Ibid., p. 261.
[5]Ibid., pp. 223–4.
[6]Ibid., p. 169.

Have American newspapers changed much since this description? Most space is still devoted to advertising; most of the writing is chockablock with unrelated anecdotes interspersed with major political stories of the day; and pieces devoted to political opinions are relegated to some difficult-to-find middle section of the paper known as the editorial page.

Tocqueville goes on to observe that "the number of periodical or semi-periodical productions in the United States surpasses all belief."[7] After even a few minutes in front of an average American newsstand, we would hardly be inclined to dispute those words—yet they were written 160 years ago. American social patterns, in other words, did not spring forth out of the blue in 1959 or 1976 or 1983. The American outlook as we know it today was not radically different in 1831—or 1731 for that matter.

Tocqueville's account of culture, society, and politics in the United States has endured for generations not simply for his trenchant observations of daily life. Observers before and since his time produced similar descriptive accounts. What Tocqueville did was to catch the essence of the American value system. He was the first to explore the relationship between American beliefs and the American form of government. In essence, he set out to explain, in *Democracy in America*, how American values provided essential underpinning for a working democracy. He said, "It is their mores . . . that make the Americans . . . capable of maintaining the rule of democracy."[8] And by "mores," Tocqueville meant what social scientists today call "cultural values." So in essence he was pursuing the same line of research as students of society today: exploring the effect of people's beliefs on the patterns of their social institutions.

To summarize Tocqueville's argument briefly, Americans in 1831 were capable of maintaining a federal system of representative democracy because they supported a set of values essential to the maintenance of that system. The primary values underpinning democracy, which Tocqueville stressed time and again, were the following:

1) A love of freedom
2) A spirit of independence and individualism
3) An orientation of common sense and a concern for the practical
4) A restless desire to better oneself, to get ahead, to acquire wealth
5) A deep-seated belief in the need for education—especially education for all and not just for an elite
6) An informality of spirit, an ease of interacting socially with people of all ranks and statuses
7) A "joiner" orientation (not Tocqueville's term); that is, a readiness to join existing groups or to get together with others to form new ones

[7]Ibid., p. 170.
[8]Ibid., p. 283.

8) A strong belief in the legal equality of all citizens and, following from that belief, a zealous attachment to the ideal of "the will of the majority"

9) A tolerance of minority perspectives

10) A deep belief in God and a strong commitment to religion and religious values

Do these perspectives sound familiar? A century and a half after Tocqueville, contemporary observers of the United States use similar words to describe American culture. The French have a phrase for it: *The more things change, the more they stay the same.*

Of course, we mustn't conclude that change never occurs. Looking over Tocqueville's list of "mores," modern observers will be inclined to add here or subtract there and especially modify the emphases. Religious commitments, for instance, no longer seem as solid as they once were, while Tocqueville saw American dedication to religion as perhaps its foremost characteristic. Yet even after years of decline in their religious fervor, Americans still hold a wide lead over the citizens in other nations when it comes to "belief in God" and support for other ideas central to mainstream Western religious traditions.[9]

Current analysts, looking at American values, might stress an increased focus on commercial materialism, and yet throughout *Democracy in America* Tocqueville made clear that an eagerness to gain wealth was rampant in the American society of that day. Of course, one of the great changes of the last century and a half occurred in the way Americans define *citizen*. The belief in "legal equality of all citizens" (see point 8 from the previous list) remains strong, but "citizens" now include women, people in the age group from eigthteen to twenty, nonlandowners, and minority groups of every type—especially African Americans, most of whom were legally regarded as chattel in Tocqueville's day.

Change, in short, has occurred, but perhaps more dramatic is how little has changed in the basic spirit of the country, the outlook of the people, and the workings of American political institutions. Does anyone doubt that Tocqueville, returning to the United States in our age, would recognize the scene?

The United States is not unique. In the institutions of all countries this persistence of social and political patterns is obvious. Discussing China, Lucian Pye argues that "two thousand years of Confucian government was an uninterrupted era of authoritarian rule."[10] Robert Putnam shows that historical developments occurring about the year 1100 helped produce the

---

[9]Comparative survey research always shows that Americans are more publicly devoted to religion than are the citizens of other countries. For a summary of evidence on the importance of religion to Americans, see Kenneth D. Wald, *Religion and Politics in the United States* (New York: St. Martin's Press, 1987), pp. 1–21.

[10]Lucian W. Pye, *China: An Introduction* (Boston: Little Brown and Company, 1972), p. 344.

famous division of Italy into two regions, North and South, with the former developing a tradition of popular self-rule and the latter a tradition of corrupt, authoritarian governance.[11] Even today, as Putnam shows, the alienated fatalism of the southern peasant and the participatory involvement of the northern worker persist, reflecting generations of cultural tradition. And of course everyone is familiar with the centuries of British support for the idea of limited monarchy, first enunciated in the year 1215 and reinforced numerous times, most prominently during the Glorious Revolution of 1688.

Therefore, cultural patterns persist and insure the persistence of political patterns. Two countries that illustrate this point well are Colombia and Russia. Any would-be Tocqueville who might have visited either country in 1831 could return there today and understand the current scene perfectly.

Colombia is well known in modern time for its social violence, a violence that spills over into the political process. Current observers often link Colombia's violence to disputes arising out of its infamous drug traffic. That approach would appear faulty, however. Colombians have never needed the excuse of drug wars to engage in political violence. The country has never, apparently, known *non*violence. In 1968 James Payne described Colombia as "a system which for a century and a half has been characterized by frequent fighting."[12] He goes on to point out:

> On a scale of political deaths per generation, Colombia has one of the highest levels of political conflict in the world. In nearly 150 years since independence the country has been racked by ten national civil wars. . . . In addition there have been countless local revolts and flare-ups. . . . Political conflict has never been low. . . . The civil wars have not represented abrupt breaks with a prior period of tranquillity. Instead they were seemingly natural extensions of an always heated politics.[13]

All this was written long before Colombia's infamous drug cartels began their notorious operations. Intense conflict among citizens is a long-standing trait of Colombian culture. A perpetual politics of armed violence is the natural result of this culture of incivility.

In Russia, too, observers over the centuries have noted the continued reoccurrence of deeply ingrained political patterns. These patterns reflect neither the American tradition of peaceful citizen influence on the political process, nor the Colombian tradition of violent and perpetual struggle for

---

[11]Putnam, *Making Democracy Work,* op. cit., pp. 121–62.
[12]James L. Payne, *Patterns of Conflict in Colombia* (New Haven: Yale University Press, 1968), p. 3.
[13]Ibid., pp. 4–5.

control of the levers of power. The Russian political tradition stresses hierarchy and order, submission to authority, and unchecked rule of the few.

This tradition of autocracy goes back for centuries. It did not spring forth fully developed in 1917 by way of Vladimir Ilyitch Lenin. As I have already shown, one can trace its origins to the devastating Tatar invasion of old Russia around the middle of the thirteenth century. As the warriors of Genghis Khan and his successors swept westward,

> the Russian land was conquered and covered with blood. Every Russian town [was] sacked and burned.[14]

Thus began a period during which Russians learned to endure absolute rule and enforced submission to superior strength.

> For two hundred years Russian principalities and city republics survived only by total, humiliating subservience to their Asiatic rulers.[15]

The barbarous behavior of Russia's Tatar rulers strains credulity. In one battle alone (Moscow, 1571) the Crimean Tatars were said to have killed 200,000 people and carried another 130,000 off into slavery. It was inevitable that the Russian successors to this cruel regime would take on a character that was similar to their former rulers.

For instance, the Tsar who became Russia's first independent, post–Mongol leader, who even helped bring about an end to Tatar rule, was none other than Ivan IV, known to history as Ivan the Terrible. His sobriquet was well earned. In the *Oprichniki* he formed the earliest equivalent of the KGB, the dreaded secret police. This handpicked group of 6,000 men roamed the countryside, marauding and pillaging. They were instrumental in helping Ivan put down his only major rival, the independent city of Novgorod. In that battle Ivan's troops slew 60,000 people. Suzanne Massie writes:

> In a century distinguished by bloodshed and atrocious cruelty everywhere in Europe, Ivan's atrocities have passed into legend.[16]

These culminated in one ultimate barbarity. During one of his mad rages, Ivan struck down and killed his own son and heir.

The succeeding centuries saw a continuing procession of autocratic Russian rulers. Peter the Great killed hundreds of thousands in his various wars. Thousands more died consequent to his whimsical decision to build

---

[14]Suzanne Massie, *Land of the Firebird: The Beauty of Old Russia* (New York: Simon and Schuster, 1980), p. 37.

[15]Ibid., p. 38.

[16]Ibid., p. 74.

the city of Saint Petersburg in the middle of a pestilential marsh. Catherine the Great also killed tens of thousands in wars and in the suppression of peasant rebellions. Most of the tsars succeeding her also behaved in despotic and tyrannical fashion, right down to Nicholas II, whose unwillingness to share power with even a puny version of a democratic legislature (the Duma) and whose insensitivity to the enormous casualties suffered by his people in World War I insured his overthrow and the coming of Lenin's communists. Stalin and his successors right up to Gorbachev behaved in a fashion similar to the previous Russian rulers. That is, they brooked no opposition, ruled in absolute fashion, and forced enormous sacrifices from a cowed and submissive people.

It is of course too early to say what will be the next development in the history of Russian politics, but given this dismal background it would take a brave seer to predict a smooth or rapid transition to polyarchy.

THE RUSSIAN PERSPECTIVE

Social and political patterns, then, persist. Once established, they take on a life of their own and endure, sometimes, for centuries. All of us recollect references to some past social pattern and are then astonished to realize that this pattern still exists. In rereading *Democracy in America* recently I was amused to see Tocqueville set out to explain that well-known (in his era) phenomenon, "English reserve."[17] How long, I wondered in the words of the old song, has this been going on?

During my four months on a teaching exchange in Archangel, I experienced firsthand some of the centuries-old traditions of Russian culture. Some of these bore only tangentially on Russian politics. I learned to endure that peculiar Russian custom of toasts involving shots of straight vodka during long and exceedingly friendly banquets. I survived the odd experience of the Russian sauna—including, to my dismay, being beaten with birch twigs. But one cultural encounter struck me especially for the light it shed on enduring features of the Russian political process.

If you stay long enough in Russia, there eventually comes a moment when you are confronted in the most dramatic way with the discrepancy between Russian reality and the image of that reality that Russian officials want you to have. That moment for me came two months into my visit, at the end of a sightseeing weekend in Moscow.

My colleague, Natasha Ivanovna, and I had arrived at Moscow's domestic air terminal to fly back to Archangel. We were undergoing the normal tribulations of travelers in Russia, when suddenly we were whisked from tawdry reality into a glossy and unreal world set up solely

[17]See Tocqueville, op. cit., pp. 540–41.

for western tourists. Before I explain what happened, I must present some background.

For centuries Russians have been aware that they are unlike "the West." Now, a sense of otherness can produce various effects. In the United States people have generally been proud of being different. Their presumed uniqueness bolstered a feeling of superiority. (e.g., "We are better than those decadent Europeans or those poor third-worlders. We represent that shining city on a hill.") For all its jingoistic overtones, this nationalistic pride also inspired a competitive self-confidence that helped drive the nation forward.

The Russian's sense of differentness produced another result: defensiveness. Especially in ruling circles and among the educated, Russian difference was historically accompanied by a deep-seated fear of inferiority. The upper classes traditionally worried that their country was backward or second-rate. This nagging worry undercut the normal psychological desire of any people to be proud of their heritage. What resulted was classic behavior: a passive–aggressive reaction. Russian policy-makers over the centuries belligerently asserted their superiority, while trying desperately to hide (even—or especially—to themselves) any societal shortcomings.

This behavior persists and can take extreme forms. At worst, people will tell you the exact opposite of what they and everyone around them are seeing with their own eyes.[18] More typical behavior consists in preventing outsiders from encountering the worst aspects of Russian life. Outright lying is then unnecessary. You just present foreigners with plush but phony versions of reality and let them assume that those conditions represent society's norm.

This tendency to sugarcoat Russian backwardness has a long tradition. A sixteenth century Greek monk who traveled extensively in Russia was never allowed to leave, because the tsar of that day feared he would tell the world what Russia was really like. He was forced to remain in Russia nearly forty years until his death.[19]

The most famous example of this Russian habit produced a name for it: *Potemkin village*. When Catherine the Great announced that she wished to travel through the countryside to see how her people really lived, her prime minister, Grigory Potemkin, set up glossy, false fronts before ramshackle huts to produce a glorified image of picturesque villages peopled by wealthy, industrious peasants. After Catherine passed by each village, the false fronts were dismantled and rushed overnight to her next destination. There they would be set up in time to fool her again. The phrase *Potemkin village* has entered the world's vocabulary as Russia's unique contribution to the scam job.

---

[18]David K. Shipler, a *New York Times* correspondent in Moscow from 1975 to 1979, provides numerous examples of this tendency in *Russia: Broken Idols, Solemn Dreams* (New York: Penguin Books, 1983); see esp. pp. 15–25.

[19]Shipler recounts this episode in Ibid., p. 18.

I encountered this syndrome countless times during my stay in Russia. Friends on the street would take me by the arm to steer me away from workmen engaged in a drunken argument, all the while talking about something else as if we were walking alone down a placid country lane. I was put up in Archangel's best hotel, complete with well-stocked cafeteria, to make me think this was a typical living arrangement. On it went.

I saw this Potemkin village syndrome most pointedly in traveling—or in trying to travel. As late as 1990 it was almost impossible for a foreigner not fluent in Russian to travel freely. Obvious foreigners were prevented from traveling as average Russians did. The authorities wanted us to see their system at its best. Or rather, they wanted us to think that what we were seeing *was* the system, when in fact it was not. It was a phony piece of puffery that had nothing to do with the system.

Since I frequently traveled with Russians, I underwent more than once a certain sequence of events that exposed the contradiction between reality and the fantasy world that authorities had created for foreigners in the vain hope that they would accept it as reality. My experience would go something like this. I would be traveling with friends, unsuspected of being a foreigner, and with them I would see how buses actually work or what waiting-room experiences are really like for average people. Eventually, I would be "unmasked" and made to accept the phony system set up for tourists and visitors. The Potemkin-village image of Russian life would be forced upon me.

A dramatic instance of this pattern occurred in mid-April, at that moment when my teaching colleague, Natasha, and I reached Moscow's airport for our return flight to Archangel. We had spent the weekend in Moscow sightseeing with friends. Having hopped a bus to the airport late Sunday afternoon, we arrived just in time to begin the boarding process. Pleased with ourselves at the apparent conclusion of a happy and successful weekend, we entered the terminal building.

The sight that greeted us would have disheartened a newly arrived Westerner. The main waiting area was like a dreary barn. It was gray, drafty, dirty, and jammed with people. Many were standing in lines (for planes, for food, for telephones). Some were sprawled on hard benches, others were sitting or in many cases lying directly on the floor itself. Wherever floor space did not directly block passageways, there would be people or their luggage. The smell of cigarette smoke was everywhere.

The people waiting formed a diverse group: whole peasant families who were loaded with strangely shaped packages of unidentifiable goods; a group of high school students, all in uniform; nondescript middle-aged men having nothing in their possession but two fully mounted automobile tires; many young men in uniform; anxious, tired-looking women with a child or two in tow; and clumps of poorly dressed Asiatic people, clearly visitors from one of the (then) Soviet Union's distant republics. All this variegated population stood or sat with that weary, patient look I knew so well. Would any of them get to leave, or would they spend eternity waiting in this bleak stable for a boarding call?

These thoughts barely registered at the time. I took in the scene and accepted it. It was simply Russia, the Russia I had come to know: earthy, drab, and utterly inefficient. I was not disturbed. I knew in any case that we would waste lots of time in the queue before boarding our plane. Lines, crowds, noise, smoke, dirt: It was just a typical public facility serving the people of the great Soviet empire. My only goal was to find the proper line for our own flight and get a place in it at the earliest possible moment.

This we proceeded to do, and after an hour or more we arrived at the check-in desk. Since all Soviet citizens then had to show internal passports along with tickets, I was forced to produce some document and handed over my American passport. The clerk stared at it with consternation. "What are you doing here?" she cried. "You can't board a plane from this section of the airport! You must go at once into the foreigners' section."

I asked, "What difference does it make?" That brought exasperated snorts. Other airline personnel were summoned, and I was unceremoniously told to get out of line. They pointed me in the direction of an unobtrusive little side door. With some difficulty we persuaded them to let Natasha accompany me. The argument, not exactly true, that I couldn't speak Russian and needed a translator convinced them. We picked up our luggage and stepped through that little door.

It was like stepping through Alice's looking-glass. We suddenly found ourselves in the world of modernity. It was like a "normal" airport. First, it was clean. Floors were polished and shiny. Much of the floor space was even carpeted. Plants and glass were major elements in the decor. Chairs were cushioned and comfortable. Soft music played from hidden loudspeakers. Only a few people could be seen; all were dressed elegantly, spoke softly, and behaved courteously. Even the airport personnel were better dressed and more polite than those I had just encountered in the bedlam on the other side of the wall. In short, we had discovered a modern equivalent of the old Potemkin village. Here was a setup designed entirely to make the visitor think that Russian airports are all "like this" and therefore exactly the equivalent of airports in technologically advanced nations of the world. Most foreign tourists passing through Moscow would see only this part of the terminal.

Why didn't they make the entire terminal like this section? Or why bother trying to fool anyone, when even the most naïve traveler will quickly see that Russia is not a modern country, despite a gleaming airport lounge here and there? The answer to the first question is simple. They didn't have the money. Or more precisely, they wouldn't allocate the money. Russian tradition, with its stress on militarism and industrial giantism, avoids spending money on consumer goods for ordinary citizens.

The answer to the second question is more complex. True, these charades cannot fool many people. Still, there is in Russian character something of a will to be fooled. Or rather, there exists a deep desire to avoid looking reality in the face. The ugly aspects of day-to-day life are ignored. Used to fooling themselves by avoiding a direct gaze at the unpleasant aspects of life, Russians may assume that others too have this will to be fooled. They seem especially hurt when they encounter Western critics, who have been trained in exactly the opposite way. We expend every effort to call attention to the discrepancy between reality and desire.

As a result of these peculiar cultural blinders, Westerners end up being more negative and Russians more positive than they "should" be. That is, the critical inclination of Americans and West Europeans leads their social observers, and average citizens as well, to find fault in situations that most objective outsiders would regard as enviable. In exactly the opposite way, Russians praise or gloss over situations that most objective outsiders would regard as pitiable.

This strange set of cultural orientations may explain why for years the American and Soviet empires were regarded by most of the world *and* by each other as essentially equivalent, on a par militarily and even economically/technologically, when it is now obvious to all that the Soviet Union was "backward" or decades behind the West in any number of ways. Americans have been besieged for decades by internal critics—jeremiahs bemoaning society's deficiencies in everything from a "missile gap" (nonexistent) in the late 1950s to a decline in "family values" in the late 1980s. Russians, on the other hand, throughout much of the twentieth century boasted unabashedly about representing "the wave of the future," about having built "the workers' paradise," about being "the most powerful nation on earth," and so on.

Remember the old axiom: If an event is believed to be real, it will have real effects. If you keep repeating an assertion long enough, loudly enough, and with sufficient conviction, people may start believing it and acting as if it were true. The tendency of Americans to criticize their own society and of Russians to exaggerate their society's achievements led the world to underestimate the substantial gap, which was never remotely bridged, between those two nations despite all the boasting of Soviet propaganda and all the carping of American critics.

One result of these cultural tendencies was a nervousness on the part of Americans leading to a greatly accelerated arms buildup in the 1980s, which eventually forced the Soviet Union into bankruptcy as it tried to keep up with its rival. Another result was the cockiness of Russian leaders, who came to believe their own propaganda (not surprisingly, since they *wanted* to be fooled about their own reality). This cockiness led to a series of dangerous, expansionist adventures, of which the Cuban missile crisis was but one example. It eventually led to an overextension of Russian resources, culminating in the disastrous decision to wage war in Afghanistan.

Although the "true" relationship between the United States and Russia may finally have become clear, the cultural blinders on both sides led to four decades of cold war and some close encounters with hot war before the reality became clear to all, namely, that the United States is vastly richer and more powerful than Russia can hope to be for decades to come.

SUMMARY

Nations generally remain true to their historical traditions. Once set in place, the cultural norms of a given society take hold and exert enormous impact on thought and behavior. Change can occur, of course, but short-run change will almost always occur within the confines of the traditional pattern. Thus, leaders do change frequently in places like Bolivia and Liberia. What doesn't change is the long-term pattern of violence and anarchy.

In the same vein the increasing enfranchisement and empowerment of more and more groups in American society over the decades fits perfectly into the polyarchal pattern that was firmly in place by the late eighteenth century. What *would* be a change in the American polyarchal system would be the establishment of a twenty-year dictatorship, say, or the occurrence of several military coups over the next decade. One hardly expects either development to come about.

It may be possible to produce rapid, substantive change in a culture, but only under highly stressful conditions. The destruction and dismemberment of Germany in the 1940s helped revamp the culture of West Germany—at least to the point where it could sustain competitive politics for several decades. Such traumatic events as World War II, however, occur rarely in a nation's history. Normally, change of the deep-seated variety necessary to alter the essential pattern of a country's culture will occur only over decades or even centuries.

The social analyst may take heart at this news. Once you know a country well, you won't need to relearn everything about it in just two or five or eight years. The broad patterns will persist. The social reformer, of course, will find this cultural persistence depressing. Despite all efforts, you are unlikely to create any fundamental cultural change in your own lifetime. If you don't like the social pattern of a given place, unfortunately, the best thing you can do is move to a land where things work more to your liking. That would be simpler and less energy-sapping than trying to reshape the values of your current society.

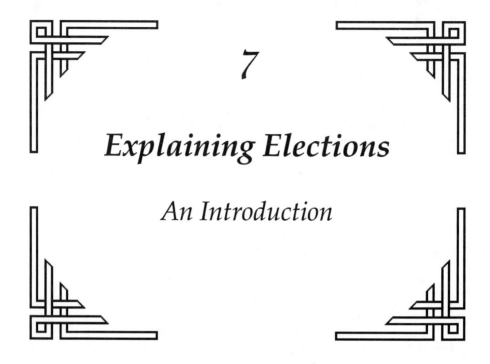

7

Explaining Elections

An Introduction

No people on earth have more opportunities to express their political wishes than do Americans. The choices available to the average American in a lifetime of elections are staggering, far exceeding the number in any other country. This cornucopia of political possibility reaches its peak in November every fourth year, when Americans get to pick their national leader, as well as a range of other officials starting with U.S. Senators and ranging downward to dogcatchers, sheriffs, and county water commissioners.

The range of choice does not stop at officials alone. Americans also get to express themselves on dozens of policy questions. These take the form of state and local referenda, bond issues, recall petitions, and so on. We may rightly criticize American politics for a number of shortcomings, but most definitely *not* for failing to allow citizen input into the decision-making process.

THE 1992 PRESIDENTIAL ELECTION: AN ANALYSIS

All of us can recall a recent opportunity for the American people to express their political preferences. In November 1992 the electorate ousted George Bush from the presidency, replacing him with his younger rival, the relatively unknown Bill Clinton. In a stunning display of independence, voters gave Bush less than three-eighths of their support, while giving an rank outsider, Ross Perot, nearly one-fifth. The vote totals among those who went to the polls are shown in Table 7-1.

TABLE 7–1 Choices of American Voters, 1992 Presidential Election

Voted for Clinton	—	44,908,233	— 43.0%
Voted for Bush	—	39,102,282	— 37.4%
Voted for Perot	—	19,741,048	— 18.9%
Voted for someone else	—	669,324	— 0.6%
Total voting	—	**104,420,887**	— **100%**

These ambiguous results brought a definite end to the Reagan–Bush era, while at the same time they provided less than majority support for the new, untried administration.

What were Americans trying to say in this election? Ever since voting day analysts have made every effort to interpret these results, to say what Americans "really" meant by their choices. The trouble is, there's no clear way to make sense of them. Different observers can see different patterns here. Let's consider just a few of the more plausible interpretations of the 1992 election.

1. *People were alienated from the system.* As in every race, they chose "None of the Above" as the most attractive option for president. That is, no candidate won more votes than the number of people who chose to stay at home and not vote at all. Nearly half the population simply refused to vote for president. (Even larger numbers failed to choose from among rival candidates for lesser offices.) Alienation and apathy would appear to be the big winners in this and most other American elections.

This point emerges clearly in Table 7–2, which takes into account not just *voters* (as in Table 7–1), but *all* the 185 million adult Americans of voting age.

TABLE 7–2 Voting Decisions of Adult American Citizens, 1992 Presidential Election

Did not vote	—	80,684,554	— 43.6%
Voted for Clinton	—	44,908,233	— 24.3%
Voted for Bush	—	39,102,282	— 21.1%
Voted for Perot	—	19,741,048	— 10.7%
Voted for someone else	—	669,324	— 0.4%
TOTAL number of adult Americans —		**185,105,441**	— **100%**

When we include all Americans of voting age in our analysis, we see immediately that the number of those who did not vote at all far exceeded the number of those who voted for the winning candidate, Bill Clinton. Also, when we add in those who voted for Perot and for "others," we see that well over half of all adult Americans refused to show up at the polls and vote for one of the two leading candidates. Fewer than half of all Americans supported the nominees of our only two signficant political parties. Nearly 55 percent either abstained from voting altogether in 1992 or supported an upstart maverick (Ross Perot). What could be a clearer sign of the electorate's disgust with "politics as usual"?

2. *People wanted conservative public policies.* This theory ignores the nonvoters, stressing that the clear majority of those who actually went to the polls (56.3 percent) opted for either Bush or Perot. Both men stood for smaller government, fewer taxes, closing the budget deficit, and "traditional" values: typical conservative positions. The electorate clearly wanted, in this view, a conservative leader.

Why didn't a conservative win? Simple. Conservatives split their vote between two candidates, allowing a liberal to squeak through to victory. A similar result occurred in the election of 1912. Woodrow Wilson, a Democrat, gained the White House with a paltry 41.8 percent of the vote. He benefited from the fact that two Republicans, Taft and Roosevelt, both stayed in the race to the end and split over 50 percent of the electorate between them. So even though a majority of American voters wanted a Republican president in 1912, they got a Democrat. The same thing occurred in 1992.

3. *People wanted moderate public policies.* Under this interpretation Perot's appeal was to centrist elements in the population. Most polls show that he appealed across the spectrum to every segment of the electorate, especially to less ideological and partisan voters. His liberal stands on some social issues (e.g., he was prochoice on abortion) and his willingness to raise some taxes (e.g., on energy) show that he was really a moderate, not a true conservative.

Most people saw Clinton as a moderate, for that matter. Thus, five-eighths of those who voted (Clinton and Perot supporters) chose a moderate alternative to conservative rule.

We could go farther and argue that many who stayed home on election day did so *not* because they were infuriated at the general direction of events or disgusted by the options presented to them. *Au contraire.* They were *content* with life in the United States and felt no particular need to register an opinion. It is the dissatisfied, after all, not the content, who take action. Staying home symbolized—for many, at least—a deep sense of contentment with the status quo.[1]

Finally, don't forget that many Bush voters saw *him* as a moderate.

[1]For evidence to support this perspective, see John R. Petrocik and Dara Shaw, "Nonvoting in America: Attitudes in Context," in William Crotty, ed., *Political Participation and American Democracy* (New York; Greenwood Press, 1991), pp. 67–88; and G. Bingham Powell, "American Voter Turnout in Comparative Perspective," *American Political Science Review* 80 (1986): 17–44.

Indeed, his lack of true ideological zeal for conservative positions is precisely where he went wrong, according to his critics from the right.

Together, these points provide strong evidence that the 1992 election represented a vast show of support for middle-of-the-road policies.

4. *People wanted liberal public policies.* This interpretation may be the most difficult to sustain, but it is hardly beyond the realm of possibility.

To start, assume that most Clinton voters wanted a liberal administration. Polls regularly suggest that 20 percent to 25 percent of the American people claim to be liberals. That puts their number between 37,000,000 and 46,000,000. Clinton's actual number of votes came to 45,000,000. That total dovetails nicely with the contingent of liberals in the populace.

Furthermore, we know that about a fifth of the Perot vote also came from people claiming to be liberal. Adding that group to the totality of all Clinton voters gives us nearly half the electorate (about 48 percent) desiring liberal outcomes from the election. In addition, one could argue that the bulk of those who did not vote *would have voted for Clinton* (the liberal option), *if* they had gone to the polls. Let us examine the reasoning here.

Most polls show that nonvoters are much more likely than voters to come from disadvantaged backgrounds.[2] They are poorer, less educated, and more likely to be minority group members than are people who vote regularly. These are precisely the people most likely to vote for Democrats (that is, for the liberal option), in those few cases when they actually do get themselves to the polls.

This liberal interpretation argues, then, that nearly half those who did bother to vote, and most of those who didn't, really wanted a liberal president. The winner of the 1992 election should logically, therefore, carry out his "mandate" to pursue liberal policies.

5. *People wanted a change.* Americans had lived for nearly twelve years under Republican presidents by the time of the 1992 election. Had they truly admired the achievements of Republican rule, this theory argues, they had a golden opportunity to state that preference loud and clear. Yet only 21 percent of the potential electorate bothered to stand up and be counted for the Republican standard bearer. Four-fifths of the nation's citizens made a choice *other* than to support the status quo.[3] What could be a clearer sign of desire for a radical break from the past?

These numbers are all the more striking when we consider how popular Reagan and Bush appeared to be during eleven of the previous twelve

[2]See the evidence presented in Raymond E. Wolfinger and Steven J. Rosenstone, *Who Votes?* (New Haven, CT: Yale University Press, 1980).

[3]Many citizens simply stayed home, of course, voting for no one. But that's part of the point here: The electorate showed no widespread enthusiasm for the status quo—that is, for Republican control of the national policy-making process. If large numbers of people *had* been ecstatic about keeping Republicans in power, they would have turned out in larger numbers than they did to support Bush—and to vote for Republican candidates for other offices, too, for that matter. Review Table 7–2.

years. In particular, the slippage in Bush support was nothing short of astounding. A year and a half before the election, Bush attained the highest level of popular support ever recorded for an American president (91 percent approval in one poll). By election day he had sunk dramatically. Indeed, one could argue that, for an incumbent U.S. president seeking reelection, Bush turned in the *second-worst* electoral performance in history.

It turns out that among sitting presidents running for reelection (starting with George Washington in 1792), only William Howard Taft won a lower percentage of the popular vote than did Bush. Taft garnered a mere 23 percent of the vote in 1912, when he had the misfortune of running against *both* Woodrow Wilson *and* a popular ex-President, Teddy Roosevelt.

It is true that other presidents were even less popular than Taft or Bush. Several presidents (e.g., Fillmore, Pierce, Arthur) couldn't stay in the White House, although they wanted to, because their party wouldn't even *nominate* them for the chance to retain the office. As a result, they didn't get as far as the general election—which Bush, at least, did. Other presidents (e.g., Truman, Johnson) realized that they had little chance of winning reelection and simply withdrew from the nomination process altogether.

So Bush was probably not the second-most unpopular U.S. president ever. Indeed, he was extremely popular during much of his term in office. Nevertheless, he was the second-most unpopular of all incumbent presidents who got as far as the November election. This point may be of some comfort to Bush supporters, but no matter how we stretch the conclusion, the 1992 results still place Bush in the lower quarter of electoral achievement for all presidents who desired to retain their office. After all, most presidents who wished to stay in the White House did so; and many of the losers came much closer than Bush did to electoral victory.

This unusually small number of votes for an incumbent president was one sign of the electorate's 1992 desire for dramatic change. A second indicator showed up in the vote for Ross Perot.

Who on earth was this man? A more unlikely candidate for the presidency can scarcely be imagined. He had never been in politics in his life, had never held political office, did little serious campaigning, had no organization to back him (until the last minute), and ran outside the established structures for gaining the Presidency (that is, the two major parties). The year was *1848* when Americans last put someone in the White House who was neither Democrat nor Republican.[4]

Furthermore, Perot struck most analysts as lacking presidential qualities. His billionaire status cut him off from the daily experience of average Americans, the people whose support he claimed to seek. Political sophisticates deemed his offbeat pronouncements odd. Some observers characterized his personality as unstable and possibly dangerous.

---

[4]The winner of the 1848 presidential election was Zachary Taylor, candidate of the Whig Party.

Despite these apparently fatal drawbacks, this untested and untried candidate, lacking all institutional backing, overcame major gaffes and produced in the end remarkable results. Few analysts have noted just how remarkable his achievement was. Perot goes down in history as producing the best attempt *ever* to take the White House, from among candidates outside the major parties.

Throughout the long history of American presidential elections (fifty-two have occurred between 1788 and 1992), only two candidates, *other* than those representing the top two parties of their day, scored a higher percentage of the popular vote than Ross Perot did in 1992. As everyone knows, "other candidates" in American elections (usually called "third-party candidates," whether they represent a real party or not) have fared badly. Typically, even "serious" third-party candidates (like Eugene Debs in 1912 or John Anderson in 1980) get between 5 and 10 percent of the vote. On rare occasions, some candidate will break through the 10 percent barrier: George Wallace did with his 13.5 percent of the vote in 1968, and so did Robert M. LaFollette with his 16.6 percent in 1924.

If we list the top-performing "third-party candidates" for the U.S. presidency since 1788, we find that Teddy Roosevelt heads the list. In that 1912 race previously mentioned, he attracted 27.4 percent of the vote. Millard Fillmore comes in second. Running at the head of the American (or Know-Nothing) Party, he captured 21.1 percent of the vote in 1856. Ross Perot follows closely with his 18.9 percent of the vote in 1992. Technically, then, Perot comes in third in this group of hundreds of people who have run for the U.S. presidency without the backing of one of the two major parties. I would argue, however, that a closer consideration of the evidence must lead us to see Perot as the most formidable third-party candidate.

Consider this: Only two people did better at the polls than he, and both were former Presidents. These well-known insiders clearly started their races with a huge advantage. Teddy Roosevelt was by all accounts wildly popular and had dominated American politics during his nearly eight years in the Oval Office. That the eccentric and inexperienced Perot ends up in the same league as this political giant is nothing short of amazing.

The Fillmore case is odd. Millard Fillmore ran for president at a time of party turmoil and transition. Of the two major parties of his day, the Whigs were dying out and the Democrats were splitting up. Fillmore helped to found a new political organization, the American Party (often called the Know-Nothings), which proceeded to nominate him for president in 1856. In that same year the young Republican Party nominated its first candidate for president. It was hardly clear at the time whether Democrats, Whigs, or Republicans had any more right than Fillmore's new party to call themselves "major." In accepting Fillmore as a "third-party candidate," I was stretching a point to be scrupulously fair. Even so, this former president, a man who spent a lifetime inside the American political process, backed by a national organization of activists and followers, could still muster a result just barely better than that achieved by Perot, who had almost no organization and no national political experience.

For these reasons I argue that Perot's achievement was by far the most impressive of any third-party candidate for president since the beginning of the Republic. The *meaning* of that achievement can be endlessly debated— why it happened, what it signifies—but certainly the first conclusion that must leap to mind is simple: Americans wanted some dramatic change from the status quo. Many, it turns out, wanted it so badly that they made an extraordinary leap of faith and voted for someone as historically unusual as the Texas billionaire.

POLITICAL BEHAVIOR AND THE ELECTION PROCESS

We have presented five theories, or five ways to interpret a dramatic political event involving millions of citizens. Even these five theories hardly exhaust the number of plausible interpretations of the 1992 American election. They do, at least, suggest something of the complexity of political life and the difficulty of making sense of it.

Which of these interpretations is correct? Who knows? Each theory contains serious kernels of truth. Politicians will stress the theory or the elements of truth that benefit them and their allies. Republicans will, for instance, stress theory number two: 1992 "really" showed voter support for conservatism. On the other hand, Democrats will stress theory number five ("time for a change"), along with theories number three and four: change toward the center and the left.

Circumspect analysts will argue that they cannot easily determine which theory is correct, but the reason is simple: Americans did not speak with a single voice in this election. Indeed, Americans never speak with a single voice—nor do any other people. To understand that point is the beginning of political wisdom.

It is true that in 1992, many Americans were alienated and didn't bother to vote. (Remember theory number one.) Many others clearly wanted dramatic political change (theory five). The "change-now" voters were divided, however, into those who wanted movement toward the center (theory three) and those eager for more left-oriented, liberal policies (theory four). Finally a large bloc of voters were either satisfied with the conservative status quo or hoped for even more conservative policies ("Back to Reaganism!") than George Bush had so far provided (theory two).

Other theories abound to explain why people vote. Many Americans in 1992 surely cast ballots based on candidate personality traits. "Perot tells it like it is." Others made choices based on individual issues of great concern. "Clinton is prochoice." And some (more than we might care to acknowledge) voted for wholly idiosyncratic reasons. "Bush reminds me of my uncle Vern."

Given the vast assortment of reasons behind the 1992 electoral behavior of the 185 million adult Americans, it takes a brave analyst to say what "the American people" really meant as they made their November election decisions. Perhaps I can be faulted for lacking that bravery. In any case I don't plan to set forth here the "correct" interpretation of this election. My aim is more perverse. I hope to show, simply, why coming to the correct interpretation of *any* election is a daunting and difficult task.

Elections involve millions of individual decisions, arrived at for a myriad number of complex and convoluted reasons. We must first understand the factors that influence these millions of voting decisions by average citizens before we can make sense of the *sum* of those individual actions, that is, the actual results of any given election.

In preceding chapters, I have treated cultures as entire entities. To simplify analysis I proceeded as if each member of society perfectly represented its dominant values. This strategy was useful when comparing one culture to another. To compare large groups one must make broad generalizations. Americans are optimistic about the future; Indians are fatalistic; Italians are cynical; and so on. This strategy breaks down as we examine only people within the same culture. The closer you look at any phenomenon, the more complex and various it appears. Within any culture we find a wide array of world outlooks. Obviously, not all Americans are optimistic. (Some of my best friends certainly aren't!) Neither are all Indians fatalists, nor all Italians cynical.

When we examine the political activity of ordinary citizens within a single culture, we find striking variety, not uniformity. And it's those *differences* among a nation's citizens that make politics interesting—indeed, possible. Diversity is what intrigues the political analyst. Differences in political behavior between individuals and groups: That's what one wants to explain.

Let us return to that 1992 election. Why does it seem so hard to tease out its meaning? Because Americans aren't one uniform people. This diverse people behaved, during the election, in bewilderingly diverse ways.

Some Americans stayed home because they were perfectly content. Others refused to vote because they were hopelessly alienated from the system. Of those who went to the polls, some wanted a victory for liberalism. Others wanted centrist or conservative results. Many didn't vote on ideological grounds at all, but on the basis of personality. Still others were swayed by partisan appeals ("Support the Republican!") or antipartisan arguments ("Reject the old, corrupt parties; vote Perot!"). And of course many voted on the basis of social, ethnic, and geographical group ties: blacks and union members for Clinton, mountain state residents and business executives for Bush, middle-aged white males for Perot.

In short, in this election—as in all elections—Americans were not united. The divisions that characterize any society become especially obvious when we pay close attention to some major political event (like a national election) in which most citizens participate. It makes no sense most of the time to generalize about what "the American people" want or think. Yes, at the broadest levels, we can say that Americans deeply believe in God, are patriotic, and express strong support for the virtues of freedom. But when you get down to specifics, the answers stop being easy. Do Americans want change? Are they liberal or conservative? Are they racist or tolerant?

A reply to specific questions like these can't take a simple yes/no form for an entire people. Instead, the answer looks more like this:

-Some are.
-Some aren't.
-Some are some of the time.
-Many change their minds from one day to the next.
-Most haven't thought enough about the matter to have an opinion.
-Many don't care in the slightest anyway.

This fuzzy and unsatisfactory conclusion is the beginning of wisdom when it comes to understanding how average citizens think and behave in politics. They find a variety of ways to express themselves, and many don't express themselves at all. Whether it adds up to anything at any given moment is wholly unclear.

SOCIAL IDENTITY AND ITS IMPACT ON POLITICAL BEHAVIOR

What is clear, however, is that the choices that citizens make concerning political involvement (whether to get involved, how to behave if they do get involved) do not occur on a random basis. That is, if 10 percent of Americans are seriously interested in the political process (as studies suggest), that does *not* mean that 10 percent of workers and 10 percent of Asian-Americans and 10 percent of Mississippi residents are politically involved. Likewise, if 37.4 percent of all voters pulled the lever for George Bush, that does not mean that 37.4 percent of investment bankers, 37.4 percent of African Americans, and 37.4 percent of Californians voted for Bush. People with different social characteristics don't behave alike—especially on matters of importance.

Social *cleavages* occur in all societies. People everywhere define themselves, or are defined by society, as belonging to certain groups and not belonging to others. People everywhere have different life experiences, which set them apart from each other. People in different groups think and act differently. Their religious practices will vary: In America, few Easterners and few bankers will be found handling snakes or jumping into water over their heads for baptism rituals. The way they dress will vary: Few people in Idaho will wear three-piece suits; Few people in Washington, D.C. wear boots. Their attitudes on key social issues will vary: Most workers will oppose free trade practices; most big-business leaders will support them.

People in one social grouping will differ radically from those in another. Think, for instance, of differences between Hispanics and Anglos, between those on welfare and the well-to-do, between Vermonters and Alabamans, even between men and women. If these different subgroups within the broader culture act and think differently in many ways, it should not surprise us that they also act and think differently on political matters.

Politics, we know, is integrally connected to the society in which it is embedded. If a value or behavior pattern is important to a group of people, they will express that value in politics or act politically to protect that behavior pattern. Since groups of people differ from each other on key values, any action by any group to support its values will inevitably produce a counteraction by other groups who think differently. The resulting conflict between these groups doesn't just *lead* to politics; it *is* politics.

We can now see why support for any particular political policy will never be distributed randomly across social groups. Rather, those from one background will be more likely than those from another background to support, oppose, or be indifferent to any given political position. On very few issues will support, opposition, and indifference be at about the same levels across all social groupings.

To understand any country's politics, then, we must start with group difference. No society is perfectly homogeneous. People are divided by age, ethnicity, race, region, religion, and gender. While there is rarely a one-to-one relationship between any individual's group membership and political behavior, the impact of group affiliation and shared experience is strong enough to create *patterns* of behavior that cannot be ignored. Both social analysts who wish to understand the world and activists seeking power in order to run the world must familiarize themselves with group political tendencies.

OPTIONS FOR POLITICAL BEHAVIOR

Different groups behave differently in politics, then, and those differences can have serious consequences. Before we can examine those consequences, we must first explore the options people have for political behavior.

The individual citizen must answer two fundamental questions concerning political activity. First, *should I get involved?* That is, is it worthwhile to engage in politics at all—even to the minimal extent of going to the polls and casting a vote? Second, *what direction should my actions take?* Should I be acting in ways that lead to the system's overthrow (radical action), in ways that suppress opponents of the system (reactionary action), or in more standard ways (voting and even working for conservative, moderate, or liberal causes)? In other words should I behave in politics as a leftist, a centrist, or a rightist?[5]

All citizens, then, (and that includes you!) must make two choices; first, *whether* to become politically active, and then *how* to express that political activism. It turns out that people of different social backgrounds answer both questions in different ways—with important consequences for the political system. Let us begin by examining the issue of participation.

Perhaps the most consistent finding in all political science research is this: *Most people are not interested in politics most of the time.* This finding always puzzles those of us who can scarcely think of anything *but* politics. Still, let's be realistic. Most people focus their attention elsewhere. They are wrapped up in the day-to-day realities of life: family, relationships, job. In their spare time, people watch television, work at hobbies, indulge in sports. The idea of voluntarily attending city council meetings or choosing to watch legislative committees at work would strike many as odd, if not downright bizarre, behavior.[6]

SUMMARY

In short, politics for most citizens ranks low on the interest scale. For sheer pleasure, it's right down there with visits to the dentist and conferences with the kid's teacher. Politics, after all, is complex, controversial, and conflict ridden. Who in their right mind would willingly get into it? Occasionally, of course, it touches us all, and we can't avoid it. But except for a small minority of zealots, most people remain outside the political arena whenever they can—which is most of the time.

Paraphrasing Lincoln, we might say that politics interests all of the people some of the time, and some of the people all of the time, but never all of the people all of the time.

Most of the time, in fact, politics in every setting involves only a small percentage of the population. It stands to reason that those people who do participate in politics are more likely than those who don't to gain political

[5]These terms are explained in Chapter 9. For a more detailed study, see Steven J. Rosenstone and John Mark Hansen, *Mobilization, Participation, and Democracy in America* (New York: Macmillan, 1993).

[6]See John P. Robinson, Philip E. Converse, and Alexander Szalai, "Everyday Life in Twelve Countries," in Alexander Szalai, ed., *The Use of Time: Daily Activities of Urban and Suburban Populations in Twelve Countries* (The Hague: Mouton, 1972), pp. 113–44.

advantage. They are the ones who shape public policy. It is they who will gain whatever benefits their political system has to offer (jobs, money, fame, power). The question is, Are those people who get involved, thereby obtaining the ability to shape political outcomes and to reap political rewards, different in any significant way from other citizens?

If involved citizens did represent a cross-section of the population, the effect of their political activism would be neutral in terms of benefiting or disadvantaging any given segment of society. If the active members of any polity are substantially different from average citizens, however, we must suspect that political outcomes will be skewed in directions favorable toward those groups in society most like the ones in power. Indeed, we would be amazed, would we not, if things were otherwise? Imagine reading this story in the *Times* tomorrow;

> In the little-known country of Ehewhon, where doctors make up a majority of the nation's legislators, parliament has just voted to cut physicians' fees in half.

Strains credulity, no? So with the presumption that it makes a serious difference as to who gets into politics and ends up controlling political outcomes, let us undertake to see just which groups in society are more likely, and which are less likely, to do this very thing.

8

Who Participates in Politics and Who Doesn't?

Consider this for a minute: Who will be seriously interested in politics? Which individuals will be so interested that they will sacrifice other activities to read about politics, listen to radio talk shows, watch TV news programs, discuss politics with all and sundry, and participate in politics by writing officials, joining groups, going to meetings, working for candidates, and even running for office? Do you know anyone like that?

Chances are you do. We have all met people like this. We also know people with only the barest interest in politics. They can't imagine spending an evening at City Hall watching politicians debate the zoning law. They skim past the C-Span channel as if it were eye poison.

Once as an Army private I casually mentioned some recent political event to a barracks mate. He cut me short. "Drop it!" he growled. "I never talk about politics." I was stunned, never having encountered such willful apathy toward the most fascinating subject on earth.

VARIABLES AFFECTING POLITICAL PARTICIPATION

How do political junkies (like me) and the haters of politics (like you?) differ from each other? The question is crucial, because the haters won't have the slightest impact on public decision making. The junkies will. What distinguishes the politically involved (who are going to gain power) from the rest of the population (who won't)?

Answering this question turns out to be far from simple. Numerous social and psychological factors influence our likelihood of being politically participatory. For simplicity's sake, let us focus only on the major determining variables.[1]

Education stands out as the single best predictor of political involvement. Every study of political participation has shown that, no matter what the setting, the more years of formal schooling people have, the more likely it is that they will engage in political activities.

This finding should hardly surprise us. Think about its impact at the extremes. We can well imagine that people with Ph.Ds or law degrees will be more politically interested and involved than people who stopped all formal schooling at age twelve. That seems perfectly reasonable, on the face of it. But it turns out that education is such a powerful force that even one more year of schooling will make you more attuned to politics than the person with one less year. If you take a group of fifty-year-old white male welders living in Sioux City, Iowa, for example, you will find that those who made it through the eleventh grade of high school (some thirty years previously) are slightly more likely to show an interest in politics, vote, and go to meetings than those who left high school after completing only tenth grade. In other words, hold everything else constant, and a little additional input of education gives you a little additional likelihood of political involvement. It follows, naturally, that a lot more education produces a much greater likelihood of political involvement.

As an aside, we can draw a simple conclusion from these findings. If you wish to increase the level of political participation anywhere, develop an educated populace. Encourage or (what the heck!) *require* people to spend many years of life going to school.

Class is another variable that affects political involvement. Other things being equal, the lower you are on the totem pole of life, the less likely it is that you will become a political activist. Unskilled workers are less likely than are business executives to read about politics, talk about politics, vote, or run for office. Middle-class professionals will be more active than people on welfare.

---

[1]The discussion that follows draws on material in the following works: Angus Campbell, Philip E. Converse, Warren E. Miller, and Donald E. Stokes, *The American Voter* (New York: Wiley, 1960); Sidney Verba and Norman H. Nie, *Participation in America: Political Democracy and Social Equality* (New York: Harper & Row, 1972); Norman H. Nie, Sidney Verba, and John R. Petrocik, *The Changing American Voter* (Cambridge, MA: Harvard University Press, 1976); David Butler and Donald Stokes, *Political Change in Britain* (New York: St. Martin's Press, 1974); M. Margaret Conway, *Political Participation in the United States*, 2d ed. (Washington, D.C.: CQ Press, 1991); William Crotty, ed., *Political Participation and American Democracy* (New York: Greenwood Press, 1991); Mark Franklin, Tom Mackic, Tom Valen et al., *Electoral Change: Responses to Evolving Social and Attitudinal Structures in Western Countries* (Cambridge: Cambridge University Press, 1992); Rosenstone and Hansen, *Mobilization, Participation, and Democracy in America*, op. cit.; and Wolfinger and Rosenstone, *Who Votes?* op. cit.

The implications for those who wish to raise the level of mass involvement are clear. Develop a dynamic, growth-oriented society that spreads wealth to the many. Before you know it, political involvement by the citizenry will be booming. On the other hand, if you are a dictator and want to keep people quiet, be sure to keep them poor and barefoot. You'll insure their quiescence for decades. (You may think I am joking, but a similar attitude prevails in any number of places: in Haiti, for example, and in Mississippi, too, not many decades ago.)

Gender is another powerful variable that affects political activism. As we have already seen, gender differences are especially marked at the higher levels of the political process. Women are in the minority, usually the extreme minority, in decision-making positions everywhere. It should not surprise us, then, to learn that nearly everywhere men are more likely than women to take those actions that we call political: read newspapers, gather in public places to discuss government affairs, vote, riot, and so on.

There is one exception to this rule, but it's critical. In a number of countries with advanced, industrial economies, women participate in most aspects of politics at about the same level as men do; sometimes at higher levels. For instance, women *vote* at higher rates than men do in the United States. The reasons for this will become clear as our discussion continues and deepens. Apart from ten or fifteen unusual countries, however, the point remains: Politics nearly everywhere is a man's world.

Two other factors—*religion* and *ethnicity*—are often thought to bear on the likelihood that people will become politically active. Certainly, they both affect our *social* behavior in a variety of ways. Their impact on political interest is complex, however, and can only be suggested here.

Perhaps the main impact of religion and ethnicity springs from their effect on your social status, or *class*. What counts is NOT your specific religion or ethnic group—but rather the relative social standing of that religion or group within the culture of which you are a part. Thus, Catholics in the United States may have been less politically active than Protestants during much of the nineteenth century—but that was not because they were Catholic per se. Catholics then were recent immigrants to the United States, poor and working class. Anyone in that circumstance would be less politically active than average, whatever the religion. Likewise, *minority ethnic and racial groups,* of whatever kind, especially those clearly despised by the majority, will be less politically active than average—but that's mainly because most minority groups are poorer and lower in social status than average, and groups toward the lower end of the socioeconomic spectrum, as we know, are normally not politically active.

In turns out, upon further investigation, that many ethnic and religious minority groups are *more* active than we would expect—*if* we hold other variables constant. Thus, American blacks vote in relatively low numbers, and we might at first be inclined to attribute this to something in black culture. On closer inspection, one notes that blacks are actually *more* likely to vote and otherwise participate in politics than are white Americans—if you hold the variable of class constant. That is, black working-class Americans vote in greater percentages than do white working-class Americans; and black middle-class Americans vote in greater percentages than do white middle-class Americans.[2]

Why, then, does it *appear* that blacks have a poor turn-out rate? It is simply that the vast majority of them are working-class or lower on the social prestige scale, and working-class people everywhere don't participate much in politics (unless they are encouraged by strong unions and strong political parties, neither of which exist in the United States).

So the participation rate of American black voters is weak, because most of them are poor, not because of their culture or their skin color. The real question to answer is why their involvement is higher than average compared to the typical white poor or working-class person. The reason has to do with *social identification.* Blacks (and minority group members in all cultures) are extremely conscious of their group identity. Most white Americans don't go around all day aware of their color. Black Americans can hardly help thinking regularly about their skin color—just as Turks in Germany are constantly reminded that they are Turks, and Kurds in Iraq, and Koreans in Japan, and so on.

Any kind of group identification makes one attuned to the way society, through its political mechanisms, can impinge on the daily life of your group—and ultimately on you. If you belong to the unchallenged majority, you take your condition for granted. Your status usually will affect your social and political choices only subliminally. Things are clearly different for minority group members. Americans blacks (and German Turks and Iraqi Kurds) *know* that politics affects them frequently and seriously. Hence, compared to complacent and apathetic majority group members, they will be better informed about politics, even ready to get involved to defend themselves and fight for improvements in their social condition.

SOCIAL INVOLVEMENT AND POLITICAL ACTIVITY

These facts show the tremendous importance of social consciousness, *social identity,* in producing political participation. Key connections between the individual and society always draw one closer to the political process. A related phenomenon that induces political activity springs from the richness of a person's group or social life. A way to summarize this complex

[2]Milbrath and Goel come to this conclusion after reviewing a number of voting studies. My discussion here and in the next three paragraphs owes much to their analysis. See Milbrath and Goel, *Political Participation,* op. cit., pp. 119–22.

variable is the term *social rootedness* or *social connectedness*. Its impact on one's likelihood of political involvement is powerful.

It turns out that the more groups you belong to and the more deeply involved you are in these groups, the greater will be your awareness of politics, your interest in it, and your involvement. It would appear that social activity has a carryover effect. The more numerous and the more active your social connections, the more political you are likely to be. This finding makes sense, since politics itself is a social activity. Involvement in the political process grows naturally out of other social activities, even if they don't appear at first glance to have political implications.

Numerous corollaries follow from this link between social connectedness and political activity. Social isolates, for example, are among the least likely members of society to be politically active. Take the extreme case: Hermits will always be uninvolved in politics. Following the same principle, shy, diffident, or retiring people won't become active in politics. Those with few social connections, who belong to no groups, who have few family ties, who live in isolated places, who are unemployed, who work by themselves or with only a few others, these people too won't be much involved in politics.

Group joiners, on the other hand, will be. The man or woman who belongs to the Kiwanis Club, the Chamber of Commerce, and the Literary Guild, who raises money for the United Fund, who volunteers for the Cub Scouts or Brownies, who coaches children in Little League sporting events—that person is much more likely to have political interests than the couch potato whose spare time is spent channel surfing at the boob tube.

The effect of social involvement on political activity is powerful. The groups to which people belong channel their attention toward politics in a variety of ways, many of which are indirect. The more groups you are in, the more people you meet. The more people you meet, the more conversations you have, and the more likely it is that a subject with political implications will arise. While having coffee with friends, someone will mention how their car's front end was just jolted out of alignment when it hit a monster pothole in the street outside. Someone else will blame the "do-nothing" mayor for "letting city streets go all to hell." A third person may chime in that it's not the mayor's fault; "those cheap city councilors are to blame." Before you know it a full-fledged political conversation is under way.

Socially oriented people, as a matter of course, discuss events of the day reported by the local newspaper and electronic media, and many of these events are politically charged. Hence, the socially active person is much more likely than the social isolate to be drawn into political discourse. This stimulus will be sufficient to induce in most people some modest political interest. Most social joiners will become interested enough in politics at least to vote. For some the frequency of talk about politics will lead them to discover an abiding personal interest, and they will become participants who devote serious time and attention to the political universe.

Groups can have a direct, as well as indirect, effect on political involvement. The more people you know, the more likely it is that someone will think of you when it comes time to appoint people to the neighborhood planning commission. Join enough groups, or stay in one long enough, and someone will inevitably ask you to help them run a campaign for their cousin's daughter-in-law, who's running for the school board. People may even appreciate your qualities enough to suggest that you yourself run for office. Unfortunately, this may not be the high compliment it sounds. Many elections are noncompetitive; the dominant party's nominee is certain to win. Yet minority parties *have* to nominate someone. Sacrificial lambs are always needed in politics, and being cajoled into that role has helped to provide many a citizen with an introduction to the political process.

Some groups are much more clearly oriented toward political issues than others. If you belong to one of these groups, you are much more likely than average to develop an activist orientation toward politics. If you belong to a local hiking group, you *might* get drawn into politics in the rare circumstance when an issue arises that touches your group's interest directly. For example, the state legislature is considering a bill to sell to timber companies the state park where your group camps out every summer. You and your group would become politically active pretty quickly in those circumstances, even though most of the time your conversations within the group wouldn't be particularly political.

If you belonged to an activist environmental organization, however, politics would impinge on your consciousness much more frequently— even if you joined out of no political interest, but simply because of a desire to "help clean up the environment," or "save the whales," and so on.

One of your social groups may stimulate your political interest, then, because something in the political environment impinges on the group's affairs and concerns. In an even more direct way, a group may induce your political participation because the group is, in effect, a political entity. Labor unions and business associations (e.g., the chamber of commerce) are perhaps the best examples of this type of group. You might belong to them originally for nonpolitical reasons, but they are likely to make you become politically conscious very quickly.

It should come as no surprise to learn that union members are much more likely than nonunionized workers to show an interest in politics, to vote, and to engage in other political activities. It should also be no surprise that in countries where labor unions are strong, working-class people are more involved in politics, better represented, and hence better treated (better working conditions, higher pay, longer vacations) than in places where unions are weak. In this regard Swedish workers (85 percent unionized) are much better off, relative to the rest of their society, than are American workers (17 percent unionized).

The ultimate example of the impact of groups on citizen involvement is the political party itself. Parties are social organizations, and their main purpose is precisely to spur political participation—participation for the benefit of the party, naturally. It stands to reason that the stronger the party organization in any given place, the more citizen political involvement will occur. Conversely, places with weak parties will have low levels of citizen involvement.

We can see this phenomenon around the world and in the United States as well. Political parties are strong in Sweden, Britain, France, and Germany. Levels of citizen activism in those countries are correspondingly high. Parties are weak in Thailand, Egypt, Peru, and Slovakia. As expected, most citizens in those places are not deeply involved in the political process. Regional differences in citizen activism abound in the United States. Where party organization is strong (Minnesota, Illinois, Connecticut), so too will you find a high level of citizen activism. Where parties are weak (Alabama), citizens will be less active politically.

THE CUMULATIVE EFFECT AND POLITICAL PARTICIPATION

We have seen many examples of the power of social connectedness. This effect of social roots on political activity shows up in a variety of other ways. Certain objectively measurable aspects of life make you more or less likely to feel like an integral, connected member of your society (hence, more likely to be political). The simple fact of *age* is one of these variables. The younger you are, the less likely you are to be a settled member of society with a feeling of investment in it and a sense of responsibility for its continuing success. Hence, you are less likely than older citizens to see reasons for political involvement.

Younger people, too, are less likely than middle-aged or older people to be group members. Most people don't join the Elks, sign up to run the church auction, or volunteer to collect funds for the local hospital until after they have finished their education, gotten a steady job, settled down in a community, gotten married, and had children. Thus, young people escape the pressures and inducements toward political activity that social group membership provides.

Other things being equal, then, young people will participate in politics much less frequently than middle-aged or older people. Indeed, if you are a purist, you will find the voting rates of young people positively scandalous. (If you're a political scientist, of course, they make perfect sense, clearly illustrating one consequence of the social connectedness axiom.)

Young people don't participate much in politics, because their lives aren't as thoroughly embedded in society as they will become in later years.

In the same way, people who are *married* and people who *own their own homes* are also more involved in politics than single people and renters. The principle is clear. The more stake you have in society and the more conventional ties you have to mainstream culture, the more you will develop those social connections that often lead to political awareness and involvement.

This point leads to one of the fascinating findings of social science, one often summarized as "the more, the more" thesis.[3] Each of the variables affecting participation has a *cumulative* effect. In most nations, as we have seen, men are more likely to be politically active than women. So too will educated people be more active than less educated people, and upper-middle-class people more active than (nonunionized) workers. As individuals attain more of these participation-inducing attributes, they become *much* more likely than average to exhibit political interest and get politically involved.

Thus, an *educated male* (two participationist attributes) is more likely than either the average male or the average educated person to show political interest. Similarly, the *educated, wealthy male* (three factors associated with participation) is *extremely* likely to become politically involved. Add a few other traits—an educated, wealthy male who is married with children, has owned the same house in the same community for three decades, and who belongs to a local business association—and you reach a near-statistical certainty that that person will be participating in politics well above the level of the average citizen.

The opposite principle holds true. The fewer you have of the characteristics associated with political involvement, the less likely it is that you will develop any connection to the world of politics. A poor, illiterate, rural woman is one of the least likely people in the world to get involved in the political process. By no coincidence, this person is precisely the least likely everywhere to benefit from the output of the political process. Governmental policies from Ghana to Georgia treat poor rural women as invisible. Politically speaking, that is exactly what they are.

UNDERSTANDING THE POWER OF VARIABLES

Education, class, gender, social connectedness: These are a few of the variables that explain why some people are more likely than others to develop an interest in politics, even to become politically active. The really interesting question is, *Why* do these variables have the effect that they do? To answer that question we must move into the realm of psychology.

[3]Dahl elaborates on this point in his classic study of power and participation; see Robert A. Dahl, *Who Governs? Democracy and Power in an American City* (New Haven, CT: Yale University Press, 1961), p. 227.

A famous axiom in social science states that individual behavior can't be understood just by considering the personality of the individual whose behavior you wish to explain. Nor is that behavior simply the result of external social forces. Rather, anyone's behavior at any given time is the product of an interaction between that person and the forces outside that person, which shape and narrow the range of possible action.

The key elements here are simple. Behavior occurs when a given *individual* facing a specific *environment* makes a *decision* about how to act in that circumstance.

This perspective can be condensed, for ease of understanding, into a simple equation. It is usually written, $B = f[OE]$, where

B stands for behavior,
$f[ ]$ stands for "a function of,"
O stands for the organism, and
E stands for the environment.

The equation can be read this way: "Behavior is a function of the interaction between the organism and its environment."[4]

In plain English this means that to understand anyone's behavior in any given situation, you must understand their attitudes, values, and personality traits *and* their personal circumstances. You can't ignore either the psychological aspects of behavior (what's in the organism's mind) or the social–economic–political circumstances (the environment) within which the organism must act.

Let's illustrate. We know that other things being equal, a college-educated, middle-class professional is more likely to vote and attend political meetings than a high-school-educated factory worker. But what if the educated person lives in a dictatorship? What if the factory worker belongs to a strong union? Other things are no longer equal. The dictatorial environment will discourage political participation by all but ardent supporters of the regime. The union will encourage participation, producing involvement by many who would otherwise remain on the sidelines.

My friend, James Payne, used to tell an amusing story to show how environment shapes human behavior. Years ago, he spent his junior year of college in Peru. When he went to movie theaters in the capital city, Lima, he noticed that everyone was smoking, despite an abundant number of highly visible No Smoking signs. He chalked this behavior up to "the wild, undisciplined nature of the Spanish temperament," and lit up his own cigarettes with impunity.

---

[4]This equation and its utility for political analysis is given extended treatment by James Chowning Davies, "Where From and Where To?" in Jeanne N. Knutson, ed., *Handbook of Political Psychology* (San Francisco: Jossey-Bass Publishers, 1973), pp. 1–27.

Then during a vacation week he traveled to a distant town to see more of the country. Having enjoyed all the local tourist sites, he dropped in one evening at the nearest cinema to take in a film. Settling comfortably into his seat, he promptly started puffing on a cigarette, ignoring as usual all the signs forbidding him from doing so. The young man to his right quickly leaned Payne's way and whispered, "There's no smoking in this theater!" Startled, my friend replied that everyone smoked at the movies in Lima. "Yes," came the response, "but here they give fines!"

Situations, then, affect behavior, and not just psychological predispositions. If you want to know why people act as they do, you must understand not only what they are like as people, but also the constraints of the situation in which they find themselves. Both environmental and personality factors must be considered in trying to understand the context in which any human behavior takes place.

FACTORS THAT ENHANCE POLITICAL PARTICIPATION

We can now summarize what we know about the conditions conducive to enhancing popular participation in politics. Education, class, gender, and social life connections all affect the likelihood of political involvement in two ways. First, they structure our environment. They shape our social setting, determine the messages we hear, and delimit the kind of people we interact with.

Second, they influence us through psychological impact. They help determine how we think about ourselves and the world. They do so for many reasons, but one stands out as vital. These variables affect our sense of *self-worth*. Every study of political participation shows that those with self-confidence, a strong self-image, and a positive view of their own potential are the most likely people to become political participants.

Self-confidence derives from many sources. Genetic factors beyond the scope of political science surely play a role. But so do the variables we have been examining. Education, for example, provides the knowledge needed to understand politics. People don't spend time on complex matters they don't understand. (When was the last time you read a medical journal for fun and relaxation?) As a subject becomes easier to grasp, you are more apt to talk about it, read about it, get involved in it. Education increases your sense of self-esteem by giving you more knowledge and better reasoning powers. It helps you understand the world better (including the political world) and thus enhances your sense of competence and self-worth.

Education affects your self-image in other ways. For one thing, it helps you understand the links between your own life condition and public policies that impinge on, perhaps even cause, your current social circumstances. When you understand causal links between public life and your own private life, you are better able to act in public ways that might lead to improvement in your private conditions. Even for those who don't undertake specific political acts, increasing education leads to an improved sense of control. Simply understanding the environment creates a sense of security and makes you feel self-confident rather than helpless.

Social connectedness, like education, also makes one feel better about oneself and increases the likelihood of becoming politically competent. Involvement in a series of groups is apt to produce friends, supportive relationships. The more social ties you have and the more friends, the higher your self-esteem is likely to be. (When we feel that other people like us, our self-image is enhanced.) Group connections produce a sense of *social competence*—a psychological variable always associated with high levels of political interest and involvement.

Social connections also increase our feelings of *political efficacy*. The more people you know, especially the outgoing types you meet in voluntary community groups, the more likely it is that you will come to know political movers and shakers. There's nothing like knowing the mayor, or a friend of the mayor, to give you a sense of potential clout.

Social connectedness also helps you understand politics by providing realistic experiences about how social groups work. Loners don't get day-to-day experience in give-and-take, argument and debate, conflict and compromise. Psychologists call this *reality testing*. It helps socially active people gain the interactional skills useful in political intercourse. Social experience also illuminates the connection between politics and community. It gives one some idea of how to operate effectively in both arenas. To the extent that group experiences help develop political knowledge and leadership skills, they also enhance self-esteem, which is vital to effective political activity.

Of course, these variables work in the opposite direction as well. The less education you have and the fewer social ties, the lower your sense of self-esteem and political efficacy. Hence, the less likely you are to be politically active.

The point suggests why class and gender affect political activism. They strongly influence one's self-worth. In most places throughout history, most men in the lower social rankings and nearly all women, whatever their status, have been taught to think poorly about themselves. Indeed, even today poor people and women in most societies learn in a thousand ways that society looks down upon them.

If others treat you with relentless negativism, it must eventually have an impact. Humans are social beings. They develop images of themselves based on the way others see them. A constant barrage of criticism weakens the ego of all but the strongest personalities. Those subjected to a steady diet of scorn can hardly avoid the development of a negative self-image. If society has castigated you for much of your life, you normally won't develop the self-confidence needed for political involvement. Rather, you will develop an *alienation* from society, a negativity, even a *cynicism*, that produces withdrawal from social commitments.

Objective social variables, then, (e.g., class, gender, race) affect political involvement by inducing or undermining the self-confidence needed for that quintessentially social action: political participation. Those people on whom society smiles most brilliantly (well-educated, successful, majority-group males) develop the inner self-confidence *and* the social connections that make political involvement easy and natural. For others, for people who are *not* told daily by society to think highly of themselves, social connectedness can help produce the same results as high social status or a good education. Close friends and group leaders stroke the ego, make one feel good about oneself. They induce those feelings of self-esteem without which political activity becomes daunting, something to avoid.

Figure 8–1 sums up what we have learned about the factors likely to induce or inhibit political participation.

We now know a good deal about political participation. The best thing about learning is applying newly gained knowledge to the real world. Based on what we have learned about the factors that induce participation,

Figure 8–1 Simplified Schema for Understanding the Causes of Political Participation

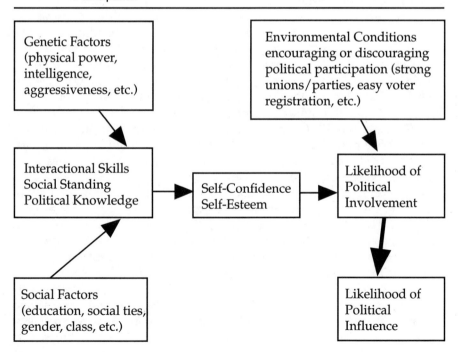

we should now be able to figure out just where on this planet citizens will become activists and, equally interesting, where they will not.

Places of political activism are easy to predict. Participation will surely be high in countries (or sections of countries) that produce a well-off, educated citizenry. It will also be high in places that encourage tolerance. Where gender, race, religion, ethnicity, and other artificial social distinctions are *not* used by some citizens to oppress others, the number of citizens with a severely negative self-image will lessen and the chance that people will feel good about committing themselves to social action will increase.

Activity levels will also be high in nations characterized by a wide variety of active voluntary social groups. Countries with strong labor, farm, and business associations will have significant citizen involvement in politics. Where political parties are strong and aggressive mechanisms of social recruitment, we will also find high levels of citizen activism. Finally, we will expect to find high levels of political participation in places where citizens are older than average (preferably over thirty) and reasonably stable in their habits (married, own property, don't move often).

Correspondingly, citizen political involvement will be lower in places inhabited by poor, uneducated people who observe a whole host of discriminatory social distinctions, especially those based on gender, class, religion, race, and ethnicity, and whose social organizations are weak to nonexistent, including the absence of economic and political organizations such as unions and parties.

These, of course, are general rules; exceptions always exist. They tease our minds as we think of them, and they lead us to expand or revise the general rules. It turns out, for instance, that participation in politics has always been high in the American state of Maine, where I live, even though it does *not* rank high on several of the variables that appear necessary for high levels of citizen activism. For instance, Maine has never ranked very high on national indicators of wealth and education.

To understand the high levels of citizen involvement in Maine, one must add one more factor to the equation for participation in public affairs. Social scientists often call it a *sense of civic duty*. This phrase delineates an attitude of obligation, of responsibility for getting involved in public affairs. "The good citizen is supposed to take part in the life of the community." To the extent that you believe in this precept, to the extent that it has been hammered home in your family, in your school, in the town where you grew up, you will act on it as an adult. At the very least, you will vote regularly, show up for the occasional public meeting, and perhaps communicate from time to time with your mayor, governor, or senator.

The opposite of civic duty is cynicism and distrust. Political scientists often label this attitude *political alienation*. If officials are stupid, corrupt, and uncaring, states the cynic, what's the sense of activism? Whoever gets into office will be concerned only with lining their own pockets, not with representing you or doing what's right. What's the point of voting or making an effort to influence these crooks? You can't have an impact, so why waste your time?

Where citizen alienation is high, one expects less political participation than in places where a strong sense of civic duty prevails. An ethos of citizen responsibility and a trust in the motives of public officials predominate in Maine, a state with a strong moralistic tradition inherited from early Pilgrim settlers.[5] By no coincidence, Maine led the nation in voter turnout at the 1992 election. (Of all adult Mainers, 72 percent voted, compared to 55 percent of all Americans.) Maine always ranks in the top five or ten states for percent of eligible citizens who go to the polls at any given election.

By way of contrast, turnout rates are much lower in Maryland, a state much wealthier and better educated than Maine and therefore "objectively" one that should produce higher turnout rates. This state, however, is characterized by widespread levels of citizen cynicism, feelings that government officials don't care about average citizens, and a belief that most politicians are corrupt and self-serving. These attitudes reflect, in the terms of Daniel Elazar, an "individualistic" culture.[6] Holding political attitudes of cynicism and distrust, many Marylanders don't bother to show up at election time. Psychological factors thus weigh heavily in explaining the Maine–Maryland differential in turnout rates.

Table 8–1 shows clearly that Mainers are not only much more participatory than people from Maryland, but also more active than New Yorkers and Californians, two other sets of people wealthier and better educated than residents of Maine. These data support the proposition that all key variables must be taken into account in trying to explain any given sociopolitical pattern. They also suggest once again the complexity of the political

Table 8–1 The Effect of Political Culture: Selected Data Comparing Maine to Three Other American States

State	Per Capita Income, 1986	Education Level*	Voter Turnout, 1988	Voter Turnout, 1990
Maine	$12,709	14.0	61.1%	56.0%
Maryland	$16,588	19.8	49.0%	30.0%
New York	$17,118	18.7	47.8%	26.8%
California	$16,778	19.8	47.1%	32.9%

* "Education level" equals the percentage of the adult population holding a college degree in 1980.

[5]Daniel J. Elazar has developed the notion that three different cultures have shaped American society: the moralistic, the traditionalistic, and the individualistic. Of these, Maine (and New England, in general) has been most strongly influenced by the moralistic traditions of the early Pilgrim and Puritan settlers. See Elazar, *American Federalism: A View from the States*, 2d ed. (New York: Thomas Y. Crowell and Company, 1972), esp. pp. 84–126.

[6]See Elazar, op. cit.

process. For those who would try to make sense of it, it provides an endless source of fascination.

SUMMARY

Political participation is a puzzle. Some people get deeply involved in politics, while others can hardly bear to think about it. Still others show moderate or occasional levels of involvement. What determines these varying degrees of political commitment has long intrigued social scientists, and after decades of study, we now know a good deal about why people do and do not participate in politics.

The clearest conclusion is this: If politics touches us directly, or is believed to affect us deeply, then we will enter the political arena. People who are wealthy know that government tax policies can dramatically affect them. Educated people understand the links between political decisions and the conditions of their own lives. Socially connected people come to know political influentials and gain firsthand contact with the world of politics. These and other obvious social circumstances help link people's individual lives to the broader institutions of government and politics. Those links make political involvement both easier and more likely.

Politics can also touch us through our environment. External circumstances can force the subject on our attention and suggest, even encourage, our participation. In countries with strong political parties and strong unions, for instance, politics touches a broad range of citizens through organized activists who stimulate mass interest and induce mass involvement. Lower-status groups thus get included in the political process, whereas they are often left out of it in societies with weak parties and unions (such as the United States).

Environmental factors affect political involvement in other ways. Closely contested elections, for example, will stimulate voter interest and turnout. And governments may set up election rules so as to make it easy for people to get to the polls. Polls may be open on weekends or holidays, government officials may register voters automatically, and so on. In the United States, on the other hand, governments have traditionally made it difficult for people to vote. Elections occur on working days, and voters who haven't weeks ahead of time taken the personal initiative to register find themselves disenfranchised at the polls in most states.

Ultimately, however, involvement in politics is a personal decision: One decides to do it or works to avoid it. Since politics is a rough-and-tumble complex world, most people avoid it. For the most part, those lacking in a strong sense of self will be discouraged from participating by both the denseness and the tension of political arguments. Societies that encourage individual self-esteem (through norms of individualism and rewards of wealth and education) will exhibit high levels of participation. Lacking these attributes, societies rich in participation-inducing organizations can also achieve high levels of political involvement. Nevertheless, politics as an enterprise will never stimulate the bulk of any population to a deep-seated commitment of time and energy. Theories that try to explain politics based on the idea of an active and politically interested citizenry are doomed to fail.

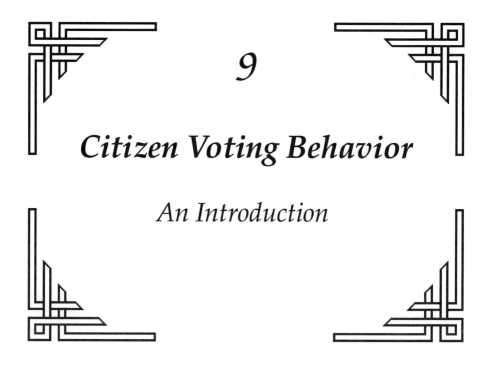

9

Citizen Voting Behavior

An Introduction

Whether to participate in politics is one question. Once you decide to enter the political arena, you face another issue. *How* are you going to act?

In theory, you can imagine a host of activities open to the political participant. You can merely discuss politics from time to time with your friends. You can move on from there to pay serious attention to politics and vote regularly. A step past discussing, information gathering, and voting is *persuasion*, an active effort to bring others to your point of view. This persuasive activity can take a serious turn: You can write letters to your local newspaper, to the mayor, even to your senator and the president. And you can get even more deeply involved, attending political rallies, helping candidates for office, becoming active in some of the hundreds of political groups ranging from the Sierra Club to the National Rifle Association. At the most extreme level of commitment, you might even run for office yourself.

LEVELS OF ACTIVISM

Although we can imagine many different political acts, most take place at one of three levels. At its simplest, at the level typical of most citizens everywhere, politics occurs only in the occasional conversation and around election time. Most citizens are neither wholly alienated and isolated from politics, nor are they wholly caught up in it either. Average citizens have a modest level of interest in politics, a modest level of knowledge about it. They will talk about political matters from time to time—when the subject comes up—with friends, neighbors, and colleagues. They will register their attitudes toward current political events in that formal societal rite we call an election. Once in a great while, usually during a crisis of some kind, they may get briefly caught up in more extended political activity. Then they may attend a political rally or write a letter to some political figure. But most of the time most citizens think little about politics and do less.

The plain fact is, most citizens just don't find political life seductive. Hence, they won't devote their attention or spare time to it. It takes serious commitment to move past the simple talking–voting activity that characterizes the political involvement of average citizens. And most citizens have little motivation to make that commitment.

At the next level of political activity, then, the number of participants dwindles dramatically. Here we find the political activists. They spend serious blocks of time following politics in the media (press, radio, TV), discussing it frequently and in detail with like-minded friends, going to political meetings, joining organized political groups, attending rallies, and donating time and money to back candidates they admire and issues they support.

It should not be supposed, by the way, that activity at this level is always benevolent, in the do-gooding sense touted by small-town American newspapers, civics-book primers, and the Mr.-Smith-Goes-to-Washington-and-sorts-out-the-mess cliché. The action of citizen participants everywhere is supremely "political." That is, like most human behavior, it is narrowly self-interested. Many who become politically active are working to promote a party, a movement, or a specialized group interest. Many have an even more basic motive. They wish to enhance their individual career prospects.

Now there is nothing automatically wrong with these motivations. In a free society we all have the right to promote our interests. Just as we shouldn't glamorize political activists ("good citizens doing their duty"), we shouldn't denigrate them all either ("corrupt opportunists using public office for selfish ends"). As political analysts, we must judge each politician individually and objectively. What does she stand for? What is he like as a person? What tactics do they typically use to get their way? How well do their operating styles reinforce or undermine the core values of their political culture? In other words, what is the objective effect of any politician's behavior? That is the question we must answer before making blanket generalizations about politicians and their impact (for better or worse) on society.

We must also note that in this group of actively involved citizens, there will always be a segment of those who engage in "unconventional" behavior, who pursue what supporters of the status quo will call "antisystem" goals. (These words stand in quotes because they represent subjective judgments.) The line between conventional and unconventional behavior, between system-supportive and antisystem activity, is fuzzy indeed. Was the American civil rights movement antisystem? Or was it intensely symbolic of the deepest and truest values of American democracy? These questions are difficult to answer.

They become even more difficult to answer when an activity begins conventionally (say, a union-sponsored strike) and moves on to become violent. Sometimes a perfectly legal workers' strike begins peacefully, then turns into a raging confrontation between activists (strikers) and symbols of authority (police). Or the government may call in troops to put down clashes between fired strikers and their replacements. One can then argue endlessly over who was "really" acting in an unconventional or antisystem manner. Was it the strikers (for interfering with the free working of the market system), or was it the government (for interfering with the workers' democratic right to strike)?

Despite these definitional issues and the problem of hard or borderline cases, impartial analysts can usually agree on what behavior goes beyond the range of generally accepted norms in any given political system. Shouting down people you disagree with, for instance, violates the idea of free speech that is central to polyarchal politics. Killing government officials you disagree with is antisystem behavior, regardless of the country.

No political system has ever been free of antisystem activity. In stable systems, especially those in widely supported polyarchies and in strong dictatorships, the number of "subversive" participants will be small—probably well under 1 percent of the population. In unstable systems they doubtless form a significant percentage of the adult population—perhaps from 3 to 10 percent. They can, for that reason alone, cause a continuing series of politically destabilizing events.

Political activity, to recapitulate, can encompass the following:

1. No action or next to no action
2. A modest level of involvement (occasional discussions, voting)
3. A serious level of commitment, involving a regular set of political actions either for conventional aims or for radical system change.

Let us imagine one more level of activism: leadership. The intensity of commitment at this level goes beyond the efforts of the average political activist just described. Political leaders devote most of their lives and most of their resources to politics. It is not something they do on a part-time, in–out basis. For years, they spend most of their waking hours in political endeavor. It is a career for them, a life's work. Their extreme level of commitment places them in a different category from that of the ordinary, garden-variety political participant.

When George Bush left politics (unwillingly at that) in January 1993, it had been nearly three decades since he began full-time political work by running for the U.S. House from Texas. Lyndon Johnson left the presidency (again, unwillingly) in 1969; he had first been elected to congress in the late 1930s. A gentleman named Carl Hayden represented Arizona in our nation's capital from the time his state was admitted to the Union in 1912 until he finally retired in 1968 at 91.[1] These examples only scratch the surface. At the level of the political elite, we find people who spend decades in public life, who live (and sometimes die) for political causes. For many of them, little in life is more important than politics.

Given this intensity of commitment, full-time activists are going to find their way to power. They will assume leadership positions at every level, from town councils to presidencies, from local citizens groups to international lobbies. Their single-minded focus insures that they will gain power and influence far beyond their numbers in the population. This group of political leaders is so important that we shall later devote an entire chapter to showing what they are like. At this point we mention them only to complete our portrait of the citizenry within most political systems.

Obviously, we have painted with the broadest of strokes here. Think of these differentiations as a foundation for the process of understanding the various forms that political participation can take in most societies.

Figure 9–1 recapitulates what we have learned. It shows that participation in politics occurs at several levels. Each level of involvement requires a much greater voluntary output of energy and a much greater use of personal resources than the preceding level.[2]

At the lowest level of involvement are citizens unwilling to invest even minimal effort in the political enterprise. They have, for whatever reason, no interest in politics. This lack of interest is closely related to inadequate political skill. These people often have too few of the resources (knowledge, money, connections) needed to make an impact on politics. They are usually not just political isolates; they are social and economic isolates as well.

At a level of energy somewhat beyond these political *refuseniks* stands a vast group of marginally involved citizens. They will, in most countries

---

[1]Arizona's Hayden served in the U.S. House of Representatives from 1912 until 1926, when he was elected to the U.S. Senate, where he remained until 1968. He gained his first public office in 1902 as Town Councillor of Tempe, thus winning his first office before the age of the automobile and holding his last office well into the age of nuclear weapons.

[2]The ideas presented in the paragraphs that follow and in Figure 9–1 rely heavily on evidence presented in W. Russell Neuman, *The Parade of Mass Politics: Knowledge and Opinion in the American Electorate* (Cambridge, MA: Harvard University Press, 1986), esp. chap. 2; Sidney Verba, Norman H. Nie, and Jae-on Kim, *Participation and Political Equality: A Seven-Nation Study* (New York: Cambridge University Press, 1978); and Alan Marsh, *Political Action in Europe and the U.S.A.* (London: Macmillan, 1990). See in particular the data presented in Marsh, p. 14 (Table 1.1).

most of the time, include the majority of the population. These people have some idea of what is happening in politics, they pay some attention to political events, and they invest a modest level of energy in political action. Those acts consist primarily of occasional political discussions, paying some attention to political developments during election campaigns and during other critical moments in their country's history, and voting.

At a much more intense level of activism, we find that set of committed party workers, campaign volunteers, interest group members, and all-around political junkies who constitute the core of membership of political groups everywhere. Depending on how liberally we define intense political activity, this group will normally include 10 to 20 percent of any country's citizenry.

Finally, at the top of the ladder we find those activists who form society's leadership pool. These are the people who devote their adult lives to politics and who, as a result, gain a disproportionate share of leadership positions and influence over policy outcomes. All existing evidence suggests that these people will always form a tiny percentage of the population—probably about 1 percent, but 2 or 3 percent is also possible, depending (again) on how liberally we define full-time political activism.

These estimates of the number of people in each category are based on a wide range of data, primarily national and cross-national surveys (known colloquially as public opinion polls). The numbers are not precise. They represent, rather, a range of possibility. That is because political involvement itself is not stable and precise. Individual participation will vary dramatically from era to era, and from country to country.

In a quiet era of stability, such as the United States experienced in the 1950s, the number of people found at the lower end of the table (the inactive and the marginally active) will be larger than it will be in a period of upheaval and activism such as the late 1960s. Similarly, the number of active citizens will be larger in countries that encourage participation and provide the resources for participation than in countries that discourage participation and fail to provide the monetary and educational resources that make participation likely and possible. Our conclusion still stands. In all places and at all times, a serious minority of any country's population, probably at least a fifth and possibly two fifths, will simply remain outside the political system, being uninvolved other than as subjects—occasionally touched by the effects of government policy, but never influencing that policy. We can label this group the Apathetics.

A larger group in the population will be somewhat more active. This group will usually represent over half the population of any country. We can label them Citizens. When conjoined with Apathetics, they form the vast majority of people in any given political system.

The people who could be called committed activists (Participants) will usually make up a tenth of any nation's citizenry, rising to perhaps a fifth of the population in wealthy, educated countries or in countries undergoing

FIGURE 9–1 The Pyramid of Political Involvement

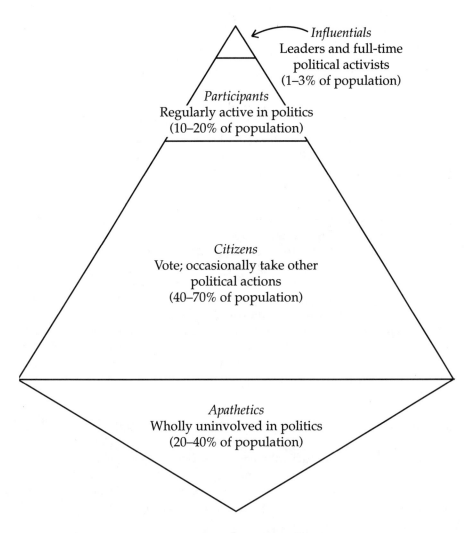

Influentials
Leaders and full-time
political activists
(1–3% of population)

Participants
Regularly active in politics
(10–20% of population)

Citizens
Vote; occasionally take other
political actions
(40–70% of population)

Apathetics
Wholly uninvolved in politics
(20–40% of population)

serious levels of political turmoil. Though always remaining a minority, their impact should never be underestimated. For one thing, their actual *numbers* can be large. Ten percent of all adult Americans, for example, equals more than 18 *million* people. No social analyst and certainly no politician will ever ignore a chunk of the population that large. In addition, people in this group are so much more active than Citizens and Apathetics that they have an enormous impact on political decision making.

Finally, the number of people at the leadership level (Influentials) will always be minimal. The reason is obvious. Humanity is numerous, interests are diverse, and career options are many. Given the myriad ways to make your living and spend your spare time, the odds are that only a small number of people will ever be attracted to any one specialized career path. Every society produces artists and actors, bankers and bakers, mechanics and lawyers, astronomers and politicians, but no society produces a profusion of any of these. Human beings have different interests, different tastes, and different skills. The number of people who both love politics and excel at it will always be small.

Evidence suggests that the number of Influentials will always be at least 1 percent of the population.[3] (You need about that number of people just to staff, and compete for, the major leadership positions in any society.) On the other hand, it will rarely get beyond the 3 percent level. For one thing, there is simply no need for that many full-time activists, so when numbers reach the 2-to-4-percent level, many people find themselves never attaining the offices they want or having the influence over political outcomes they seek. They are likely then to slip back a level or two in political commitment (becoming Participants or just plain Citizens), while finding another way to spend their free time and pursue a career.

Unsuccessful political candidates, for instance, often return to the fields of law or business from which they sprang. They usually retain enough interest in politics to keep active at the Participant level. They will go to meetings, contact public officials about policy matters, and work for other candidates in elections. But unlike Influentials, these former candidates will no longer be working full-time at politics. Particularly disillusioned former candidates may even drop out of politics altogether and, like Citizens, do little more politically for the rest of their days than vote.

SOCIAL FORCES INFLUENCING CITIZEN POLITICAL BEHAVIOR

Two of the groups just described warrant detailed examination. Because they have such an ongoing and continuous impact on the political system, Influentials are further examined in Chapter 11. We begin here by scrutinizing that other crucial group for understanding politics anywhere: Citizens.

Although they often remain quiescent for long periods of time, the large number of Citizens alone would keep us from ignoring them in our effort to grasp how politics works. Beyond that, we must pay close attention to their behavior, because when it does occur, it comes at momentous moments in a nation's history and produces policy and personnel decisions of the greatest significance. So the question becomes, How does that 40 to 70 percent of a nation's citizens behave when they do enter and join the

---

[3]Milbrath and Goel, *Political Participation*, op. cit., pp. 98–102; see also Marsh, op. cit., p. 14.

political arena? To simplify a response to this question, let us restrict the focus to a single action: voting. Although most Citizens engage in other activities (attend the odd political meeting, write the occasional letter to some official), voting is the one act they all undertake regularly. It is their one action with collective impact upon the political system. What factors determine the way this large and crucial group will behave in any election?

To answer, we must recall our old friend, the $B = f[OE]$ equation. People's behavior results from what's inside their heads *and* the situations in which they are called upon to act. Let us begin with the psychological or attitudinal side of the equation. Why do people develop the attitudes toward politics that cause them to vote as they do?

We already know about the power of early-learned norms and deeply-ingrained cultural expectations. Those attitudes we absorb while young, almost by osmosis, through unquestioning acceptance of the outlook of everyone around us, will have the deepest impact and longest influence on our way of thinking. What forces will have a special power to shape our world outlook?

Obviously there are many influences on our attitude toward life. It turns out, however, that a handful of social forces have significant influence on the way people interpret and comprehend the political world. These factors can be summarized in the key words: culture, class, religion, race, ethnicity, gender, region, and age. Sociologists usually call these *demographic variables.* Each term implies a set of common experiences that people delineated by the term have undergone. These experiences, social analysts assume, have had a formative impact in shaping the world outlook of the people being described.

To illustrate, few would dispute that gender has something to do with how you think and behave. If you don't believe this, imagine how different your life would be if you woke up tomorrow as a member of the opposite sex. If your imagination is weak, go to your friendly local video store and rent *Tootsie, Yentl, Switch,* or *Victor, Victoria,* among many other films on the subject, to get an idea of how people get treated differently, and then start acting and thinking differently, when they are believed to be male instead of female, or vice versa.

Likewise, imagine how different your life would be if you were born into a different racial group, or into a different class, religion, or region. Even age has a serious impact on our perspectives. I, for example, think about many subjects quite differently now in my fifties than I did when I was a carefree twenty year old. As a youth I scoffed at the idea of buying insurance, getting tied down to a mortgage, and putting money aside for retirement. Those ideas seem eminently sensible to me today! (In the same vein an elderly U.S. senator once said, "When I first came to Congress, I thought the seniority system was a disastrous and undemocratic abuse of power, but the longer I stay here, the more reasonable that system appears to me.")

These variables, while not the only influences on our world outlook, have all played key roles in shaping our life perspectives. In particular, they affect our basic attitudes toward politics.

DEFINING TERMS: LEFT VERSUS RIGHT

One more simplification is needed before we can see how these influences affect voting behavior. For reasons of time, space, and energy, we simply can't investigate the way each variable affects the way each citizen votes in each election in each country that allows a reasonably free form of political expression. We must find a way to make broad generalizations about electoral behavior. We need to find a simplifying principle that summarizes, and avoids distorting, what happens in real-world political elections. The most fundamental principle that helps make sense of how people vote in any particular election derives from the notion that most (or at least, many) political preferences can be located somewhere along a continuum of political belief known as the traditional left–right spectrum.

The traditional left–right spectrum. What exactly does this mean? The phrase is vital for an understanding of modern political processes. The words left and right—along with some natural supplementary terms like center, extreme left, extreme right—constitute part of a common language, a shorthand, for political activists throughout the world. They help participants situate themselves in the political arena. They allow politicians to identify potential friends and enemies. And they help observers like us make some sense of the Byzantine world we call politics.

Although the left–right spectrum *fails* to explain at least as many political events as it illuminates, it has become such a universal method of political rhetoric by both participants and observers that one simply must know the vocabulary before pretending to understand political life.

Knowing how the terms originated helps clarify their meaning. The words left and right were first used during the French Revolution—that cataclysmic event, which in many ways, signaled the birth of the modern world. When the king called the Estates General into session in 1789, that body had not met for well over a hundred years. It had no established traditions and few precedents to guide its operations. One of the many questions it had no immediate answer for was who would sit where. As it turned out, the more radical members of the assembly, those most eager to upset the old order of things, began sitting, purely by chance, on the left side of the hall—that is, to the Assembly President's left as he looked toward the chamber from his central podium.

Now where would you sit if you supported the status quo? If you backed the king and aristocracy, accepted the power of the Catholic Church, scorned the "upstart" middle classes, and feared the "unenlightened" peasantry, where would you sit? Naturally, you would want to put distance between you and the "radical loonies" over there on the left side of the meeting room. You and your buddies would move far away. You would want, in fact, to sit on the far *right* side of the hall, as distant from the radicals as you could get, which is exactly what happened. Radicals sat to the Speaker's left, reactionaries to his right. Naturally, moderate legislators had little choice but to sit somewhere between the two warring factions. They ending up taking the center seats and quickly became known as centrists.

These seating arrangements occurred first by accident, then by choice. Finally, they became a long-established tradition. For decades in French politics you could pinpoint any legislator's exact degree of radicalism or conservatism by observing just where in the legislative chamber that person ended up sitting. The power of the French Revolution was such that not only did these terms sweep around the world and retain their significance in the political discourse of most nations today, but these very seating arrangements (a semicircular hall with parties seated left to right to indicate their degree of radicalism) can still be found in many places.

So much for history. What do these old terms left, right, and center mean today? To answer, we must first recall what they meant at the time of the French Revolution. They meant, roughly:

LEFT — *A radical change in the status quo.* ("Off with their heads!")

RIGHT — *A rigid adherence to the status quo.* ("Keep the masses in their place!")

CENTER — *Modest reforms within the existing system.* ("Can't we all sit down and talk about this?")

Their meaning has changed little in the intervening 200 years.

Before we can apply these terms to current world politics, however, we must clarify two key issues. First, what exactly do the words status quo mean? Second, are these three positions the only ones available? Answering both questions will enhance our understanding of modern political processes.

The term status quo usually refers to the structure of things as they have existed for some time and continue to exist. When status quo is applied to an entire society, it usually means *the social order as it has existed during the last few decades.*

Now the social order of any given society at any given time always works to the advantage of some people and to the disadvantage of others. The social order in 1788 France benefited aristocrats and high officials of the Catholic Church. It worked to the disadvantage of merchants, laborers, and peasants. In a similar way the status quo in the American South of 1850 benefited large landowners, while working to the disadvantage of small landowners and most especially blacks (who were so far down in the social and legal order as to be slaves). The status quo in America today benefits those who are highly educated or technically skilled. (It also rewards those who are extremely adept at handling round objects of one kind or another—baseballs, basketballs, etc.). It undervalues people with low levels of education and few skills.

Wanting a change in the status quo means wanting to undermine or even abolish the advantage society gives to those who benefit from the current social order. It means wanting instead to provide advantage to other people who currently don't enjoy societal benefits. It does not simply mean wanting to cut off the King's head (there aren't that many kings left) or give land to poor peasants (there aren't that many poor peasants left, either, in many countries). The left position in the modern world has taken on a more general meaning, although it begins with that original sense of wanting to take power and wealth from the strong and wealthy and give it to those who are weak and poor.

The simplest way to understand the left position today is to see it as advocating *a redistribution of values.* In every country, leftists are those who want to give the "have-nots" more, usually at the expense of the "haves." At its most radical, the left wants to overthrow, abolish, or simply kill the "haves." In less radical formulations leftists are content simply to narrow the gap between the "haves" and the "have nots." In all cases, their sympathies lie with the disadvantaged, that is, those folks who have less—usually a lot less—of the goodies that society has to offer.

Rightists, of course, take the opposite perspective. They usually believe that the current structure of society represents an ideal setup. It may be the product of wise, rational, and benevolent decision making by legendary historical figures. It may derive from the successful social evolution of a sensible society. It may represent God's will for humankind. For whatever reason, conservatives generally approve of society in its current form.

Conservatives usually benefit from the status quo, so they will naturally want to support it, but it's not that simple. They don't support the existing system *just* because "it's good for me, and after all, my job is to look out for number one!" They come to believe deeply in the moral and efficacious properties of the status quo. Hence, they often support it with a zealous fervor, convinced that God meant things to be this way. Supporting the status quo represents, for them, the only morally correct choice for an ethical human being. This rationalization of current social structures is what sociologists often call *acceptance of the reigning or legitimating ideology.*

Centrists, of course, stand somewhere between these two factions. They are willing to accept some change in the status quo, but they don't want to go too fast or too far. They will accept incremental, marginal reforms to help the disadvantaged. They may be willing to chip away at, but they don't want to destroy, the position of the wealthy.

One can't emphasize enough the depth of the left–right schism over *the redistribution of values*. The term values means anything a given society holds in esteem: honor, piety, power, wealth, cows, and so on. In every society in every era, some people have more than others of what society values. Leftists want to redistribute those values: More to the many, less goes to the few. Rightists want to keep intact the existing distribution.

Leftists usually think that the haves got their rewards illicitly: in a corrupt, underhanded, cheating manner, through naked power plays (force and suppression), or in some otherwise undeserved fashion. Hence, it is moral and proper to take their ill-gotten gains away from them. Rightists think that the haves reached their position because they deserved it. They were the most competent, or they pleased the Lord, or "the market works that way," and so on. Hence, the morally correct action is to leave things well enough alone; they are working just fine, thank you.

This concept of the redistribution of values is powerful. It explains the difference between right and left on a vast array of current issues. Take, for example, one of the most salient of current issues: the treatment of women. What has the feminist movement been all about? Simple: it has supported a redistribution of societal values—*from* men, *to* women. Until the last decade or two, men (compared to women) had vastly more power, status, money, legal rights, and even the psychological self-confidence that goes with the knowledge that you are favored. At first feminists (one segment of the left), and then leftists in general, came to decry that lack of balance as unfair and unjust. They wanted to redistribute values, so that women could make more money, have better jobs, and gain better treatment all around.

Rightists, of course, reacted angrily to any suggestion that the status quo (of around 1970, idealized in their eyes as looking like 1950) was anything other than just, moral, natural, and a product of God's will. Women were "supposed" to stay home, make no money, and change diapers all day. Nature (and the Lord) apparently intended separate and unequal gender roles .

We all know the arguments on both sides of this issue. This is not the place to rehash them. Rather, you should see them in a new light—as relevant to the debate between left and right, between prostatus quo and anti-status quo forces, between those seeking to redistribute values and those opposed to a redistribution.

Once you understand the left–right continuum and the principle on which it is based, you can see that a large number of issues that formerly stood by themselves in your mind, needing individual explanation, can now be placed in a context and given perspective. For instance, you now have no trouble (do you?) understanding what Rightists and Leftists think of labor unions or the civil rights movement and why.

As a general rule, then, any group challenging the status quo for depriving it of rewards, which it claims to deserve, will be considered as

existing somewhere on the Left side of the political spectrum. Some examples of such groups would be handicapped people, gays, ethnic minorities,
and feminists. Any group resisting change and defending its currently held
advantage will be considered as occupying a Right-wing political position.
Business leaders, landowners, and entrenched church hierarchies would
typify such groups.

THE LIMITATIONS OF LEFT VERSUS RIGHT

Of course, the political world is complicated. This discussion is an introductory primer to the convoluted subject of group political positioning. Visit
your library for further instruction on this subject. We cannot leave this
topic, however, without adding one or two additional points.

First, things are never as simple as just saying that there is a right and
a left side to all issues. Remember that Right and Left exist on a continuum.
People shift back and forth on that continuum, depending on the issue and
their own circumstances. Often they fall into a gray area toward the center.
Relatively few people take the extreme position at one of the far ends of the
spectrum on all issues.

In most stable political systems (especially the polyarchies), people
cluster near the center, moving from there mostly to the moderate left or
moderate right. In stable, centrist-oriented systems, debate takes place
within the center. Policy proposals with the most serious chance of adoption
will fit somewhere in the space between moderate left and moderate right.

The typical pattern is NOT that party A wants complete redistribution
of values and party B wants to keep power concentrated in the smallest
number of hands possible. Debate more typically takes place at the margins
of the status quo. Should we take a little more from the rich, and give a little
more to the poor, or vice versa? Should we have somewhat stronger affirmative action laws, or should we pay somewhat greater attention to
"reverse discrimination"? Should we make abortion a little harder or a little
easier to obtain? Those who take extreme positions make the most noise,
but rarely get taken seriously.

Many current policy debates can be placed in a left–right, redistributionist context. Once we understand that context and know which groups
are likely to take one side or another on any given issue, we are well placed
for understanding the give-and-take of political discourse at the elite level.

One final warning about the utility of the left–right perspective on politics: It doesn't explain everything. Some issues cannot easily be placed into
this schema. The intergroup hatreds and conflicts that arise from religious,
ethnic, and racial difference may not be entirely divorced from redistributionist issues (usually one group resents another for having more), but they
are more deeply rooted in the kind of psychological bias we have already
examined: People who are different from us are automatically distrusted.

Other issues also fail to fit neatly on the left–right spectrum: the ethics of public officials; questions of war and peace; some policies involving public goods, such as a national system of parks and campgrounds, along with environmental issues in general; and lifestyle questions, such as the legalization of marijuana. Of course an ambitious theoretician could always "prove" that even these issues could be understood through a redistribution-of-values lens, but a common-sense approach would acknowledge that these and a number of additional matters simply don't fall into that framework of analysis. They must be approached with a different set of intellectual tools.[4]

SUMMARY

Thus, the concept of left and right—the habit of seeing political issues on an ideological spectrum ranging from extremely radical (far left) to extremely reactionary (far right)—has its limitations. It is not a panacea. Yet it serves as a significant beginning for insight into the ongoing set of political debates at the elite level everywhere. To the politically active and influential members of all societies, the terms left and right, and companion terms like liberal and conservative, mean something. They structure elite perspectives on politics. They form central elements in elite discourse. That is important for the rest of us, since these people structure *our* political environment, narrow our range of options from which, at election time, *we* are allowed to choose. The rational voter should have some idea of what these elite debates are all about—for self-protection, if nothing else. (See Figure 9-2 for a simple diagrammatic summary of the left–right spectrum and the points of view most frequently associated with each position on the continuum.)

FIGURE 9–2 The Left–Right Spectrum: A Diagram for Understanding Political Positions in the Modern World

Left	Center	Right
Extreme Left	Center- Left Center- Right	Extreme Right
Communists (Greens)	Socialists Liberals Moderates Conservatives	Reactionaries (Fascists/Nazis)

[4]See the discussion of this point by Stokes and DiIulio for one way to make sense of an election outside the left–right framework. Donald E. Stokes and John J. DiIulio, Jr., "The Setting: Valence Politics in Modern Elections," in Michael Nelson, ed., *The Elections of 1992* (Washington, D.C.: CQ Press, 1993), pp. 1–20.

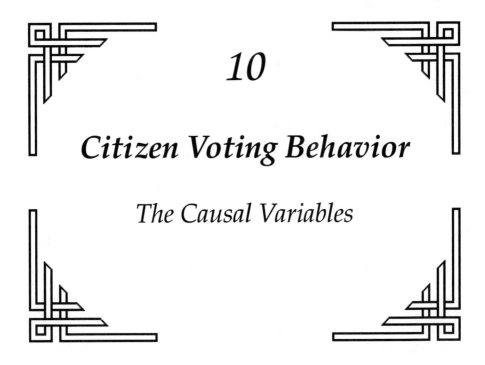

10

Citizen Voting Behavior

The Causal Variables

We are now ready to pull together several strands of analysis and to answer central questions: How do people vote, and why do they vote that way?

We know that crucial demographic variables influence how people think and act. We know that voting is the major political act most people ever undertake. And we know that at election time in any polyarchy, voters get to choose from among parties, candidates, and issues that differ from each other on the basis of distinctions rooted in the left–right continuum.

Whenever you cast a vote, then, whatever you intend by it, you are at the least choosing between a more left and a more right outcome.

The question that political analysts have been asking for decades is, Which groups are more (or less) likely to vote left (or right)? Every conceivable variable affecting social behavior has been examined over the years, so we now have a good idea of what the key influences on voting actually are.

THE CLASS FACTOR

Let us begin by remembering the basic difference between a left and a right position. The more leftward a point of view you adopt, the more you want to redistribute the values that your society at that particular moment holds dear. Those who have less of what society values at any given time will benefit, presumably, from any redistribution.

A logical inference follows: Those who have less of what society values *and* who will therefore benefit from a redistribution of those values will therefore *want* that redistribution to take place. They will advocate it and work for it—or at the least support those who do advocate and work for it. In a democracy voting is one way—minimal, to be sure—of showing support for a position. We can therefore postulate, from this set of arguments, that in elections those who have lower than average social status will be more likely than average to support left candidates, parties, and positions. Or to put it another way: *Class affects one's attitude toward left positions; specifically, the lower one's socioeconomic status, the more likely one is to vote for left-oriented parties.* What this axiom tells us is that wherever you go in the world you will make money by betting that the local working class will vote more to the left in any given election than the local middle class. If you can find some poor deluded souls willing to bet good money on the contrary position, you will soon take possession of that money and be able to start planning for early retirement.

The number of examples of this general rule can be multiplied indefinitely. In the 1992 election, for example, 59 percent of those whose family income was under $15,000 voted for Clinton, while only 36 percent of those in families making over $75,000 voted for him. To reverse the point, 48 percent of voters in wealthy families (over $75,000) voted for Bush, but only 23 percent of the poorest voters (from families making under $15,000) did so. Indeed, if voting in the United States in 1992 had been restricted to people from families making at least $50,000 a year, George Bush would have been reelected handily.[1]

The class factor can be seen even more dramatically in Great Britain. There, 54 percent of working-class voters opted for the Labour Party in the 1983 election, but only 28 percent of them voted Conservative. In France, 72 percent of the working class voted for one left-wing option or another during the 1981 presidential election, while only 17 percent voted for a rightist candidate. And this same pattern can be found nearly everywhere one looks.[2]

Class, of course, is not remotely all one needs to make predictions about the outcome of any election. For one thing, recalling again the $B = f[OE]$ equation, we know that the *environment* within which an election takes place also affects how people vote in that election. Note, for instance, that disadvantaged voters in America vote only as far left as Bill Clinton, whereas disadvantaged voters in Bologna, Italy, have frequently voted much further left—for socialists and even communists. In Peru those eager

---

[1] See data in the *New York Times*, November 5, 1992, p. B–9.

[2] On working-class voting patterns in Western nations, see Russell J. Dalton, *Citizen Politics in Western Democracies: Public Opinion and Political Parties in the United States, Great Britain, West Germany, and France* (Chatham, NJ: Chatham House, 1988); note, in particular, Table 8.1 (p. 155).

for a left option support an even more radical alternative: the violent revolutionary group, Shining Path.

The less well-off in any society will vote left, then, but just how far left they vote varies dramatically from place to place. To understand how far left workers and poor people will go in any given election, you must know something about the *culture* of that place and the *options* available to the voters in that election. *You must understand the environment.*

American culture is so centrist and moderate that proponents of even the mildest form of socialism haven't a chance of gaining more than a tiny fraction of the electorate in any political campaign. In some cultures, however, socialism and communism have been perfectly respectable options that are able to garner widespread support in a number of the world's elections.

What this means is that a left vote in the United States means something entirely different from a left vote in France, say, or in India. Nevertheless, note the overall axiom: Wherever elections take place, the lower your social status, the more likely you are to vote left, *whatever* that happens to mean in your particular environment. As a corollary, the lower your status, the *farther* to the left you will vote—if you have options among several plausible left parties. Thus, well-paid, skilled workers in Europe are likely to vote socialist, while poorly paid, unskilled workers are more likely to vote communist.

THE SUBJECTIVE FACTOR

A second caveat is needed to put into perspective the axiom that class affects voting. Remember that in discussing the variables that induce or inhibit participation in politics, we began with objective factors (gender, level of education) and found it necessary to move on from those to *subjective* ones. What really determines someone's behavior is not "objective" reality, but that individual's *view* of that objective reality. In other words, behavior is governed by the individual's own, or subjective viewpoint.

Social psychologists have long known of this phenomenon. Its central point is best illustrated by a simple aphorism: "Ideas which are believed to be true will have true consequences." If you believe that David Koresh is God on earth, you will follow his every command with blind zeal. (Whether he *is* or isn't God is irrelevant; you will behave as though God had commanded you.) If you believe that people of different skin color are inferior to you, you will behave in a racist and discriminatory manner. If you believe that people are free to choose their own fates, you will denigrate low-income people, because they *could* get a job and "make something of themselves," if they only chose to do so.

What matters in social life is not what is "true" (since there are very few widely agreed upon truths about human behavior), but what people in any given culture in any given era *believe* to be true. Throughout history, people have been willing to kill others (and accept the risk of being killed) over what seem, to outsiders, the most minuscule, even incomprehensible, differences of opinion. What exactly, for instance, is the difference between Sunni and Shiite Muslims? Or between Catholic and Protestant Christians? A Nepalese Buddhist (or a Martian anthropologist) might have a hard time understanding. And yet millions of people have died (and are still dying today), because many *believe* that these differences are crucial for obtaining eternal salvation and avoiding the path of damnation. "My way is God's way," the line seems to go; "other perspectives personify evil, and those who hold to those other perspectives must either be put to the sword or converted by the sword."

So our supposedly objective social circumstances are less important in determining our behavior than our subjective evaluation of those circumstances. A sociologist's flat statement that Jacques is a member of the "working-class," while Gertrude belongs to the "bourgeoisie," helps little in understanding the behavior of Jacques and Gertrude if *they* don't define themselves that way also. Indeed, individual behavior in the real world often drives sociologists crazy. It may turn out that Jacques, the worker, is a conservative, admires business acumen, and votes right wing in each election, while Gertrude, the rich man's daughter, sympathizes with the underdog, reads Marx regularly, and travels around the world organizing demonstrations for Greenpeace.

Objective variables, then, take us only part of the way toward understanding human behavior. They can predict a good deal about how people will act, but they never predict perfectly. Sometimes people behave in entirely different ways from what we would expect on the basis of "objective" evidence. To understand how people will behave, we must always look beyond the surface of things. Focus not just on "reality," but on how people *interpret* reality.

For example, we normally expect, as we have seen, that people in working-class circumstances will vote left—that is, in a radical, antibusiness direction. In France this pattern holds quite well—until one comes upon workers in the industrial areas of Alsace-Lorraine. These laborers, it turns out, have a long tradition of voting for Gaullist and other conservative politicians. "What is their problem?" a union organizer might ask.

It appears that these workers are deeply religious Catholics, people who live in an area that has long accepted Church ritual and teachings. One of those teachings stresses humility and submission to secular authorities, including one's boss. Workers raised in these beliefs are unlikely to be attracted to the radical antisystem doctrines pushed by French leftist parties.

In short, beliefs about reality, our social opinions and attitudes, are essential for understanding behavior. Workers in Alsace-Lorraine are, by

any standard, "workers." They "should," according to sociological determinists, be voting socialist or communist. Radicals may tear their hair and
bemoan the hopelessness of these besotted individuals who can't understand their own "self-interest;" Marxists may say these people have developed a "false consciousness" about their true social position; but dispassionate analysts (such as we are *trying* to be) must understand that without
grasping the psychological dimension that underlies human behavior, we
will never understand human behavior at all.

Besides, just to provide a balanced perspective, we can find numerous
cases around the world of middle-class (or higher) citizens who (in a sense)
identify downward—that is, they act politically as if they were members of
the working class. Intellectuals are perhaps the best illustration of this point
of view. Think about the people who make their living through the written
or spoken word (teachers, professors, journalists, writers, media personalities). What's the best way to describe the socioeconomic circumstances of
these well-educated, white-collar, middle-income influentials? *Middle-class
professional* is the usual term, one which lumps these thinkers and writers
with lawyers, doctors, accountants, insurance executives, computer experts,
and other such worthies of our postindustrial age. And since middle-class
professionals in modern societies make better than average incomes, we
would *objectively* expect to find most of them over on the right, or at least
center–right, side of the political spectrum.

The evidence generally upholds that modest assumption. Yet middle-
class professionals who *think of themselves* as intellectuals behave in quite
different ways politically from those middle-class professionals who think
of themselves, in fact, *as* middle-class professionals. Those who see themselves as intellectuals sympathize with workers—and with the less well off
in general. They even develop a self-image congruent with the normal
expectation for a lower-status person. That is, they resent their supposedly
scorned social position, believe they aren't appreciated enough (especially
in monetary terms), and work for policies that would have the effect of
redistributing values (especially income and prestige) from those who currently have them to those who don't (in which number they include themselves). Needless to say, they will vote left much more often than we would
ever expect on the basis of their actual income or social status.[3]

In short, those who consider themselves intellectuals think and
behave politically not unlike the way workers do, even though objective
tests would hardly place them in the working-class category. Once again, to

---

[3]I first encountered this idea in an essay by Seymour Martin Lipset. See his "American
Intellectuals: Their Politics and Status," in Lipset, *Political Man: The Social Bases of Politics*
(Garden City, NY: Doubleday & Company, Inc., 1960), pp. 332–71. When I was a college student in the late 1950s, a campus wag coined a term for those middle-class students who wore
scruffy clothes and spouted Marxist diatribes against the middle class. He called them *'les nou-
veaux pauvres."*

understand social behavior we must look beyond objective social facts to subjective interpretations. For every worker who supports "the system," we will find a middle-class malcontent who opposes it.

We now know something vital about voting behavior. In looking at the way any objective variable affects voting, we must first make sure we understand the *subjective* impact of that variable. Only then can we explain how that variable affects political behavior. Only then will we be able to make predictions about group voting patterns with a reasonable likelihood that these predictions will, upon investigation, prevail.

When we move from class to the next key variable, *gender,* we see even more dramatically the profound effect of the subjective on political behavior. The impact of gender on political orientation should, in theory, be obvious. In all societies throughout history women have had less of what is valued than men. That is still true. Women everywhere get worse societal treatment than men do. In short, here is a group that is everywhere disadvantaged by the status quo. A redistribution of values (in the direction of more respect, more money, and more rights) would benefit women everywhere. One could hardly find a clearer case. Any self-respecting Martian sociologist, having just arrived here and learning these facts, wouldn't hesitate an instant before predicting that women around the globe will be much stronger advocates of left positions than men will be.

Unfortunately, our extraterrestrial sociologist will be dead wrong. What do we see as we look around the Earth, when it comes to gender and politics? In all but the most industrially advanced nations, women are generally more conservative than men and more inclined to adopt right-leaning positions. But perhaps even more important than that fact is that men and women everywhere tend to agree on most political and social issues. This pattern occurs because (a) people get married to people who are like themselves, and (b) spouses who live together and share similar experiences come in time to share similar outlooks on the world, including politics.

So the dramatic difference that we might have expected does not occur; and where modest differences do occur, they occur in the opposite direction from what our theory would predict—except in places like the United States, Sweden, and Norway, where the women-to-the-left tendency does exist, but only in a marginal way, with male–female voting differences expressible in terms of a tiny number of percentage points only.

How can we explain this surprising and nonobvious, though nearly universal, pattern? We must seek the answer in subjective factors. For any number of reasons women over the ages have learned to take a conservative outlook on life. First, they suffered more than men for any nontraditional, aggressive, or risk-taking behavior. Women who refused the standard female role of looking for male protectors (fathers, brothers, husbands) were open to various forms of male violence (rape, beatings, forced prostitution, and even murder). Women who accepted the standard role of mother and child rearer were rewarded with at least a modicum of social respect, and were at least sometimes protected from the worst forms of male violence against women. (Why only "sometimes"? Because even those women who accepted the traditional role were not always protected; individual husbands could and often did beat their wives with legal impunity.)

Women learned quickly that the hurts they suffered from the status quo were nevertheless better than the devastation they would suffer from any attempt to change that status quo. This made them natural candidates for the conservative position. Remember too that people come to internalize beliefs that suit their interests. Declaring your pride in being a wife and mother helps make you feel better about yourself and allows you to get on with the job with a better attitude. Others *may*, therefore (though not always), treat you better, seeing you play your assigned (if low-prestige) social role at a high level of competence.[4]

A final reason why women often take a conservative perspective on life is that society has dictated their role as bearer of the traditions and conserver of the culture. Like all human beings, women everywhere came to internalize and psychologically absorb the roles they are expected, even required, to play. Women have, in overwhelming numbers, been the teachers of children. They raise and shape young people from the day of their birth until some time after puberty. Think: At what point in your life were there more men than women in your immediate environment? If you answer, "At age two," or "seven," or "eleven," you will be unusual. It is women everywhere who raise children and teach them the basic elements of their culture: its norms, its values, its expected patterns of behavior. (Who taught you not to say "ain't"? Who taught you to wash your hands before supper? Who taught you to say "please" and not grab for things? And who taught you to say grace before eating?)

Women, in other words, pass on a culture's way of life from one generation to the next. Naturally, someone in that vital role, conserver of the past and teacher of the traditions, will absorb the outlook and perspective of that role: namely, that the way things have always been done, that is, the long-time status quo, is the best way to carry on and should be questioned only at one's peril. Women will be strong supporters of the status quo, then, and that should make them, by this reasoning, right or center–right proponents. That turns out to be the case in the vast majority of countries.

Indeed, what must now be explained is why many women in advanced industrial countries have *dropped* their conservative outlook and

---

[4]Accepting a low-prestige social role while maintaining a positive outlook toward it is a sound psychological mechanism. It helps you maintain a healthy orientation toward life. I remember taking this attitude when I was a private in the U.S. Army, where I tried to do as good a job as I could at being company clerk. It helped me get through a boring three years in a low-status position and still maintain a reasonably positive outlook on the world.

become more radical, more left oriented than their male counterparts—because that too is the case. The answer is complicated and extensive. To simplify we can go a long way toward understanding by returning to the causes that first made most women conservative.

Life in the United States or the United Kingdom or Sweden is no longer dangerous (or at least not nearly as dangerous as it used to be) for those women who try to break out of the traditional mold and compete in society without their standard male protectors. Second, society no longer forces all women to spend all their lives in the home. The reasons are directly related to scientific advances. Society no longer needs women to be pregnant all the time to insure that they produce at least two or three children who will grow to adulthood, replenish the race, and support parents in their old age. Raising the one, two, or three children that most women are now likely to have (or none for that matter) is hardly a full-time activity, let alone a lifetime's occupation. Suddenly, the things that women were always expected to do hardly need doing any more.

Concurrently with that development, the things that men traditionally did (hard labor, hand-to-hand combat) that women supposedly couldn't do have also changed drastically. There is no longer any genetic reason why women can't do the jobs that modern society demands and rewards: Women can be lawyers, computer programmers, accountants, and business executives as well as men. They can sell insurance, issue junk bonds, and give political speeches as well as men. In other words, there's no longer any physical or biological argument against women doing the work most valued in a modern, postindustrial society. And once women start doing that work, they will start asking why their contributions to society, now exactly the same as men's, continue to be valued at a lower level. *That* is the point at which the radicalizing, left-oriented outlook of modern woman begins.

Societies moving toward true gender equality will inevitably pass through the phase that economically advanced nations currently occupy: somewhere between the situation where women are treated truly as second-class citizens, kept from even imagining that their status could be any different, and that situation where men and women who do the same work will be treated in exactly the same way and given the same money and respect for doing it. Many women in modern countries now behave as we originally conjectured they would. They see themselves in less-than-equal circumstances, see that a change in the status quo toward redistribution of values would benefit them, and adopt positions consistent with support for redistributionist (that is, left-oriented) political policies.

Not all societies, of course, will advance toward gender equality at the same rate. Again, the subjective factor plays a major role. Where the culture of a place strongly promotes a traditional relationship between the sexes, women's likelihood of bursting forth toward some reasonable level of equality with men remains doubtful. Japan, for instance, an economically advanced society if ever there was one, lags far behind the nations of northern Europe and North America in its views on gender equality. (Women there, for instance, aren't expected to continue in the paid labor force after about age twenty-eight. Many are simply fired after a few years of work, if they haven't quit the job on their own to get married and become full-time homemakers.) And countries with an Islamic tradition or an Hispanic macho culture also seem likely to take a long time before arriving at a semblance of male–female equality in social relations.

We can predict that *the more traditional a country's culture, the more likely it is that women will take a conservative attitude toward politics.* As women shed traditional roles and enter the paid labor force throughout the world, they will become radicalized and move leftward. We can further predict that this development will happen more slowly in countries where current cultural norms strongly enforce traditional gender-role expectations. This same principle also applies within countries. Sections of nations where the most traditional attitudes remain strong will find the greatest number of conservative, as opposed to liberal or radical, women. Thus, it will not surprise us to find large numbers of conservative women in Southern and rural areas in the United States, whereas women in the North, in the West, and in urban areas exhibit more liberal orientations.

THE RELIGION FACTOR

As with class and gender, the other variables that affect voting behavior are the same ones that structure our overall life perspectives. *Religion* springs to mind as an obvious influence. In any society, religion affects political behavior in two major ways. First, in line with previous points, the more conservative or traditional a religion, the more its followers will adopt conservative perspectives on all life issues, including social and political ones. Second, no matter what your religion, the more zealously you adhere to it, the more conservative you are likely to be in politics. To put it another way, the more religious you are, the more you are likely to support political conservatism.

The general rule is: *Religiousness correlates with conservative orientations to life.* Those who are religious will be political conservatives. This rule, as with all generalizations about social behavior, must always be preceded with that famous weasel phrase, "other things being equal." In other words, if you hold all other variables constant and take two people who are exactly the same in all other respects, it will turn out that "most of the time" (another weasel phrase) the more religious person will also be the more conservative person. Think about this in terms of your friends and relatives. Does it work? Do the religious ones also take conservative stands on political issues?

"Other things," of course, are not always "equal." Take the well-known phenomenon of Catholicism and politics. In most countries where Catholics exist in any number, they are more conservative than people of other religions (Protestants, Jews) and much more conservative than nonbelievers. We see this pattern clearly in France. Nearly all French people are nominally Catholic—that is, most of them are baptized, married, and buried by priests. In fact, however, half the population is "nonpracticing," almost never attending mass, hardly ever taking communion, rarely going to confession—and generally not behaving like "good Catholics" are supposed to behave. The other half of the country is serious in its devotion and performs its religious duties regularly.

It is precisely in those parts of France where Catholicism is weak, where deeply devout Catholics who attend mass regularly are few on the ground, that socialists and communists (that is, the left) have traditionally secured the highest percentage of votes. In contrast, where the Catholic Church is strong in France, there too is support for conservative politicians high.

That is the expected universal pattern. However, the pattern in the United States violates this expectation quite dramatically. Where Catholics have been numerous over the years, there the Democratic Party has been strongest. In other words, historically Catholics (supposedly the most conservative of the major American religious groups) have voted Democratic (that is, left) in much larger numbers than they voted Republican (right) and in much higher percentages than members of the supposedly more liberal religious group, Protestants.

Indeed, if only Protestants had voted in the 1992 presidential election, George Bush would have been reelected. Clinton, the most left of the three major candidates in 1992, owed his victory to strong support from American Catholic voters.

How can we explain this apparently aberrant political behavior? Is the theory about the relationship between religion and politics simply wrong? No. What we must remember is the vital caveat: other things being equal. (Unfortunately, it sometimes appears that others things are *never* equal!) If you think for a minute, you should be able to figure out for yourself why Catholics in the United States have traditionally supported the Democratic Party and not the Republicans.

O.K. Your minute's up. Let's look at the answer. What particular Americans over the years have actually been Catholic? Up to about 1950, the great bulk of them came from three major ethnic groups: Irish, Italians, and Poles. Other Catholics represented, in smaller percentages, Americans of French or Hispanic origin. (Lately Hispanic numbers have dramatically increased, but until the 1970s they were a tiny group.)

Now what do all of these American Catholics have in common? They are today or were in the past what many sociologists would call "underprivileged ethnic minorities." At the minimum they were known as "working-class ethnics," but members of the dominant majority had more pejorative names for them. (You know what they are.) In other words the population already in place, with its value system culturally shaped by British origins, despised these newcomers because they were not English, or Protestant, and definitely not middle class.

Catholics were treated, in other words, as second-class citizens, people to whom society doled out less than average amounts of status and money and good jobs—and respect. (Not long ago signs announcing, "Room for rent; no Irish need apply," were perfectly common in northeastern American cities. And even more recently "Polish jokes" were common—anecdotes implying an exaggerated stupidity on the part of all Poles.) What do we know about people who have fewer of the values society offers and who would benefit from a redistribution of those values? They turn to left-oriented solutions, to people and parties advocating redistributive policies.

American Catholics, then, have been more left leaning than expected because they have been more likely than expected to occupy working-class and ethnic-minority-group status. Devout Catholics in Ireland, Italy, and Poland, as well as in France, Spain, and Latin American countries, do *not* find themselves in the minority. Neither are they left oriented in those countries. The theory linking religion to conservatism holds generally. We must simply remember that religion is not the only variable affecting human behavior. *Class and ethnic minority status can sometimes combine to overcome the impact of religion.*

In addition, *level of religious commitment* must also be taken into account. Catholics in the United States have never been as conservative as Catholics in other countries, because they have inevitably absorbed, over time, the dominant values of the broader liberal American culture in which they find themselves. That constitutes another reason why American Catholics are not as conservative as their foreign counterparts.

ETHNIC AND RACIAL FACTORS

The point about ethnic minority status leads to the next key variable that influences political behavior at the mass level: ethnic and racial identity. We now know that people everywhere take group identities seriously. The rule is simple: *people identify with people like themselves.* "Human nature" is another of those weasely phrases that can be used to explain anything you want to believe, but in this case, we may be close to something of an iron rule. Most of us distrust people who differ from us—and the more different they are, the more we invent reasons to dislike and even fear them. There's a large literature in social psychology on something called "mirror-image misperception."[5] Studies find that close-knit groups see a host of negative traits in their enemies—and those enemies see exactly the same negative traits in return. Group differences, it would appear, almost always create group animosities.

"Differences," of course, is a relative term. As a general rule the differences between people that matter most, that produce the largest degree of resentment and hostility, are those that stand out dramatically at first encounter. These differences include appearance (what you can see) and manner of speaking (what you can hear). Those who look and talk differently from the way we do are immediately seen as "the other" (i.e., a foreign group of people), with all the negative connotations that those words imply.

People in different ethnic and racial categories automatically bring negative perspectives to bear on each other. These people almost always turn out to exhibit some obvious difference—one that can be seen or heard at first encounter. They often look different from each other. They may simply wear different clothing. Or body type differences can be dramatic. Average members of group A may be short and dark, for example, while Group B members will, on the whole, be tall and light skinned. At the most dramatic, skin color will clearly set group members apart from each other.

Appearance is only one way whereby group members differentiate themselves from others. *Language* too has a significant bearing on group identification. In many places (India, Yugoslavia, New York City) people who speak entirely different languages live in close proximity to each other. In a less dramatic manifestation of this phenomenon, members of an ethnic minority group may speak the language of the majority, but with an accent—sometimes quite pronounced, sometimes just slightly different, but clearly recognizable (African Americans, people from Brooklyn, white American southerners).

Of course, beyond these obvious differences go many others associated with race and ethnicity. People of different nationalities living within the same territory often live in extremely different ways. Or to put this in modern "Americanese," they adopt radically different lifestyles. *Lifestyle* is not easy to identify at first, but if some of your neighbors start sacrificing chickens at their weekly religious ceremonies, while you and your friends think that the only sensible way to worship is through handling poisonous snakes, it won't take long before you identify the "chicken killers" and treat them with contempt. (Of course, it won't be long before they come to

[5]See, for example, Urie Bronfenbrenner, "The Mirror Image in Soviet-American Relations: A Social Psychologist's Report," *Journal of Social Issues* 17 (1961): 45–56; William Eckhardt and Ralph K. White, "A Test of the Mirror-Image Hypothesis: Kennedy and Khrushchev," *Journal of Conflict Resolution* 11 (1967): 325–32; and José M. Salazar and Gerardo Marin, "National Stereotypes as a Function of Conflict and Territorial Proximity: A Test of the Mirror Image Hypothesis," *Journal of Social Psychology* 101 (1977): 13–19.

despise the "snake handlers," and before you know it, a full-fledged War of the Animal Worshippers has broken out.)

Nearly all countries are composed of a number of ethnically separate peoples, so the potential for intergroup conflict remains high everywhere. The conflict will take quite different forms, depending on whether or not one group dominates the others. In countries where a number of different ethnic groups exist and none clearly stands out as most powerful, the potential for violence is great. Yugoslavia, Lebanon, and even India come quickly to mind.

A second pattern is found in nations where one group clearly dominates (usually in both numbers and status) and creates the norms and values of the broader culture. In this setting, lesser groups are treated with contempt by the dominant group, usually being subjected to discrimination and oppression. (Examples such as the Kurds in Turkey, blacks in the American South, Turks in Germany, and Koreans in Japan come quickly to mind.) In these circumstances how are disadvantaged minority group members likely to behave in politics?

Operating from the theorem that the more you desire a change in the status quo toward a redistribution of values that will benefit you, the more left a position you are likely to take in politics, we can quickly see that disadvantaged minority group members will more often find themselves on the left side of the spectrum than in the center or on the right. Naturally, a disadvantaged minority group does not imagine itself benefiting from the status quo. Naturally, they believe they would be better off if a redistribution of values took place, one that accorded them more respect, better jobs, and more rights than they currently hold. So naturally they are more likely to vote for whatever left options the political process in their time and place allows them to choose.

We can see this pattern in a hundred places. American black voters, for example, have for decades overwhelmingly supported Democrats over Republicans. In any given election the Democratic candidate starts the race by assuming that at least 75 percent of the black vote is secure. That number often reaches the high 80 percent or low 90 percent figure by election day.

Similarly in British elections the minority Scots are three times more likely than their English compatriots to choose one of the clearly left parties (Labour or Scottish Nationalist) over one of the center or right parties (Liberals or Conservatives). In Brazil Native-American peasants are among the most leftist groups in the culture. In Peru, these same peasants support the radical guerrilla group, Shining Path. North African immigrants in France have been strong supporters of the Communist Party.

Of course this statement about the likely radical political behavior of ethnic minority groups, like all other generalizations, carries on its back the Other-Things-Being-Equal stamp. A particular religious minority group, like the mullahs in pre–Khomeini Iran, may in fact incline more to the right than to the left of the spectrum. Or a minority group that happens to be reasonably satisfied with the status quo (Chinese Americans come to mind) may show no sign of sympathy for the left. Like all variables, the race/ethnicity factor stands as just one element in the political behavior equation. But when other factors are held constant, the chances are excellent that we will find any given ethnic minority in any given country taking a left outlook on most political matters.

THE REGION FACTOR

Where people live has a decided impact on how they think about politics. We have already seen that our place of residence affects our likelihood of participation in the political process. Likewise it affects the substantive direction of that participation. However, the actual impact is complicated, and easy generalizations are few, when one investigates the impact of *region* on political behavior.

A traditional way to divide people by region is to postulate an urban–rural split. Life on farms or in small towns seems so clearly different from life in the urban metropolis that sociologists everywhere imagine that world perspectives, including political viewpoints, will also vary from place to place. They hypothesize, specifically, that *rural people will be more conservative than urbanites.*

Generally speaking, this conclusion holds even though it seems to violate our previous expectation that those who have less of life's desired outcomes (rural people, in this case) will want a rearrangement of the status quo in a redistributionist (i.e., leftward) direction. Why it holds is not entirely clear. Is there something inherently conservatizing about simply living on or near farmland? It would appear so. Whether the explanation lies in the lack of exposure to innovation and renewal that city residents are constantly privy to, or in the necessary adaptation to the ever-repeating rituals of farm life imposed by nature itself and the inexorable flow of the seasons, we would be hard put to say. But if you compare farmers (and rural residents generally) with their exact counterparts in urban areas, holding income, gender, religion, ethnicity, and so forth constant, you will find that city dwellers vote more to the left and hold more radical viewpoints than do rural folk.

As always, dramatic exceptions can be found. Peasants can be radicalized, as the Viet Cong discovered—to their advantage. And North American farmers whose land is about to be taken away from them can be radicalized pretty quickly too. Prairie left-wing parties have played significant local roles in both Canada and the United States. The Non-Partisan League in North Dakota, the Farmer-Labor Party of Minnesota, and the Cooperative Commonwealth Federation in Saskatchewan have all played vital political roles in their state or province since the 1930s. Again, however, we must recognize that exceptions don't destroy a rule. They merely force us to confront the complexities of political life and the perils inherent in any attempt at generalization.

Generally speaking, rural areas tend toward conservative traditions, urban areas toward liberal or radical ones. A new factor in this equation entered political life some time after World War II, symbolized by the Levittown phenomenon in the United States: namely, *the growth of suburbia.*

Just as people from rural areas everywhere flock to the city to improve their miserable fortunes, so eventually do many urban people, especially from the middle and upper-middle income strata, leave the city—not exactly to return to the countryside, but to create an artificial, carefully controlled countryside kind of place, with grass and trees and bushes and sometimes even minuscule, artificial farms ("gardens") that provide many of the benefits of country living (fresh air, safety, beauty, community), but none of the drawbacks (grinding poverty, difficult working conditions, an unsanitary lack of modern conveniences, and insecurity).

This artificial safe haven, outside the city yet wholly dependent on it, came to be known as "suburbia." Lately the invention of the enclosed shopping mall, the development of superhighway systems, and the computerization of the world economy have come to insure that suburbanites no longer need depend on a nearby city at all. Postindustrial suburbanites just don't need cities, as they did in the early days, for work, for shopping, for entertainment. Or if they decide that they do need cities, they build their own from scratch. Joel Gaveau coined the term *edge city* to describe this latest social development: the shifting of wealth, power, and population from the traditional urban centers to the green ring areas beyond the old city boundaries.[6]

At first these developments were quintessentially American—based on a culture of individualism, wide-open space, and widespread automobile ownership. Now they have spread or are spreading around the globe. We can assume that they will occur in advanced economies everywhere. In the United States, ever at the forefront of world social development, the largest bloc of Americans now lives not in the city and certainly not in small towns or the countryside, but in suburbs.

What political consequences arise from this phenomenon? It creates a host of problems that we can't begin to examine in this introduction to politics. Not the least of these problems is the enforced separation of the various segments of society from each other. People in the suburbs live radically different lives from those in the cities, where poorer people and ethnic minorities cluster. These different groups live in radically different worlds. This separation of middle and well-to-do people from the problems of the less well off in society gives them less perspective on those problems and

[6]See his description of this phenomenon in *Edge City: Life on the New Frontier* (New York: Doubleday, 1991).

makes them less sympathetic to redistributionist proposals. Those in the suburbs see themselves as doing all right. The status quo looks good to them. City dwellers are more likely to face bitter economic problems. Someone running for office on a program of redistributing economic benefits will look good to them. As one would expect, suburbanites vote in a more conservative direction than urban dwellers.

In short, rural *and* suburban residents, for somewhat different reasons, will be more conservative, more oriented toward the Center-Right or Right, than urban dwellers. Oddly, on social (as opposed to economic) issues, suburbanites tend to be *more* liberal than urban voters—largely because they are better educated. Education, it develops, makes one more liberal on social policies, though less liberal on economic ones.

It will not have escaped your attention that the rural-urban-suburban cleavage may owe little to the simple fact of place and much more to the obvious fact of class, or socioeconomic status. Especially the political difference between urban and suburban follows the expected differentiation of middle-income (and higher) citizens from those in the lower-middle to working (and lower) classes. We can't easily disentwine the exact cause-and-effect relationship. Does place of residence have an independent impact on voting behavior, or is it simply an artifact of the class phenomenon? We can't answer that question here. Let us simply bear in mind, as we leave this introductory examination of geography and politics, that a nearly universal pattern exists (for whatever reason), and politicians everywhere absorb this knowledge with their mother's milk. To find conservative voters, go to the suburbs, towns, and farms of the nation; to find liberal or radical voters, head to the cities.

Beyond this obvious point it is difficult to generalize about political patterns based on geography. We simply cannot say, for instance, that the citizens living in "the South" of their country (any country) will usually be conservative (or liberal). One country's South may be conservative (the United States, Great Britain), another's may be radical (France), and in still another country the term South may hardly have a meaning at all (in Canada nearly everyone lives in the South—more than three-quarters of Canadians live along a narrow strip of land within 100 miles of the United States). Attempting political generalizations based solely on geographical direction is, on the face of it, absurd.

Before we abandon entirely this notion of a geographical effect on politics, however, we must make one vital point. *No country exists without at least one distinctive region.* (In the former Yugoslavia *all* regions, apparently, were distinctive!) The political process in a distinctive place follows its own rules, creating special practices that strike citizens in other parts of the nation as odd, if not downright incomprehensible.

The United States, for instance, has its South, where people supported Democrats for 100 years after the Civil War, regardless of whether they accepted the national Democratic Party's stand on major policy disputes. (Much of the time they did not.) In a small part of the United Kingdom (Northern Ireland) Protestants and Catholics are still fighting the wars of religion, a struggle long since forgotten by the rest of the population. In Sicily, the most powerful local leaders are not government officials, but members of the Mafia. And on it goes.

Each distinctive region has a flourishing subculture of its own, one whose patterns clearly differentiate it from dominant national trends. Each regional subculture reflects a complex set of historical developments unique to that nation. One subculture will produce conservative effects (the U.S. South), another radical effects (wheat farmers in Saskatchewan), and a third will simply produce high levels of intergroup violence (Northern Ireland). Under these circumstances, generalizations based on region prove next to impossible.

We must, however, be prepared for *the inevitability of regional distinctiveness*. No matter how homogeneous and deeply rooted the cultural pattern may be in any country, people in one of its sections will behave in some strikingly different manner from that of the dominant majority—and you won't understand politics in that country until you understand that dramatic regional exception.

For instance, the American political outlook is often said to exemplify the thinking of eighteenth and nineteenth century European liberal philosophers.[7] Yet clearly, "the mind of the South" (to use a phrase made famous by W.J. Cash[8]) must be sought in a different set of philosophical roots.[9]

The British tradition is often said to exemplify a peaceful, compromise-oriented, incremental approach to dealing with the strife inherent in political interactions. Yet clearly the way people work out their differences in Northern Ireland (through violence) forces us to note at least one glaring exception to that pattern.

All countries have their distinctive regions. Politics in those regions will differ from politics elsewhere in the land, as will voting patterns. The student of politics must be alert for these regional differences. Without understanding why they exist and how they affect national political patterns, you will always fall short of grasping how the overall political system of any nation actually works.

To illustrate this point let us examine a country that most readers of this text know well: the United States. The effect of the distinctiveness of the

---

[7]The classic expression of this statement can be found in Louis Hartz, *The Liberal Tradition in America* (New York: Harcourt, Brace, 1955). See also Samuel P. Huntington, *American Politics: The Promise of Disharmony* (Cambridge, MA: Harvard University Press, 1981).

[8]Cash's is the first book you must read to understand the American South. W.J. Cash, *The Mind of the South* (New York: A. Knopf, 1941).

[9]For another influential view on differences between the South and the rest of the United States, see David Hackett Fischer, *Albion's Seed: Four British Folkways in America* (New York: Oxford University Press, 1991).

South on American politics can hardly be exaggerated. We will ignore the obvious effects: the Civil War, the decades of segregation, the Civil Rights Movement, and other well-known historical developments. Let's just look briefly at the South's effect on the political party system of modern America.

What voting patterns would we normally expect in a place like the post–Civil War South? The answer is simple: support for conservative, right-of-center parties and candidates. The reason is also simple and can be stated in axiomatic form:

> Where the majority feels threatened by a minority group, it will support right-wing, pro-status-quo, conservative positions.

Two corollaries follow:

> (1) The larger the minority group and (2) the greater the status gap between minority and majority, the more conservative, even reactionary, will the majority's political position become.

The reasoning here should be clear. Any majority, by definition better off than a disadvantaged minority, benefits from continuation of the status quo. It will naturally take a conservative attitude toward redistributionist change. If it faces a large and especially poor (or despised) minority group that would benefit by major (even radical) change, this beleaguered majority will by a natural reaction move far to the right; that is, it will vehemently resist any change in the existing state of affairs.

These simple principles explain why white Southern voters for 100 and more years have taken consistently conservative political positions. So far no surprises. What does shock the initiate to politics, upon first learning it, is this: Over that same period of time (from the Civil War to the present), white Southerners have overwhelmingly voted for the more left of the two American political parties—that is, for Democrats. Are they dim, perverse, unclear on the concept, or what?

The answer, again, is simple for anyone who knows why the South is America's distinctive region. This is the section of the country that lost the Civil War. That matters a great deal. It used to be said of the United States, until Vietnam, that the country had never lost a war. Even Vietnam is a dubious example of a military "loss." (How would you like to have been the "winning" North Vietnamese—gaining victory after losing a million dead out of perhaps 20 million citizens and inheriting a devastated, bankrupt country to govern?) In any case one can still say that the United States has never been invaded by a foreign power, defeated, and occupied. Yet that statement too is untrue. The devastating psychological consequences of military conquest and foreign rule *did* occur to some Americans: precisely to those who lived in the Confederate states between 1861 and (roughly) 1877.

The effects of foreign defeat and occupation on the Southern psyche can never be underestimated. The burning hatred that white Southerners came to feel toward their Northern "oppressors" overrode all other attitudes that might normally develop in the course of a people's history: attitudes based on class or gender or age or similar variables. For decades, whenever white Southerners had a chance to express themselves politically, they chose to opt for a vehement rejection of that party associated with causing the shame and sorrow of their military defeat in the Civil War. That party was of course the party of the detested Abraham Lincoln, the Republican personified. Naturally, white Southerners opted for the strongest alternative to the hated Republican Party. Hence, over the years they voted Democratic at every chance. The staunchness of their Democratic support was such that the entire region came to be known as "the solid South." One never had to ask how Southern states voted in any given election. Every single one of them voted for Democrats. Period.

Once again we see the importance of psychological factors on political behavior. White Southerners should "normally" have been voting Republican all these years. That is to say, based simply on their objective class characteristics, we would expect them to vote for the more conservative of the two major options allowed by the American political process. What went on in the heads of white Southerners, however, insured that they would never do that. They developed a clear and strong set of psychological identifications: *against* Republicans, *for* Democrats. This made no sense in left–right logic, but it made a good deal of psychological sense.

The major impact of Southern support for Democrats was twofold. First, it diminished Republican strength at the national level. Even though Republicans dominated American politics from the Civil War to the Depression, they would have been even more securely in control of political power had the South voted for them, as it "should" have. Second, it kept Democrats at the national level split in nearly schizophrenic manner, assuring deep Democratic divisions over the years both in Congress and in national party structures (especially at national nominating conventions).

Since the Democratic Party in all other sections of the country represented standard left-of-center liberalism, its members in Congress and at conventions felt themselves cursed to be saddled with that large and extraordinarily conservative minority of members representing the traditional South. Yet the party couldn't simply oust this faction from its ranks. That would insure it forever of being *the* American minority party. What liberals had to do for generations was to find accommodation with their conservative regional colleagues.

This necessity insured that politics within the Democratic party was noisy and interesting; yet it also reinforced the accommodationist, minority-focused, compromise-oriented side of American culture. Major national policies couldn't be made without taking into account the wishes of that key minority group: white Southerners. Not until the 1960s, when another powerful minority, blacks (also within the Democratic Party) started becoming a vocal force on the political scene, did Democratic efforts to reconcile the two wings of their party, liberals and Southern segregationists, come to a stunning and final failure.

The South's impact on modern American politics makes a fascinating story. We cannot delve further here into the high drama of this historical anomaly within the broader liberal culture of America. Enough has been said, however, to illustrate our general point. Regional subcultures within all nations play key roles in shaping the national political process. The effect of *the distinctive region* on the way people behave is a variable that serious political analysts overlook at their peril.

THE AGE FACTOR

One final variable that many believe affects the direction of political voting is *age*. The impact of this factor, however, is less dramatic and more complex than is often supposed. In its baldest formulation many superficial observers assume that the younger you are, the more radical you are likely to be. Conversely, you become more conservative as you age. The hoary adage goes: "If you are twenty and no radical, you have no heart; if you are forty and no conservative, you have no head." One would expect, then, that young people everywhere will be leftists and old people rightists. By this reasoning, presumably, middle-aged people will be centrists.

That pattern is much too neat and simply fails to find support in any evidence. One reason for the minimal impact of age on political behavior is that the other variables we have examined are much more powerful. Working-class and upper-class youth are more divided by class differences than united by some supposed generational unity. A young, white Southerner and a middle-aged white Southerner often find more in common politically than a young white and a young black Southerner, or a middle-aged white and a middle-aged black Southerner. Yes, being the same age as someone else provides a modest commonality, but similarities of outlook can quickly be undermined by ethnic, gender, and religious differences, which overwhelm the fragile bonding that similar age attainment can produce.

Different socialization experiences also help to undermine age unity. People of the same age grow up in wildly different family settings. Under normal conditions people adopt the values and behavior patterns of the family they were raised in. A person raised in a rural, conservative, Christian Fundamentalist household isn't going to have much in common with someone raised by Jewish liberals in a New York City, Upper-West-Side apartment—even if they are both twenty years old and members of "the younger generation."

Is our widespread belief that young people are more "radical" than old people just stereotypical nonsense? Not entirely. The kernel of truth here is that young people *are* less set in their ways than older people. Hence, they are also less predictable and less attached to age-old traditions. But that doesn't mean they will all move automatically left of Center. If the "tradition" in their locale involves voting left, it is entirely possible that they will break tradition by moving right—not by voting even further to the left. Thus, young Americans in the 1980s moved toward Reagan (the right) in reaction to the failed (in their eyes) traditional pattern of voting left (that is, for Democrats).

Only one safe generalization concerning the political impact of age appears reasonable. *The older you are, the more stable your political loyalties become.* Whatever political tendencies you develop in your first decade or so as a citizen (roughly, eighteen to thirty), those are the tendencies you are likely to stay with all your life. People settle into consistent patterns as they grow older. If you voted Democratic throughout your twenties, you will probably remain a lifelong Democrat. If you worked actively for Ronald Reagan in your twenties, you will become a lifelong Republican. One fixes on a perspective early in life and stays with it.

This pattern can help explain the apparent anomaly of quite elderly people voting for strong liberals. The majority of Americans who came of political age during the Depression, those in their twenties during the 1930s, developed into zealous supporters of Franklin Roosevelt and of Democrats in general. Those people were entering their seventies and eighties during the Reagan era—yet they continued to vote for liberals and Democrats. The supposedly conservatizing effect of age didn't move them from the left to the right side of the political spectrum. It simply kept them anchored (frozen?) in the original voting pattern they adopted as youths.

In a similar vein we can expect that young Americans exhilarated by the "Reagan Revolution" of the 1980s will still be voting Republican and conservative in the year 2040! To understand the way any generational cohort votes, then, we must carefully examine the conditions that shaped their first decade of voting behavior. The age-creates-conservatism hypothesis is much too simplistic to take us very far.

ASSESSING POLITICAL IDENTIFICATION FACTORS

Class, gender, religion, race, ethnicity, age, place of residence, and region are some of the key factors that determine how average people will behave in politics. Specifically, they are key influences on voting, that one significant and most common act at the mass level. These variables, powerful as they are, by no means exhaust the forces that shape political outlooks. We can imagine many others: one's state of health, one's sexual orientation, the experience of military service, and so on. To predict how any one person will vote, we need to know all this and more.

We must also remember, as we have seen, that each variable can either *reinforce* or *undercut* the impact of the others. Reinforcement occurs when we find a *working-class* person, who is also a *woman*, who also lives in the middle of a large *city*, who also happens to be a member of a disadvantaged *minority* group—and so on. The overwhelming impact of all these variables reinforcing the natural tendency of each is to insure that people with those combined characteristics are *extremely* likely to behave politically in a predictable manner. In this example the woman will surely be voting in a left-wing direction.

Real-world data supports that conclusion. In the United States in 1992 an astounding 89 percent of African-American women voted for Clinton. That is, nearly all of this group chose the most left option of the three available in that year's presidential election. That is a rare and striking figure in the fuzzy, iffy world of social behavior, and it shows the clear impact of *reinforcing variables*.

In a contrary manner, those people whose social experiences reinforce first one outlook on life, then an opposite one, are much less likely than others to exhibit a clear pattern of left or right support. If you were born female, for instance, into a working-class Irish family, but grew up to become a lawyer and marry a wealthy businessman, you might be torn between a leftward orientation induced by your gender status and family background, and a rightward orientation induced by your current upper-middle-class professional position and family wealth. You might vote sometimes right and sometimes left. You might occasionally abstain and even vote for an Independent (centrist) candidate if one came along. On the whole, your voting behavior would be less consistent and less predictable than that of someone in more consistent circumstances.

Political sociologists call this latter pattern one of *crosscutting cleavages*. It usually leads to moderate, centrist-oriented political behavior. Often, it causes a complete withdrawal from politics. That is because it's psychologically taxing to reconcile divergent forces. Should you follow one's spouse and vote left, or follow colleagues at work and vote right? It may become impossible to adjust these contradictory claims, and withdrawal from the political fray may become the best solution. By escaping from politics you eliminate the pressure of having to make some difficult personal decisions.

To predict how voters will behave, we need a final piece of information: the *psychological impact* of each variable, its *intensity* for each individual. Class identification, for example, is felt strongly by some, hardly at all by others. It will naturally have a greater impact on those who feel it deeply. Workers who definitely see themselves as "working-class" will vote more clearly to the left than workers who don't—even if they make the same money, do the same job in the same factory, and live in the same neighborhood. Unions play a crucial role in instilling working-class identification. In all countries unionized workers are more radical (left oriented) than workers who belong to no union.

This concept—*psychological self-identification*—is perhaps the most significant factor in voting decisions. If you think of yourself as an X, you'll dress like an X, live in the X neighborhood—and vote like an X. In this regard, political scientists have discovered that of all the predictors of voting, the strongest is one called *party identification.* Simply stated, it means that those who *think of themselves* as Republicans, or Socialists, or Greens will usually end up voting for Republicans or Socialists or Greens.

That may seem obvious, yet the strength of party identification in any polity has an enormous impact on its pattern of politics. The more deeply implanted party loyalties become in the minds of a nation's citizens, the more stable the system is likely to be. Where stable party identifications occur, each party can count on a basic reservoir of support from election to election. Consequently, wild voting swings, which could bring new, destabilizing movements rapidly to power, become unlikely.

Of course, those dissatisfied with the current state of affairs may chafe at this stability of party fortunes, which results from longlasting party identifications. Reformers may see this stability as debilitating. For them it's an archaic drag on progressive developments, forcing the system to reflect outmoded party divisions of a prior generation, preventing it from facing new issues and problems with innovation and creativity.

Whatever one thinks personally of the value or drawback of strong party allegiances, the political analyst must recognize the explanatory power of this variable. If you want to know how people will vote in any given election, the simplest thing is to ask them what party they normally identify with. Much more often than not, that's the party they will be voting for. *The pattern of party identification* in any given country is one of those crucial pieces of information that the political analyst *must* have in order to make an intelligent assessment of political processes in that nation.

SUMMARY

We now know the ABCs of voter behavior. Merely learning the alphabet does not allow one to read Shakespeare, but it does represent a minimal precondition for advancing to the Bard. If you have followed the argument thus far, you know some basic information about mass political action. This firm foundation will help you start to make sense of mass political developments in most nations. It should also provide you with a sound perspective for absorbing the new information you will constantly be exposed to about the way most citizens everywhere behave in the realm of politics.

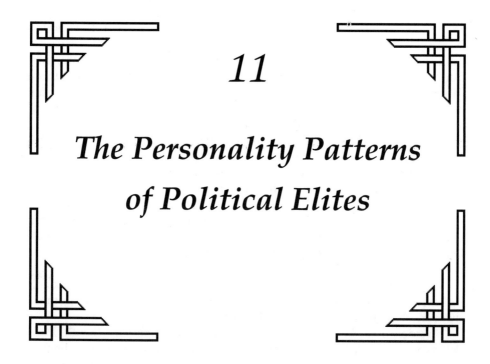

11

The Personality Patterns
of Political Elites

What are politicians really like? This question has intrigued social observers through the ages. A second question, however, casts doubt on the value of the first. Does it matter what politicians are like?

To raise that question is usually to assume that the answer is no. Many analysts downplay the importance of personality in politics. They seem to imagine that the political process obeys some universal laws. These laws, apparently, operate independently of the people actually involved in the political enterprise. For instance, those who overstress the impact of culture on politics are called *cultural determinists.* Those who overstress the impact of economics on politics are known as *economic determinists.* (Marxists typify this latter group, but they are by no means the only ones.)

UNDERSTANDING THE POLITICAL PERSONALITY

People who view politics as determined by exterior forces, don't really care *who* operates a country's political system. Whoever the leaders are, they will inevitably behave in the manner predetermined by those cultural, economic, historical (or whatever) forces that underpin political patterns everywhere.

These rigidly deterministic approaches fail to take account of human nature. Politicians, real people with complex personal traits, have an enormous inpact on how politics is conducted in any setting. What's more, they don't all look and act alike. They differ radically from each other, and these differences matter. Underlying the argument of this chapter is a simple point: *political elites have an enormous impact on how politics is conducted, and since elites differ from place to place, so too do political patterns.*

Political conflict, as we know, is normal and can be found everywhere. But whether that conflict degenerates into violence, is stifled by repression, or is channeled into compromise depends, to a significant degree, on the men and women active in the political system at any given time.

Let us return, then, to the question. Who participates in politics and what are these people like? We have already seen one way to dismiss this question—by downplaying the impact of personality on political events. Others discount it for a second reason. Why (they ask) bother to examine politicians? They're all alike anyway, so why study the obvious?

"Politicians are all alike." Everyone has heard this claim. Trite though it may sound, citizens in many parts of the world take it for wisdom. Is there anything to the claim? Should we give it credence?

Widely held beliefs are rarely devoid of some kernel of truth. Politicians *are* "all alike" (and different from members of the general public) in a few obvious ways. They all seek, or are at least willing to accept, a role in the public life of their society. Most people, as we know, shun all but sporadic political activity. In this sense politicians will be, almost by definition, more gregarious than average, more public minded than average.

Politics is, after all, quintessentially interactive. It cannot be conducted alone. Those happy to work by themselves or in small groups (at home, in isolated office cubicles, on farms)—those people will never be politicians (short of undergoing personality transplants). Likewise, people who fear leadership roles, who prefer to melt into the background of any group—those people too will find political life uncongenial. Politicians must act as leaders, even when their activity takes place in modest settings such as neighborhood self-help groups or town council subcommittees.

One can doubtless think of other traits of the political personality. Most politicians will have some verbal skill, for instance. A tongue-tied, shy, coarse, or ungrammatical citizen will rarely get far in the world of politics. It is, after all, preeminently a world of *words.*

Still, the traits we have mentioned—gregariousness, leadership qualities, verbal skills—are hardly the ones most people have in mind when they utter the old cliché: "Politicians are all alike." You know what people mean by this statement, and they don't mean it as a compliment. They mean that politicians are all alike in being the scum of the earth! People who use this phrase think of politicians as self-serving, opportunistic and untrustworthy. In taking this perspective, they join the majority of American citizens who usually rank politicians right down toward the bottom of the social status ladder, along with another unpopular group: used-car salespeople.

Naturally, some politicians conform to this stereotype. Bad apples are found everywhere. But shallow clichés rarely produce good analysis. Anyone who has had the slightest contact with real politicians knows that this tired generalization conveys little of what they are really like.

Let us consider some people who have actually been politicians. Adolf Hitler was a politician. He created the German National Socialist Party (the Nazis) in the 1920s, got himself elected to the Reichstag and named Chancellor in the early 1930s, and went on to gain notoriety as one of history's greatest tyrants and killers.

Jeannette Rankin, a Western radical born in 1880, was also a politician. A lifelong pacifist, she became the first woman ever elected to the U.S. Congress, winning a seat from Montana in 1916—before women could even vote in national elections. She arrived in Washington just in time to cast a vote against Wilson's proposal to take the United States into World War I. Ousted at the very next election, Rankin spent twenty years in the political wilderness, getting finally re-elected to Congress in 1940, just in time to cast another vote against war—this time against American entry into World War II! She thus became one of those little-known footnotes to history: the only person who voted against American involvement in both World Wars. (She also marched in anti-Vietnam peace rallies in the 1960s, giving her something of an antiwar hat trick.)

The bloodthirsty Fuhrer and the peaceloving feminist—what, if anything, did these two politicians have in common?

Consider other contrasting figures who have been political leaders. The crusading, assertive, and ideological Mao Zedong was a politician who led a revolutionary movement that turned China upside down; its international repercussions have not yet played themselves out. Warren Harding was a politician. This timid, dependent character had few political beliefs and no leadership skills. He did what others—including his wife and his political cronies—told him to do. Now he has disappeared into the maw of history, leaving no trace unless it's the privilege of being widely regarded as "the worst American President."

We could spin out these contrasts forever. In just the small group of men who have been American presidents, we find the gregarious Teddy Roosevelt and the retiring Franklin Pierce; the heroic Abraham Lincoln and the inept Ulysses S. Grant; and (biggest contrast of all) George Washington, man of probity, versus Richard Nixon, the dishonest.

These variations do not apply only to American politics. Everywhere, we find politicians who differ radically from each other in temperament and style. The British have, in recent years, been ruled by the caustic Margaret Thatcher, the affable Harold Macmillan, and the aloof Edward Home (all Conservatives, by the way). Russians have lived under the paranoid Stalin and the frank, open Gorbachev. The Japanese have been led by the rabid fanatic, General Togo, and more recently by a dreary succession of political bureaucrats. And the Philippines went from the autocratic brutality of Ferdinand Marcos to the placid nurturance of Cory Aquino.

Naturally, these examples of contrasting political personalities merely scratch the surface. You can easily make your own contribution to this little exercise. Think of any two politicians—starting with your local city council or school board. Or consider three politicians you surely know something about: those who ran for the U.S. presidency in 1992. Are Bill Clinton, George Bush, and Ross Perot really the same type of person? Chances are, you can think of many personality differences to distinguish them from each other.

To further grasp the point, go to some political meetings in your area. (You will find a dozen possibilities each month, if you make the slightest effort.) Watch how the politicians behave. Go up and talk to five or ten of them. It would be astonishing if you came away still thinking that "'all politicians are alike."

I have spent over two decades in activity of this sort: tracking down politicians in a variety of settings and talking to them about their political activities. What emerged from my interviews were clear personality differences. Even political activists who hold the same position and share many objective characteristics talk and act in radically different ways. This leads to an obvious conclusion. If you want to understand why political elites act as they do, you must understand something about their psychological make-up.

These points can be easily illustrated. Let us look at two "average" state legislators. They are both women: Betty Gardner and Joan Moore. On the surface, they are remarkably similar. Both are middle-aged, middle-class Republicans. Both were state legislators, members of the Maine House of Representatives, when I interviewed them in the summer of 1984. Both lived in small towns, had had years of involvement in local government, and planned no career beyond the Maine legislature at the time of the interview. Despite these outward similarities, a few minutes with these women tell us that they could hardly be more different.

Betty Gardner is nervous and timid. She can't quite understand what she is doing in the state legislature. It's all beyond her. She was "amazed" when her party's town committee asked her to run for a vacant seat.[1] When she actually won the election and reached Augusta, she felt "all alone." Her first day on the floor of the House appalled her. She thought, "I'll never understand what they're saying. What have I gotten myself into?" Self-confidence is hardly Gardner's strong suit.

---

[1] In this chapter all quotes attributed to Maine political activists derive, unless otherwise indicated, from my interviews with them during the summer and fall of 1984, when I was undertaking research for a study on gender and political personality. The names I have given these politicians are all pseudonyms, and I have otherwise made every effort to disguise their true identity.

In fact, this fearful woman needs constant reassurance from others to bolster her flagging self-esteem. Toward that end, she works at being friendly to everyone. It is crucial to her that others like her. When people accept her, welcome her into their social circle, it alleviates, even if temporarily, her deep-seated fear of rejection. This desire for social acceptance leads her to see the people in her environment as congenial and pleasant— even when they aren't. She needs to perceive other legislators as warm, welcoming people, or her chance of being surrounded by a comforting cocoon of friendship will vanish. Thus, she describes political peers in an extremely positive light.

> The other [legislators] are really great. I knew only one other person in the legislature [before the session began]. But everyone came up and shook my hand; they were all friendly and nice. They're a great bunch.

Not all activists think of other politicians as optimistically. Gardner's need for support from others leads her to see them all as "great," whatever their actual traits. She can't be objective, because being liked by all these "great" people is her central goal. She even finds Governor Brennan, leader of the opposing party, a warm, congenial figure—an especially odd assessment, since most observers of the day found him cool and restrained, if not downright distant.

This tactic of seeing the best in others has a payoff. By focusing on their positive traits, Gardner does make people like her. Her own friendliness insures that they will view her amicably. Thus, she avoids the criticism her weak ego dreads. Her eagerness to please shields her from hostility. At the same time, it prevents her from ever being a leader or having any serious impact on the issues of the day. Any clear stand on an important policy matter would earn her opposition from somebody. So would any attempt to seek higher position. (She'd have to compete against others to achieve it.) Striving never to give offense, Gardner avoids assertive behavior. Her need to please others produces a follower mentality and a passive behavior pattern. She was recruited for the legislature (much to her dismay), but will surely never go beyond it.

In vivid contrast to Gardner stands Joan Moore, her Republican colleague. A woman of boundless energy and enthusiasm, Moore exudes self-confidence as she heartily describes her numerous political activities. "I tend to be a doer," she says. "I like to get involved and get things done."

Moore leaves little doubt about the accuracy of this statement, as she describes issues she has pursued in city government. Bird sanctuaries, sewer problems, the spending of HUD money, historical landmarks, housing starts—these are just some of the policies she's eager to talk about in our conversation. As a state legislator, she is proudest of her work to reform the state's education system. Problems and solutions form the focus of her attention. Moore shows no interest in speaking of anything but policy matters. By way of contrast, Gardner hardly spoke of policies at all, her focus being on personal relations with others and on whether or not they like her.

As opposed to Gardner's hesitant speech pattern, Moore talks rapidly and with vigor. Her dynamism is impressive; her enthusiasm is contagious. As for politics, "I love it. I get up every morning, and I can hardly wait to look at the newspaper." She claims to be "a very organized person," who is "never floored by anything." No one who has met this ebullient woman could doubt the truth of that last statement.

The self-confident Joan Moore stands in sharp contrast to the mousy Betty Gardner. The two women differ also in their willingness to take strong stands on controversial issues and in their inclination to wield power. Moore doesn't hesitate to say what she thinks about current policy matters. Gardner prefers to avoid thinking about them. Moore chairs a legislative committee. Gardner couldn't imagine holding a leadership post. No one would ever mistake one of these women for the other.

Personality differences hardly confine themselves to women. Contrasts between male politicians are equally striking. Compare Maine State Representatives Roland Giguere and Will Maddox. Their objective similarities aren't quite as obvious as those linking Betty Gardner and Joan Moore. At sixty, Giguere is twenty-five years older than Maddox. While Maddox represents a rural area, Giguere represents an urban one. Still, both are male state legislators, Democrats, and lifelong residents of a small, sparsely populated, relatively homogeneous state. If "all politicians are alike," these two should turn out to be similar in character.

In fact, they are anything but similar. Giguere is a dogmatic moralizer, while Maddox is an ambitious riser out to make a name for himself. Let's take a closer look. Giguere seems almost a Lancelot figure. He focuses on doing the right thing, promoting his principles. "I try real hard," he says, "not so much to please everybody, but to do what is right." As is often the case, "doing what is right" means taking strong stands that will anger others. The thick-skinned Giguere doesn't mind in the least. "I do take a stand," he declares, and goes on:

> I've taken some very strong stands on law and order and on . . . moral issues. I am an opponent of the E.R.A. [Equal Rights Amendment] because I believe that the E.R.A. will work *totally* against the good of the woman.

Giguere proceeds to criticize welfare cheats, to castigate liberal judges, and to denounce the moral decline of modern society. This strong-minded man sees the world in black and white terms. He and his supporters are "clean-living, hard-working, and pure." Those who oppose him are "weak characters," have "shady backgrounds," and "lead immoral lives."

Being an outspoken conservative in a liberal party bothers Giguere not a whit. He simply must express his indignation at the creeping rot he sees everywhere. No wonder he finds himself always in the midst of political turmoil. His uncompromising support of controversial positions makes him a likely target for abuse. His personality almost naturally creates enemies. Giguere stands light years away from Betty Gardner, whose personality automatically produces friends. What's more, he surely destroys one political stereotype. Those who think that politicians are all mealymouthed and wishy-washy have never spoken with Roland Giguere.

Will Maddox is another sort altogether. This guarded young man works hard to hide his true sentiments on anything. After listening to him talk for an hour, I had trouble defining exactly where he stood. Was he a liberal or a conservative? Or even a moderate? I still don't know. I did learn something about him, however. Maddox is eager to go far in the world of politics. His career is the one topic of abiding interest to him.

Even though he won't talk about current issues enough to indicate where he stands, Maddox can recount in some detail his early campaigns for the legislature. He doesn't hesitate to express his desire for a committee chairmanship post in the next legislative session. He also makes it clear that he won't be content to accumulate power gradually in the Maine House of Representatives. His real aim is rapid national recognition.

> If [serving as committee chair] is a successful time, I see some possibilities for advancement. I mean a real advancement. I don't see myself as . . . assistant majority leader, majority leader. . . . I guess the only dream or the only goal that may be possible, it would be down the road, ten years down the road. It would be to run for Congress.

Maddox is self-absorbed: a careerist and a little more.

This focus on moving up quickly, on personal success, leads him to be deeply suspicious of others. Their ambitions could get in the way of his own. Therefore, he trusts no one, thinks well of no one. In politics, he says, "you meet with a lot of people that have large egos." His caustic cynicism surfaces time and again. "You can't trust very many people in the legislature," he claims. "Politicians are pretty much out for themselves." It is hard not to see these statements as psychological projections. Maddox himself has a large ego and is pretty much out for himself. He doubtless finds it easier to accept those traits in himself, by coming to believe that they characterize everyone else in the world as well.

Ultimately, Maddox is a tense, worried loner. Wrapped up in his struggle for a place in the sun, he loses sight of political reality. Issues, moral questions, the positive qualities of fellow legislators: He just can't focus on these matters. His own drive for glory takes all his attention and energy. Maddox is as different from the moralistic Giguere as "lean and hungry" Cassius was from the "honorable" Brutus.

A fifth member of the Maine state legislature exhibits still different personality traits from those of the four already described. Ray Roberts loves politics for the sheer sport of it. He revels in the competition, taking almost childish delight in explaining how he developed a winning door-to-door campaign strategy. Here is how he presented himself to a potential voter:

> I did not invite a debate or make it easy for a person to discuss issues. My purpose was to get a vote, not to debate or argue. I made it a point to *observe*, before I went into a house. If I'd see a beagle, I would ring the doorbell, and let's say the man answered, I'd say, "Oh, I see you've a beagle out there. How's the rabbit hunting?" Not even bring up politics immediately.

Roberts tunes in to the needs of others, not like Betty Gardner, that is, so that they will like him, but to manipulate them into helping him win a political contest.

The manipulation, however, is low-key and not vindictive. Roberts wants to maintain allies, the better to win future victories. His happy, optimistic air is well suited toward that end. He is a naturally likable fellow. You can't help but enjoy his company and his stories, especially his rules for playing the political game successfully. He is a calculator, but one who operates on the rule of "enlightened self-interest." A good calculator by that rule won't use people too obviously or hurt them needlessly, because you never know when you may need them again. Treat everyone well today, and you will have allies tomorrow: This seems to be his motto. Roberts expresses this idea of moderation in political life when he stresses that "'the art of legislating is to work out compromises." He may be a clever player of the political game, but he's also a team player. Ray Roberts plays to win, but in doing so he won't make waves and he won't make enemies.

We could expand these examples indefinitely, but let's avoid overkill. Surely, the point is made. If you take personality at its most fundamental level, politicians are hardly all alike.

HOW PERSONALITY IMPACTS POLITICAL BEHAVIOR

Why, a skeptic might still ask, should we wish to know about the personality of politicians, even if they aren't all alike? Won't the *circumstances* they confront, not their political personality, govern their behavior in the real world? The answer to this question should be clear from the preceding portraits. The diversity of character represented there should also be reflected in a diversity of action. *Politics is a world of choice.* Political roles aren't clearly defined, as they are in an office typing pool or an Army basic-training camp. In these latter circumstances it doesn't matter what you are like as a person. When the boss gives you a memo to type, you type it. When the sergeant tells you to run the obstacle course, you run it. But what do you do once you've been elected to the legislature? Do you go around making friends with everyone? Do you give press conferences every day and try to make the evening news reports? Do you spend all your time promoting one key policy reform, or do you get up on the floor and give a firm opinion about every issue that comes before the legislature? There are no clear answers; legislators will settle each question in their own individual manner, and we can well imagine that Betty Gardner, Joan Moore, Roland Giguere, Will Maddox, and Ray Roberts will answer each question differently, carving out quite different roles for themselves in the process.

Personality matters, then, because in a world of options, people will choose to behave in ways that suit their individual personality. No one will expect the insecure Betty Gardner to end up Speaker of the House. Equally, no one would anticipate that the combative Roland Giguere will be found masterminding delicate compromises on legislation of controversy and dispute. We need to know about the personality of politicians because they will behave one way or another, depending on their motives, drives, needs, and desires. Knowing the character of political participants will help us understand and even predict their actions.

If the belief that politicians are identical is erroneous, there is an equally erroneous, though opposite, point of view. It holds that politicians, like all people, are unique individuals. Each is different from the others. They must each be analyzed on an individual basis. Attempts to label or categorize them are doomed to fail.

This perspective, like its predecessor, is not without merit. Of course, none of us is exactly like anyone else. Furthermore, we all wish to be treated as special, not as part of some group. But this perspective, fine as a moral precept, lacks analytical power. If we wish to make generalizations that help explain the world, we must devise categories for people who share common characteristics.

Furthermore, the "everyone is unique" perspective fails on empirical grounds. Large groups of people often do behave in very similar ways, even if the individuals within each group are marginally different. We have already seen that working-class people vote differently from middle-class people. Class differences cause a wide range of other behavioral differences. Almost everywhere, for instance, working-class people eat their evening meal before middle-class people do. The latter in turn dine before most upper-middle and upper-class people. (In the United States, working-class people will eat "supper" between five and six P.M., middle-class people will eat "dinner" between six and seven P.M., and yuppie types will get around to a "late dinner" between seven-thirty and nine P.M., if not later.)

An old sociological axiom goes something like this:

> In some ways each person is unique.
> In some ways each person is like all other people.
> In some ways each person is like some other people.

It is the third of these aphorisms that interests us. Study of "the unique person" lies in the realm of psychiatry and biography. It also appeals to historians of the "Great Man" school: A few great leaders have shaped history, molded events to their will. The study of "all people" belongs to physiological psychology. The core of the social sciences takes its focus from the idea that one *group* of humans behaves one way, while another *group* behaves in quite a different way. Explaining why these differences occur and what their consequences will be is the central task (and the exquisite fascination) for students of human behavior.

When political scientists look at politicians, then, what strikes us is *not* that each one is unique (though in a trite sense this is surely true), nor that they are all the same (they are—in a few, though not terribly interesting ways, as we have explained). What fascinates us, rather, is that we see a small number of clear personality types. Each type exhibits a number of significant similarities, but differs dramatically from all the other types. This finding opens the way to some profound insights into the way politics works. Once we know what type of politicians we are dealing with, we can understand not only why they behave as they do but how they are likely to behave in the future.

My own research focuses on this topic of political personality. It forms part of an approach to the study of elites begun by James L. Payne and labeled "incentive theory" in his 1968 book on Colombia.[2] That theory was developed in various books and articles by Payne, myself, and others, culminating in a joint 1984 publication, *The Motivation of Politicians*.[3] The theory evolved from our observation of politicians in such diverse settings as Colombia, Venezuela, Brazil, the Dominican Republic, France, and various American states.

---

[2]Payne, *Patterns of Conflict in Colombia*, op. cit.

[3]See in particular James L. Payne, *Incentive Theory and Political Process: Motivation and Leadership in the Dominican Republic* (Lexington, MA: D.C. Heath and Company, Lexington Books, 1972); Oliver H. Woshinsky, *The French Deputy: Incentives and Behavior in the National Assembly* (Lexington, MA: D.C. Heath and Company, Lexington Books, 1973); and James L. Payne, Oliver H. Woshinsky, Eric P. Veblen, William H. Coogan, and Gene E. Bigler, *The Motivation of Politicians* (Chicago: Nelson-Hall, Inc., 1984). For other reports on the findings of incentive research, see our bibliography in *The Motivation of Politicians*, pp. 203–4.

Our approach fits squarely into a political science tradition, which might be termed "the psychology of political types." An early advocate of this method was Harold Lasswell.[4] James D. Barber and Rufus P. Browning, among others, have conducted work in this area.[5] Michael Maccoby in 1976 completed a study of businessmen that reaches conclusions similar to those of our incentive studies.[6] Incentive theory, in short, fits into a broadly recognized niche of the social sciences and is backed by a wealth of empirical evidence gathered over the course of many years.[7]

The theory begins with a seemingly obvious question. Why do people engage in politics? Straightforward though the question may be, those who study politics often avoid it. Most political scientists prefer to focus on what politicians say and do. They study how politicians win nominations and elections, what policies they propose and support, how they vote in the legislature, what coalitions they are likely to build—tangible, objective, measurable activity. Rarely do scholars ask a more basic question. Why do people become politicians in the first place? Why do they stay in politics? These motivational questions may be difficult, but they are worth the effort to investigate, because the answers tell us much about why politicians behave as they do.

Incentive theory begins with the proposition that what drives people into politics will shape what they do in politics. To understand political behavior, we must understand the motives underlying that behavior.

To grasp the power of those motives to shape political action, we must first remember a basic reality. Most people *don't* get involved in politics. Few social facts have been better documented: Average citizens just don't enjoy political activity.[8] This fact helps illuminate something important about political activists, those who do spend much of their life in politics. They find serious rewards from this activity, while the rest of us simply do not.

[4]Lasswell was among the first of those social scientists who stressed the impact of psychological factors on political behavior, advocating this approach as early as the late 1920s. See his groundbreaking *Psychopathology and Politics*, op. cit., and his later work, *Power and Personality* (New York: W. W. Norton, 1948).

[5]See James David Barber, *The Lawmakers: Recruitment and Adaptation to Legislative Life* (New Haven: Yale University Press, 1965) and *The Presidential Character: Predicting Performance in the White House* (Englewood Cliffs, NJ: Prentice-Hall, 1972); and Rufus P. Browning, "'The Interaction of Personality and Political System in Decisions to Run for Office: Some Data and a Simulation Technique," *Journal of Social Issues* 24 (1968): 93–110.

[6]Michael Maccoby, *The Gamesman* (New York: Simon and Schuster, 1976). Maccoby discovered, among businessmen, personality types similar to those described by Barber, Browning, and those of us engaged in incentive research.

[7]I elaborate on this point and discuss a number of related studies that suggest the value of this approach in *The French Deputy*, op. cit., pp. 2–12; see especially Table 1–2, pp. 7–9.

[8]For confirmation of this point, along with a detailed discussion of who does and who doesn't participate in politics, see Milbrath and Goel, *Political Participation*, op. cit., esp. pp. 5–34. See also Verba and Nie, *Participation in America*, op. cit., esp. pp. 25–101. See also my discussion of this point above, Chap. 8.

Why isn't politics more popular? The reasons are many. For one thing, most people find other pursuits more compelling: work, sports, family, hobbies, love life. For another, political activity always entails costs. Politics, after all, is a conflict-ridden, complicated, time-consuming, thankless, frequently boring, and sometimes dangerous endeavor. Devoting yourself to it full time is not most people's idea of fun.[9]

Yet in every social setting, a small percentage of people devote most of their waking hours to politics. They live and breathe politics. They seem almost intoxicated by it, addicted to political life. They will "miss meals, neglect children, and lose sleep for politics."[10] Politics, for them, becomes practically an obsession. They *must* be involved in it; to be kept out of politics would represent a severe psychological deprivation for these ardent enthusiasts.

How else can we characterize what is going on here, other than to speak of the desire for political involvement as a drive, a compulsion? Involvement in political life fills some deep inner need for these committed activists. The profound emotional rewards they find in politics compensate them for the drawbacks that keep the rest of us out. They willingly put up with the hazards and pain of the political role because of the intense set of satisfactions they find in it. The rest of us see in politics only the drawbacks and few of the benefits.

PSYCHOLOGICAL MOTIVATIONS FOR POLITICS

Payne labeled this motivational force, which induces long-term political activism, as a politician's *incentive*. Since the incentive is clearly a powerful drive, we expect it to influence behavior. Other things being equal, "political participants behave in a manner consistent with their incentives."[11]

Our research has so far uncovered seven incentives—that is, psychological motivations for politics. Each incentive induces full-time, long-term political commitment, and each produces a distinct set of attitudes and behavior. Those who have one incentive behave alike in many ways and differ dramatically from those with another incentive. There is a cohesive-

[9]For an extended discussion of this point, see Payne et al., *The Motivation of Politicians,* op. cit., pp. 1–5.

[10]Payne and Woshinsky, "Incentives for Political Participation," op. cit., p. 519.

[11]Ibid., p. 518. Incentives, of course, are hardly the sole factor to influence political behavior. Politicians are obviously affected by the situations they face, the norms of their culture, the traditions and role expectations of the office they occupy, and so on. We are not arguing that incentives explain everything—merely that they explain *some* things, and matters of real importance at that, so they must be taken into account in any comprehensive attempt to explain political behavior. See Payne's discussion of this point in *Incentive Theory and Political Process,* op. cit., pp. 7–15.

ness to each type, a certain logic: The incentive each holds produces behavior of the sort you would expect or predict based on knowing the original motivation. We can sense this in the descriptions of each type.

Politicians with a *program incentive* get "satisfaction from working on public policy."[12] They are problem solvers. Like Maine State Legislator Joan Moore, program types enjoy "collecting information, analyzing consequences, drafting measures, and bringing about desired changes."[13] They are open to compromise and know how to work cooperatively with others to achieve their goals. They focus on the details of policy making. They are workers, focusing on the job to be done while avoiding emotion-inducing rhetoric. In personality they are neither diffident nor self-promoting, but rather stable, self-confident, and secure.

Politicians with a *conviviality incentive* want "to be accepted by other people and to engage in harmonious interaction with them."[14] Like Betty Gardner, these participants are insecure. They seek to bolster a weak ego by merging into a group of warm, approving colleagues. They are joiners—but followers, never leaders in the organizations they join. These conviviality types focus on getting along, making themselves liked, being helpful. Never self-starters or self-promoters, they will adopt passive, spectator roles in the political arena.[15]

Politicians with a *status incentive* seek fame and glory. They need "to *be* somebody."[16] Like Will Maddox, they are preoccupied with rising quickly, with becoming a success. They focus on career achievements and on marks of social recognition. Prizes, awards, publicity, and public office are the rewards most coveted by status types. Because they project their own climbing orientation onto other politicians, they are cynical about their colleagues. Status types are uncooperative, work poorly with others, frequently make enemies, and are seen by others as untrustworthy. Uninterested in the details of public policy, they remain content to echo popular clichés rather than study complex issues in any serious depth.

Politicians with an *obligation incentive* are obsessed by a need to follow their conscience, to do what is right. Like Roland Giguere, their lives are governed by a strict set of moral imperatives. They strive to behave correctly and do their duty, no matter what the consequences or whom they might offend. Obligation types preach the need to act by principle, denouncing those who don't as ethical lepers. These moral purists see politics as a dirty world populated by corrupt politicians, people who are unprincipled and who lack backbone. Since obligation types view each policy matter as a

---

[12]Payne et al., *The Motivation of Politicians*, op. cit., p. 49.

[13]Ibid.

[14]Ibid., p. 79.

[15]Barber, in fact, used the term "Spectator" to describe this political personality. See his description in *The Lawmakers*, op. cit., pp. 23–66.

[16]Payne et al., *The Motivation of Politicians*, op. cit., p. 19.

question of ethics involving a right and a wrong side, their discussion of issues is characterized by rigidity and dogmatism. Their strong and frequently expressed biases make them difficult people to work with.

Politicians with a *game incentive* seek competitive interaction with others to demonstrate their own manipulative prowess. They tend to be robust, assertive, and enthusiastic. Like Ray Roberts, they think of politics as fun. They love its strategic and tactical side. Trying to be skilled players, they become maneuverers and manipulators. Still, game types respect other politicians. Politics is a game, after all, not a struggle for jungle survival, as it is for the status type. Other players are to be treated with dignity, not fear or contempt. Game types stress the importance of *being a team player* and *sticking to the rules*. Without cooperation and rules, you can't have a game and then politics would no longer be fun. Game types are objective political analysts. They must be, in order to compete intelligently and win. This objectivity extends even to themselves: They can step back and discuss their own strengths and weaknesses with dispassion.

Two incentives types are less commonly found in American political culture than the previous five. Politicians with a *mission incentive* need "to be committed to a transcendental cause that gives meaning and purpose to life."[17] They attach themselves with religious zeal to some political movement. As dedicated movement supporters, mission types become preoccupied with matters of the cause's doctrine and ideology. They are ever eager to promote the correct party line. Life, for them, is an all-consuming struggle to promote the movement and its truths. Conversely, they must also work to destroy the enemies of their faith. They view other participants in a dichotomous light: They are *either* comrades-in-arms *or* evildoers who must be obliterated. This all-or-nothing attitude makes them dangerous opponents and difficult allies. You must be an unquestioning follower of their movement, or they will view you with suspicion.

Politicians with an *adulation incentive* seek "praise and affection."[18] They want "to be loved; . . . to experience the outpouring of popular gratitude."[19] Adulation types need admiring followers around them at all times. Being surrounded by throngs of well-wishers, accepting lavish praise from fawning supporters, receiving thanks from grateful recipients of favors— this kind of personal reinforcement is what adulation types crave. They are forceful personalities, almost outrageously self-confident. And they never shirk from conflict. If others rob them of their desired acclaim, they will fight back with unmitigated antagonism.

Most politicians, our research shows, can be characterized by one, and only one, incentive. Newcomers to incentive theory often question this find-

---

[17]Ibid., p. 163.
[18]Ibid., p. 165.
[19]Ibid.

ing. Aren't "double" or "mixed" incentives possible? Couldn't someone be driven by a need for both status *and* conviviality, for instance?

It turns out empirically that such occurrences are rare. Fewer than 5 percent of all respondents reveal multiple incentives.[20] This finding may seem puzzling, but the theory does suggest an answer. It postulates that sustained political activity is unpleasant and full of drawbacks. If people hold one intense need that *must* be satisfied (that is, an incentive) and find that politics satisfies that need, they will accept the sacrifices necessitated by political activism in order to reap the intense psychological rewards that the activity also provides. *It is this single, burning drive, in short, that induces political involvement.*

The rest of us—average personalities, so to speak—hold mixed motives. We have a variety of needs; not one of them is dominant. Since no drive is particularly strong, the rewards that politics could offer in satisfying any given drive are relatively insignificant. Its disadvantages, however, remain as strong as ever. The average citizen, therefore, finds little motivation for long-term political commitment. He or she may dabble in politics from time to time, but will rarely remain active in it for long, rightly reckoning that the drawbacks of politics well outweigh the benefits. Only single-minded activists, incentive types, are likely to stick with politics long enough to rise to the middle and upper levels of political influence.

HOW INCENTIVES AFFECT POLITICAL BEHAVIOR

The strength of the incentive does more than just keep participants *in* politics. It affects how they will *act* as politicians. Each drive produces a different pattern of behavior, as participants seek the psychological satisfactions that brought them into politics in the first place. Status types, for instance, push themselves aggressively forward toward the limelight. Program types, on the other hand, work on policy problems in a businesslike manner behind the scenes. These different styles have given rise to a well-known distinction in political science literature: the difference between legislators who are "show horses" and those who are "work horses." The other incentive types, likewise, have their own distinctive styles of action.

These dramatic differences in behavior affect the nature of political institutions. A setting dominated by status types will resemble in few ways one packed with program types. Our research has found that politicians with a status incentive cause high levels of political instability. Obligation, adulation, and mission types also have this effect. All four treat opponents with contempt, see little value in temperance, and raise the political temperature by exaggerated, rhetorically overblown charges against their enemies

---

[20]See Payne's discussion of this point in *Incentive Theory and Political Process,* op. cit., pp. 157–59.

and against "the system" as a whole. Naturally, the combined effect of their activity induces citizen discontent, alienation, and cynicism, thus fueling demands for radical change and undermining mass support for the existing regime.[21]

Program, game, and conviviality politicians, on the other hand, help lower the intensity of political conflict. Where they predominate, political discourse is couched in temperate and rational language. Tempers rarely flare, politicians get along with each other, and the public is not constantly roused to a fever pitch of hatred by crowd-pleasing orators. Public problems may even find resolution, especially if the number of program types is high. Thus, comes a lowering the potential for violent confrontation between groups discontent with the pattern of government policy.[22]

Knowing the incentives of the dominant political actors thus helps us understand something about the nature of politics in any given place.

HOW INCENTIVES AFFECT POLITICAL CAREER PATTERNS

Incentives explain another crucial difference among politicians: their career patterns. Status types move forward quickly, eager to gain prestigious positions as rapidly as possible. They turn out, on the whole, to be considerably younger than other participants in any given setting. For instance, of the twenty youngest U.S. Senators or British MPs (members of parliament), it's a safe bet that the majority will be politicians with a status incentive. Of those who don't become senator or MP until later in life (e.g., after fifty-five or sixty), almost none will be status types. That is because people with the status drive have a climbing orientation. They take an "up or out" approach to their careers. If they can't rise quickly, they feel frustrated—thwarted in their need for recognition. They tend to give up politics altogether and move into other arenas of life—law, business, writing—where they may have a better chance to gain the rewards of prestige and recognition that they so desperately seek.

Adulation and mission participants, for different reasons, also enter politics at a fairly young age. Conviviality types, in contrast, hold back. Their lack of self-confidence means they don't jump quickly into the political fray. When they do get into politics, often in middle age or later, they tend to stay put at the lower levels, fearing the increase in conflict and personal criticism that inevitably occurs with political success. Thus, older men and women in town councils everywhere stand a good chance of being conviviality participants.

---

[21]We present this argument in extended form in Payne et al., *The Motivation of Politicians,* op. cit., pp. 173–79.
[22]See our discussion of these points in Ibid.

Program and game politicians get into politics somewhat later than status types and move forward less quickly, but not for lack of self-assurance. They find politics fascinating at any level. There are always problems to solve or games to play. They don't see staying in place and learning to be effective as "stagnating," the term a status type would use. Other things being equal, then, game and especially program types in any institution will be a few years older than status types and have a few more years of lower-level experience.

Obligation types too have their distinctive career pattern. They can enter politics at any age, but they stay in it for markedly less time than the others. They do so, first, because they enjoy politics the *least* of all potential participants. They see it as a corrupt, evil world, in need of the purifying reforms they intend to impose on it. Once they realize that politics can never be restructured to their high moral standards, they leave in disgust—preferring to keep their own hands clean and to avoid being sullied by the dirty world of the political arena.

A second reason why obligation participants don't have long political careers centers on their rigid, accusatory personalities. Their unyielding operating style rubs many the wrong way—voters and politicians alike. They make enemies, and they often make fools of themselves as well, taking dogmatic and unpopular positions with little heed as to whether or not those stands fit the desires of the populace and the accepted wisdom of the day. To make a long story short, they are often forced out of politics by those outraged at their self-righteousness and distressed at their harsh, unbending moralism.

PREDICTING BEHAVIOR: AN UNCERTAIN PROPOSITION

This brief introduction to political motivation can only skim the surface of this complex and fascinating subject. Incentives are not as easy to identify in practice as they are to describe in theory. It is always fun to speculate about the personality structure of well-known political leaders, but be careful. You need a good deal of training to be able accurately to identify politicians' incentives. Just because a senator is young doesn't mean he is a status type. Just because a Governor smiles a lot doesn't mean she is a conviviality type.

Still, it's amusing and even good analytical practice to try to dope out a politician's incentive from the variety of clues available to us. If a given senator turns out not just to be young, but "the youngest senator in the country" and prior to that "the youngest governor in the country," and prior to that "the youngest person ever to be awarded a law degree in the state of North Massafornia," then the evidence begins to *suggest* a status incentive. If, furthermore, you learn that this senator has appeared on the Today show more times than anyone else in the past year, is famous for accusing other senators of corruption and dereliction of duties, and is known among colleagues as something of a loner, then you can (still tentatively) start postulating that this senator may well be a status type. Finally, if you read that the senator is known among peers as terribly ambitious, as a "difficult" person to work for, and as someone who rarely goes to committee meetings or "does homework," then you can become a little more confident that the status label may be accurate. But you must always consider this a working hypothesis until you have amassed a wealth of additional indicators.

The ideal way to identify incentives is through in-depth interviews.[23] If you can't conduct these yourself, you can sometimes find personally focused, autobiographical accounts of their lives written by the politicians themselves.[24] Portraits presented by journalists are usually less effective devices for uncovering incentives, because journalists seem to assume that all politicians are status motivated and structure their interviews accordingly. Occasionally, however, a good piece of journalism will make a politician's personality profile crystal clear.

To gain a shorthand perspective on each incentive type, turn to Table 11-1. It operates as a kind of pocket guide to the seven leadership styles. The last column will be particularly useful. It provides the phrases that colleagues, acquaintances, and observers use to describe politicians within each category. When you hear people depicted in these ways, you have a clue that may unlock the puzzle of their personality. Bear in mind, however, that this table must necessarily simplify; political leaders are much more complex than we can suggest here. If the subject intrigues you, delve deeper into it by exploring sources mentioned in this chapter's footnotes.

Fun though it may be to identify famous leaders' incentives, it is more important to use incentive analysis for understanding *group* political patterns. Knowing the incentive of an individual, no matter how powerful, tells us nothing about the pattern of politics in that participant's setting. Besides, predicting how any one person will behave, no matter how good our knowledge appears to be, is an uncertain proposition. I know myself better than I know any politician, and I can't predict what I'm going to do tomorrow. How well can I predict what Bill Clinton will do tomorrow?

Any single case may be an anomaly or an exception. (We know that smoking causes lung cancer, but we can't say that any given smoker will get lung cancer.) Besides, rarely does one person have a lasting impact on the overall style of politics in any system. What we need to examine are group patterns, not individual idiosyncrasies. Any particular politician

---

[23]We explain this process in Ibid., pp. 185–90 (Appendix I).
[24]See Ibid., pp. 30–31.

Table 11–1 An Introduction to Political Personality: The Incentive Types Classified and Described

Political Type	Image of Politics	Focus of Attention	Words That Describe
Mission	War	Enemy, truth, doctrine	Militant, extremist, ideologue, fighter
Obligation	Moral crusade, duty	Moral precepts, proper ethical behavior	Opinionated, rigid, dogmatic, uncompromising
Program	Hobby, puzzle	Problems, solutions, details, facts, results	Problem-solver, businesslike
Game	Fun, a game, a complex, structured competition	Strategy, tactics, techniques for winning	Robust, flexible, wily, a game-player
Status	Jungle	Personal success, prestige, recognition, fame	Loner, aloof, arrogant, opportunistic, untrustworthy, cutthroat
Conviviality	Club; family	Getting along; friendship with others; and relationships in general	Good old boy; good-time Charlie; Miss Congeniality; follower; spectator
Adulation	Theatrical stage	Being at the center of a throng of admiring followers	Ham; life of the party; self-dramatizer

may be an exception in one way or another. One status participant might be less ambitious than the others, another might be more friendly than average, a third might be more studious than expected. But if we compare a group of 100 status politicians to 100 program politicians and 100 conviviality politicians, we can be sure that these individual differences will cancel out and that each group will exhibit the expected characteristics: The status-dominated group will be racked with conflict, the conviviality-dominated group will be seen as a friendly but do-nothing institution, and the program-dominated group will be seen as work oriented and businesslike.

To illustrate the power of incentive theory for explaining long-term institutional trends, let us apply what we have learned to an analysis of recent changes in the U.S. Congress.

There can be little doubt that the way Congress operates has changed. The House and Senate of our time differ dramatically from the House and Senate of the 1950s and earlier. In that era (roughly, 1920–1960), Congress was a reasonably businesslike, collegial institution, which conducted its affairs with civility and stood fairly high in the estimation of the public. Symbolic of the Congress of that day were the norms that all members were expected to observe. These included the following:

    Hard work
    Apprenticeship
    Expertise
    Reciprocity
    Courtesy
    Compromise
    Institutional patriotism[25]

In other words, legislators were expected to study issues, keep their mouths shut until they actually knew something, speak only on matters they knew something about, respect the expertise and integrity of other legislators, give and take on any issue, not expecting everything to go their way all the time, and take pride in (rather than criticize) their political institution.

These are simple and sensible requirements for behavior within any organization. They may indeed be essential to insure any group's effectiveness, yet norms like these don't come about willy-nilly. No societal law insures their occurrence. Indeed, many institutions have quite different norms, which encourage conflict and animosity.

We can postulate, in fact, that norms of the type associated with Congress prior to the 1970s were developed and sustained by a solid coterie of program participants. These norms fit perfectly the program politician's needs and operating style.

Program types wish to work on and influence policy. They know that to achieve that end they must spend long hours studying policy matters. That insight leads them to respect those who have already gone through the process and gained expertise in some issue area. Not wanting to cut themselves off from potential support on legislation they plan to back, program types try to get along with their colleagues. In pushing pet projects, they are willing to engage in give-and-take bargaining, preferring through compromise to gain some of their policy ends rather than risk losing all their goals by pushing intransigently for extreme positions. They stand up for, or at least refuse to criticize, Congress as a whole, knowing that denigrating national institutions weakens the political sys-

---

[25]A number of classic studies of the way Congress worked in the 1950s and 1960s found that these norms were widely held and played a central role in structuring legislative behavior. See in particular, Donald R. Matthews, *U.S. Senators and Their World* (New York: Vintage Books, 1960); Charles L. Clapp, *The Congressman: His Work as He Sees It* (Washington, D.C.: The Brookings Institution, 1963); Donald G. Tacheron and Morris K. Udall, *The Job of The Congressman* (Indianapolis: Bobbs-Merrill, 1966), pp. 173–76; Nicholas A. Masters, "Committee Assignments in the House of Representatives," *American Political Science Review* 55 (1961): 345–57; Richard F. Fenno, Jr., "The House Appropriations Committee as a Political System: The Problem of Integration," *American Political Science Review* 56 (1962): 310–24; John F. Manley, "The House Committee on Ways and Means: Conflict Management in a Congressional Committee," *The American Political Science Review* 59 (1965): 927–39; and Herbert B. Asher, "The Learning of Legislative Norms," *The American Political Science Review* 67 (1973): 499–513.

tem and hence their own likelihood of gaining public support for policies they wish to achieve.

This "traditional" behavior pattern of Congress would appear, in short, to reflect a group dominated, or at least heavily influenced, by program participants. One would hardly argue that all members of Congress in, say, 1949 held a program incentive. But one can surely say that a large fraction of those legislators (at least a third?) held that incentive and doubtless only a small number (surely less than a fifth) held the status incentive.

CHANGING TRENDS: THE NEW POLITICS

Notice what has happened to Congress in recent decades. The norms described previously have declined, and some have completely disappeared.[26] The atmosphere is tense in both houses. Hostility runs high among members. Some time ago John Rhodes, a Republican representative from Arizona and also House minority leader, put it this way (and things have only gotten worse since he wrote):

> The atmosphere in and around Congress is far more acrid than at any time during my career. The Members are louder, more uptight, hostile and devious. . . . Today's Members—particularly many of the newer Members—have failed to master the art of disagreeing without being disagreeable. . . . The average Congressman of yesteryear was congenial, polite and willing to work with . . . colleagues whenever possible. Most important, his [*sic*] main concern was attending to . . . congressional duties. Today a large number of Congressmen are cynical, abrasive, frequently uncommunicative and ambitious to an inordinate degree. In their eagerness to draw attention to themselves—and advance politically—they frustrate the legislative process.[27]

[26]This is a principal theme in James L. Payne, "The Changing Nature of American Congressmen: Some Implications for Reform," paper delivered at the 1977 meeting of the Midwest Political Science Association, April 21–23, 1977. I elaborate on that theme in Oliver H. Woshinsky, "Donald Riegle and the Changing American Congress," a paper delivered at the 1980 meeting of the Northeastern Political Science Association, November 20–22, 1980. Other scholars who have noted the decline of the "'traditional" congressional norms include Herbert B. Asher, "The Changing Status of the Freshman Representative," in Norman L. Ornstein, ed., *Congress in Change: Evolution and Reform* (New York: Praeger Publishers, 1975), pp. 216–39; Nelson W. Polsby, "Goodbye to the Senate's Inner Club," in ibid., pp. 208–15; and Norman L. Ornstein, Robert L. Peabody, and David W. Rohde, "The Changing Senate: From the 1950s to the 1970s," in Lawrence C. Dodd and Bruce I. Oppenheimer, eds., *Congress Reconsidered* (New York: Praeger Publishers, 1977), pp. 3–20.

[27]John J. Rhodes, *The Futile System* (Garden City, NY: EPM Publications, Inc., 1976), p. 7.

Even discounting the political motives that Rhodes might have had for these charges, the knowledgeable political observer is struck by the accuracy of his description. Anyone familiar with incentive analysis knows exactly what Rhodes is complaining of: It would appear that status participants have been entering Congress in recent decades and displacing program types.

If that hypothesis is correct, we would expect a number of formal and informal changes to occur. A new set of norms, habits, and rules, congruent with the status participant's outlook and aims, would eventually take hold. This development has indeed come about. Several trends in congressional operating procedure are perfectly explained by hypothesizing an increase in the number of legislators with a status motivation and a corresponding decrease in the number of legislators with a program incentive. These trends include:

1. *Decline in the power of leaders.* The change from a strong Sam Rayburn or Lyndon Johnson to a laissez-faire Mike Mansfield or Carl Albert was symptomatic of a general weakening of congressional leadership. Committee chairs no longer wield enormous power. Even very junior legislators now snipe at party leaders and refuse to cooperate with them. A huge number of formal leadership positions now exist, giving everyone easy access to the prestige of office but increasing the number of important players, so that it becomes impossible to reconcile all interests and create a cohesive and coherent set of national policies. These changes are consistent with the status type's desire for position, resentment of those with power, and nonchalance toward the development of rational policymaking procedures.

2. *Weakening of the seniority system.* The famed seniority system has been undermined in many ways. That development would be expected after an influx of status types. A strict seniority system in the past, coupled with a small number of key congressional committees, kept most legislators from achieving prestigious jobs. As status types got elected to Congress, their discontent with seniority grew apace. Eventually, they created a system combining a wide-open leadership selection process with a large number of formal leadership posts (e.g., roughly 130 subcommittee chairmanships in the House). That way, everyone can be a chief—or at least stand a very good chance of becoming one.

3. *More talk, less work.* Status participants allocate their time to attention-getting activities and avoid spending time on the study of policy matters. As status types increase in Congress, one would expect more members to give speeches throughout the country, either before live audiences or on radio and television shows. Conversely, they will be less well informed than previously on the details of national issues. Power in policy matters, as a result, would devolve to congressional staff and to experts in the execu-

tive branch. Most observers believe that developments of this sort have clearly occurred.

4. *More publicity.* The amount of behind-the-scenes committee work appears to be on the decline. This trend would follow from an increase in status participants. These members gain no psychological benefit from work done behind closed doors. They want as many of their actions as possible performed in an exciting, dramatic atmosphere likely to generate publicity. As status types gain power anywhere, we expect to see an increase in the number of open, well-publicized, even televised political meetings. That trend could hardly go any farther in Washington. Both House and Senate are now televised, and 97 percent of all congressional commitee meetings are open to the public and often televised as well.

Our surface inclination is to rejoice in this "openness of the new politics." A more judicious perspective notes that the effect of openness is not always to enhance the prospects for rational or responsible policy making. When performing before a mass audience, politicians can do little more than take symbolic stands and strive to present them eloquently. If they use that forum to try out new, perhaps iconoclastic, arguments, or to present detailed evidence and complex logic, they will not only get nowhere but may even hurt their political career chances. Besides, in highly publicized proceedings no opportunity exists for the give-and-take, bargaining, and mutual adjustment that must accompany any bill of major impact in a complex modern society.

The formality of public debate excludes all skills but those of the orator. Those are precisely the skills cultivated by status participants. We can see why they yearned to "open up the dark halls of secret congressional meeting rooms," and "let some air into the closed congressional system"—as they would put it, using effective but shallow journalistic clichés. We can also see why program participants would disagree with these aims.

5. *More internal conflict.* Any increase in the number of status types anywhere engenders a predictable increase in the level of intragroup hostility. Members will begin to castigate each other in public and personalize their issue disagreements. In the past, depersonalization of conflict was a major congressional norm. Legislators were supposed to disagree over policy without getting into personalities. This norm contributed to a working, cooperative spirit and a dampening of tension. It also insured a certain flexibility in the lawmaking process; members disagreeing on an issue today would not be so alienated from each other that they could not re-form into a different coalition on another issue tomorrow. This norm also served the aim of rational policy making. If members 'speak only to the issue" (not to personality, not to the galleries), then other members—even those on the

opposite side of that issue—can listen calmly and perhaps take some of the better points into account as they work on amending and improving the bill.

Status participants gain little from norms aimed at lowering the level of tension and enhancing the policy-making process. We expect those norms to decay as status participants rise in legislative influence. Cynical of others' motives and resentful of competitors and higher leaders, status types will make biting personal references to opponents during ordinary policy debate. The personal hostility they bring to policy discussion poisons the general atmosphere and makes the forging of compromise legislation on major issues (e.g., health care) all but impossible.

6. *More perquisites.* As more status participants reach Congress, we expect to see more stress placed on the status-enhancing aspects of the job itself. Legislators will receive more money, more staff, new office buildings, better travel allotments, and assorted other perks like free haircuts and gym privileges. By way of contrast, money formerly spent on functions that enhanced the policy-making process (e.g., the Library of Congress) will be drastically cut back.

STATUS MOTIVATION: THE RISING CONGRESSIONAL FORCE

There is little doubt that status types have come to replace program types as the dominant force in Congress. Those key changes of the past three decades outlined previously can be explained by this hypothesis. But why has it occurred? What is there about the politics of our era that favors the election of status-motivated politicians to high office?

Payne suggests several factors that, added up, give an electoral edge to status participants over potential rivals, especially over rivals with a program incentive.[28] These factors include the following:

> An increase in the *number* (not necessarily the percent) of people voting in congressional elections, due to an influx into the electorate of young people (those eighteen to twenty have been allowed to vote), baby boomers, recent immigrants, and African Americans (many of whom were effectively disenfranchised before the Civil Rights Movement)
>
> An increase in geographical mobility among Americans (consequently, fewer people know much about local political leaders)
>
> A decrease in the proportion of the electorate with personal or in-depth knowledge of the candidates in any election (a result of the two previous factors)

[28]Payne, "The Changing Nature of American Congressmen," op. cit., pp. 6–10.

The growth of the electronic media as an influence in politics

The rise of the primary as the principal means for obtaining party nominations, giving an advantage to "outsider" campaign styles over "insider" political skills

The combined effect of these developments, Payne argues, is to create *a new political environment, which favors politicians adept at appealing to and impressing large, distant, relatively uninformed audiences.*

When politicians must become popular with a mass electorate that knows little about them, those skilled in image manipulation become advantaged. Status types will do well under these circumstances. They want to gain mass appeal. Hence, they work at making themselves attractive, and we have already seen how important for one's career it is to be attractive. They also work hard at mastering speech-making techniques, including the art of the sound bite. They frequently go so far as to hire professional actors and speech specialists to coach them in the skills of debate and rhetoric.

A few decades ago candidates were picked by party leaders who knew them intimately, then ratified by a fairly small number of nontransient voters who knew these local nominees reasonably well. In those circumstances program participants would normally have a good chance at winning. Close up, one can appreciate their profound mastery of subject matter and their studious, responsible character. From a distance (on a far-off podium, on a television screen), program types—citing numbers and examples, avoiding the provocative if exciting phrase—appear colorless, lacking in verve, and even downright boring.

The current condition of American politics clearly disadvantages those give serious benefits to status types and disadvantage program types, as these different participants seek to gain higher elected office. No wonder the number of status types in Congress has been rising, no wonder the political process in that body has been transformed—and no wonder that body has never been held in lower esteem than it is today.

SUMMARY

What goes on within political institutions doesn't simply reflect the impact of external, environmental forces. The simpleminded determinism of that viewpoint ignores the fact that politicians have both power and personalities. The power they have allows them leeway in their behavioral choices. They can't ignore their environment, of course, but neither are they robots or puppets, unthinkingly reflecting the outside world. They are free to range widely, making decisions well to the left or right of any supposed national consensus. They are also free to set up a range of policy making procedures and adopt any number of operating styles within the corridors of power. Just how they decide to behave in this world of choice will depend a good deal on what kind of people they are and what personality profiles they exhibit.

It pays, therefore, to know something about the psychology of a nation's elite. Incentive theory is not the only approach to this topic, but it is a powerful and a useful one. Once we know the basic distribution of incentives within any elite group, we can predict a good deal about how that group is likely to behave, and what institutions it will create and sustain. Motivational analysis, it appears, can provide us with some crucial clues for piecing together the puzzle of political life.

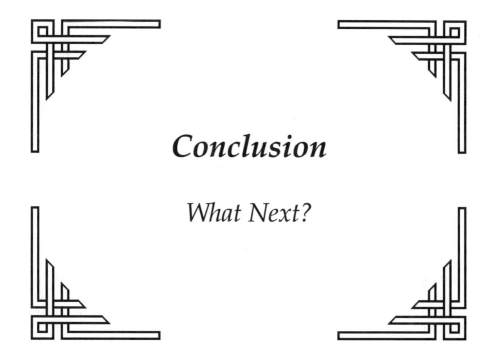

Conclusion

What Next?

We have focused most of our attention in this book on what social scientists call "mass political behavior." We have addressed the question, What is the relationship between citizen norms and political processes? We have seen that the two are inextricably connected. Democratic politics is unlikely to occur in an authoritarian culture. Attempts to impose democracy on authoritarian citizens stand little long-term chance of success. In the same way, attempts to impose dictatorship on a democratically inclined people will ultimately come to naught. To understand any system's politics, then, you must start with the deep-seated values of the general population.

Having said that, we must add a crucial modification. The underlying culture does not tell us much about the day-to-day activity of full-time political activists. Yet it is they who determine what politics looks like in the short run. They dominate the headlines, set policies, and run government offices. How high tariffs will be, how many new bridges will be built next year, at what age one will be allowed drink alcohol are some of the mundane yet vital questions that touch us all and which political leaders are constantly asked to decide.

It is at this elite level that *politics*, as most of us conceive it, is happening. We simply take for granted the long-term setting: our culture. "Real" politics, for most of us, is the day-to-day set of decisions undertaken by the thousands of individual members of our society's political elite. We must know something about those people if we are to understand the ongoing process of policy making, which affects us all.

To understand politics in the long-term, then, we need to know the underlying values of an entire population. To understand politics in the short-term, we must understand what the *leaders* of the culture look like. To be sure, the culture itself will influence the types of leaders that arise. Still, their psychological makeup stands as an independent variable in its own right. Governing elites affect the political process in myriad vital ways. We can't neglect this crucial influence if we wish to make sense of the overall political system.

Mass *and* elite, then: An understanding of both is crucial for the attainment of wisdom about the political process. Yet the values of the mass and the incentives of the elite are ever in flux, ever changing. We have set ourselves a lifelong task, if we wish truly to grasp how politics works at any given time, in any given place. Luckily, politics is a lively business, and its study provides hours of endless fascination. Those who wish to understand political life will never be bored. Good luck as you forge ahead on this exciting venture.

Index